THE NAMES OF TOWNS
AND CITIES IN BRITAIN

Compiled by

MARGARET GELLING, W. F. H. NICOLAISEN,

and MELVILLE RICHARDS

Edited and introduced by

W. F. H. NICOLAISEN

B. T. BATSFORD LTD London

FIRST PUBLISHED 1970

© MARGARET GELLING, W. F. H. NICOLAISEN
AND MELVILLE RICHARDS 1986

FIRST PUBLISHED IN PAPERBACK 1986

ISBN 1 7134 5235 8

PRINTED IN GREAT BRITAIN BY BILLING & SONS LTD, WORCESTER
FOR THE PUBLISHERS B. T. BATSFORD LTD
4 FITZHARDINGE STREET, LONDON W 1H 0AH

CONTENTS

INTRODUCTION

I

In 1963 there appeared a little German publication called *Namen deutscher Städte* in which four members of the Leipzig group for name studies set out to give short accounts of the names of the largest German cities. At its annual meeting in the University of Nottingham on 13 March 1965, the 'Council for Name Studies in Great Britain and Ireland' examined this booklet and, encouraged by it, instructed three of their own members to compile a similar dictionary of names for Great Britain. Indeed, the brief was to aim at something a little more ambitious than the slim paperback the German scholars had produced and to include a certain number of towns in addition to all the cities. This book is the result of that brief, and although it may fall short of its ideal realisation, it can nevertheless claim a number of 'firsts' in the field of name research in this country.

In the first place, it is the first book to have been published for 60 years in which place-names of England, Scotland, and Wales are being investigated systematically, together. More than that, it is the first book ever in which a group of British place-names has been presented in dictionary form. It is also the first time that scholars from the three countries concerned have co-operated in the production of a book on place-names, and it is finally, we would claim, the first publication in which the selection of names to be included has not been dictated primarily by linguistic considerations but by extra-linguistic criteria.

Let us look at these various claims in turn. The time has been ripe for many years now for a substantial onomastic publication which would ignore the present boundaries between the three countries and treat an aspect of the place-nomenclature of Great Britain as a whole. Of all the languages known to have been involved in the shaping of Britain's linguistic history only two— Pictish and Cornish—were spoken in their own limited territories

5

without penetrating to any noteworthy extent beyond the boundaries of these areas; and even these two languages can, in a way, be said not to be as isolated in their impact as this statement might suggest since closely related other Celtic dialects had a wider influence. All other linguistic strata, however—English, Norman French, Norse, Danish, Gaelic, Welsh (and its ancestors), and possibly an Indo-European forerunner of all these, termed 'Old European'—were spoken in more than one of the three countries, and sometimes in all three. For this reason, it has always been very unsatisfactory for Scottish readers to find English onomastic studies, especially those investigating the geographical distribution of a certain name-type or element, finish at the present-day Scottish-English border since there is normally no indication whether the distribution continues into Scotland at all and, if it does, how far and how densely. The same, of course, applied to equivalent Scottish publications. Similarly, the often rather puzzling problems concerning pre-English Celtic names of England are not seldom much more easily solved if one takes the place-nomenclature of Wales into account, and even for Scotland and Wales there is room for co-operation if one thinks of a category like the place-names beginning with *Aber-* (like the Welsh Aberaeron and the Scottish Aberdeen) which is only to be found in these two countries but not in England. For these and for many other reasons a publication dealing with the names of all three countries was therefore desirable and long overdue.

It was tempting to cast such a publication into the form of consecutive narrative and to discourse on a number of aspects—linguistic, historical, geographical, social, etc.—in turn, giving under each heading, or in each chapter, relevant examples from all three countries. The main objection to such a presentation was not simply a question of practicability, particularly from the point of view of three different personal writing styles flowing together to make a satisfying and convincing whole, but in a more positive sense the experience that usually a reader's chief interest lies in getting information quickly about a particular name, and its associations. Such ready-made availability of information is, in the writers' opinion, only to be found in a dictionary with proper cross-references, and an alphabetical arrangement has therefore been adopted for the main part of this volume, with a separate alphabetical list of Greater London names at the end. Under each name, not only the location as to county and country is given but also the known or supposed meaning and the most significant early spellings, the latter being a necessary and accepted part of all place-name investigation. The sources of such spellings, however, are only indicated in particular instances, especially when a name is mentioned in an important source such as Ptolemy, or the Antonine Itinerary, or Bede, or the Anglo-Saxon Chronicle. Otherwise no identification of sources such as charters, pipe rolls, boundary descriptions, Domesday Book, etc. has been attempted since such detailed information was judged a hindrance rather than a help in this context. Quite clearly, the average reader will not follow up such direction to the original manuscript or printed version anyhow but rely on the integrity and ability of the scholar as to the correctness of the forms quoted. Those readers, on the other hand, who do want to go back to the original source, its nature and context, can usually do so without too much difficulty by consulting the standard reference works, particularly in England where Ekwall's *Dictionary* and the publications of the English Place-Name Society have laid such firm foundations for onomastic scholarship.

The main feature of this book, however, lies in the fact that it does not simply stop here and consider the answer to the question 'What does this name mean?' as the end and purpose of all place-name research. Sometimes, admittedly, once a name has been ascribed to a particular language and its meaning has been given (always with due regard to the early documentation of the name in question and to its modern pronunciation), there is very little else to be said, and place-name investigation has, in such cases, been a purely etymological-linguistic exercise. This is a valid approach and it is also basic to all name study, but the proper onomastic inquirer will want to take these foundations and build on them, treating names as *names*, and not merely as linguistic units, as *words*. In most entries, therefore, something more is being said about the nature of the name; the actual feature on the ground from which it must have, or may have, arisen; its relationship to other names of the same type or containing the same

7

element; its position with regard to possible earlier names for the same place; its historical implications, distributional context, social significance; its place within the linguistic stratum to which it belongs; etc., etc. Not every facet is covered for every name, because sometimes the information required is not (yet) known or irrelevant, or both. Whatever is adduced, however, is given in full sentence form with a minimum of the linguistic scholar's shorthand employed in most publications in this field. There is no reason why a popular reference book should not be authoritative; and a readable, authentic account of all names has therefore been aimed at, making use of the most up-to-date publications in each field.

Accounts of this kind, with equal authenticity and standards of scholarship for all three countries within Great Britain, could not have been written by any one scholar. The study of place-names has become such a specialised art that it is difficult for one person to deal adequately with all types of names belonging to different languages, periods, regions, and social strata, even of one country. To do justice to the names of three is nowadays well-nigh impossible. One of the main reasons why the 'Council for Name Studies' was created in these islands was the wish and necessity for co-operation and co-ordination in this very special field of research. In a way, it is in fact the very existence of this Council which has made this book possible, and it was only natural that the task of preparing it should have been given to three individual scholars, all experts in the place-names of their own country. Dr Margaret Gelling was entrusted with the English section. Her own two volumes on the *Place-Names of Oxfordshire* have already appeared in the county series published by the English Place-Name Society, and her systematic account of the place-names of Berkshire is ready for publication in the same series. Obviously her contribution is the most voluminous, with more than 600 entries, but she has had the good luck of being able to fall back on the 43 volumes so far published by the English Place-Name Society, as well as on that remarkable example of single-handed achievement, Eilert Ekwall's *Concise Dictionary of English Place-Names*. To the best of our knowledge, this work has no parallel in any other country, certainly not in Europe. Professor

Melville Richards of the University College of North Wales at Bangor, author of many articles and papers on Welsh place-names, undertook to prepare the Welsh entries, numerically far fewer but nevertheless not less time-consuming because of the absence in Wales of anything remotely equivalent to Ekwall's *Dictionary*. Most of the Welsh material, therefore, stems from Professor Richards's own collections and archive, and is here published for the first time in systematic form (another 'first'). For the Scottish section, the Introduction and the overall editing, the services of Dr W. F. H. Nicolaisen, Head of the Scottish Place-Name Survey in the School of Scottish Studies of the University of Edinburgh, were requested. His task seems to have lain, with regard to the degree of difficulty, somewhere between those of Dr Gelling and Professor Richards, in so far as the Scottish Place-Name Survey has built up an extensive place-name archive over most of the last two decades. There are also some good books on certain aspects of Scottish names, especially Celtic names, but also one or two county volumes. The only 'dictionary' of Scottish place-names in existence is, however, totally unreliable and should be treated with care. Much of what is being said about Scottish names in this volume is therefore also presented in this form for the first time. The responsibilities within this unifying framework of co-operation are consequently clearly divided but also interdependent. Although a serious attempt has been made at making the layout and style of all entries as uniform as possible, individual characteristics, interests and areas of knowledge will nevertheless still be noticeable without, we hope, making the presentation too uneven. Any discrepancies which may appear may, of course, also be ascribable to the differences in the nature and reliability of the background literature available in each of the three countries.

That this book is not trying to rival Ekwall's *Dictionary*, however much it may be indebted to it, need not be stressed. Not only does it incorporate Welsh and Scottish, as well as English names, it also differs in its aims in two other main respects. One of these we have already discussed, and that is the treatment of names as *names* and not simply as *words*; this is an onomastic and not a purely etymological dictionary. If it is wider in scope in these two

9

respects, the geographical and the interpretational, it is more limited in the third, although this is closely linked with the second: the selection of names. The decision to confine this volume to names of towns and cities was not simply imitative of the German publication mentioned at the beginning. It was in reality born out of its own philosophy, which in turn made the German booklet so attractive ('One should do this kind of thing for Britain one day!'). The names in this volume have not been chosen for linguistic reasons or because they show a significant geographical distribution or because they illustrate a particularly interesting or dark period of British history or prehistory. They have also not been chosen because they are quaint and curious or demonstrate some particular principle or may serve as examples for an exercise in the study of place-names. They have been chosen for one reason only: they are the names of those places—towns and cities—in which most people in Great Britain live to-day. They have therefore, in this sense, been accidentally thrown together because this is their only unifying factor. That, within this (extra-linguistic!) category they should share certain other traits and show certain systemic patterns is another matter and not surprising. This does not, however, to any extent reflect similarities in the respective processes of naming but is rather due to the fact that people over the ages have tended to build settlements which in the course of time gained some importance, in certain selected, favourable and congenial places, as we shall see later (p. 25).

The chief difficulty in the selection of names within the stated framework of this volume lies in the application of suitable criteria to assess what constitutes an *important* settlement, even if one agrees that *importance* is in fact the overriding and operative quality. For obvious reasons one has no trouble with cities in this respect, but towns are more difficult to classify. For the purposes of this book, we established three main criteria: size (population), status, and other qualities (like historical importance). With regard to size, it was decided that for England most towns of more than 10,000 inhabitants should be included. In order to have a fair representation, this figure had to be 5,000 for Scotland and also, nominally, for Wales. In England, only two county-towns which had given name to counties were below the 10,000 mark.

These two (Buckingham and Huntingdon) were included, but the three small county-towns of Appleby, Bodmin and Oakham were omitted. In Scotland and Wales, however, the situation was quite different. Even after all burghs and towns over 5,000 inhabitants had been listed, some county-towns or towns at least partially fulfilling the role of county-towns had still not been included: Kirkwall ORK, Golspie and Dornoch SUT, Portree (Skye) INV, Nairn NAI, Banff BNF, Stonehaven KCD, Kinross KNR, Lochgilphead ARG, Wigtown WIG, Kircudbright KCB, Jedburgh and Newtown St Boswells ROX, Duns BWK, and Linlithgow WLO. These were therefore all added. Similarly, in Wales a number of county-towns, which had not qualified because of lack of size, had to be included for 'status' reasons, as well as some centres of Urban District Councils, like Menai Bridge AGL and Nant-y-Glo MON, important market towns like Narberth PEM, and one or two tourist centres. In all these cases, a criterion of size was, however, applied in so far as no names were admitted which applied to settlements of under 1,000 inhabitants, the lower limit for a settlement called a 'town' in census terms. Practically always the figures used were taken from the 1961 census, except in the cases of New Towns which have grown far beyond their 1961 size since then, or perhaps did not exist at all at that time.

Most troublesome in the fair and proper application of the basic criterion of size were the large conurbations in which it is sometimes difficult to establish whether a 'place' with the required number of inhabitants, or many more, is an independent unit in the sense of the term 'town' or not. Whereas suburbs were by definition clearly excluded, areas like Greater London, Liverpool, Birmingham, Manchester, and Glasgow did not always easily admit to such clear-cut distinction. It has therefore been our policy to make individual decisions, as to what was to be included and what not. Frequently, the interest of the name as a *name* was the decisive factor, and even with the best will in the world a certain unevenness and unfairness could not be avoided. The only big exception has been Greater London, where we decided to list the names of places of required size now within that administrative unit in a separate section under Greater London at the end of the main dictionary (p. 193). Ideally, all London boroughs should,

11

of course, also have been included but the scope of the book regrettably did not allow any further expansion.

From the foregoing it is therefore clear what the general intention of those who planned, wrote, and published this book was: To discuss, by making use of the latest results of modern scholarship, in a readable, comprehensible, and authentic way the names of Britain's towns and cities, i.e. the places where the majority of the population lives to-day, and to treat these names not so much as words, as lexical items, but rather as names, as onomastic units, with all the special qualities these have, compared with mere words.

II

The main quality attaching to names, particularly place-names, which ordinary words do not normally have, is a 'power of survival' which not only allows them to live on when the words which have gone into their make-up have become obsolete but also when the very language which coined them has died out. This special quality is due to the fact that names can function quite adequately and meaningfully as names, even when they have become quite meaningless as words. Indeed, it is questionable whether names can be handled better or more efficiently if their meaning is apparent or known. Do names like Nottingham, Glasgow, and Cardiff really function better as names once we know them to mean 'village of the followers of Snot', 'green hollow', and 'fort on the River Taf', respectively? One might claim that the opposite is true and that the most naïve approach to a name is also the best and that unintelligible names fulfil their role most directly. Perhaps a neutral point of view should be adopted in this matter, simply stating that a meaningful place-name is not better than a meaningless one. The purpose of this book must therefore not be regarded as making provision, or giving guidance, for the better use of the names of our towns and cities.

Nevertheless a quality which, in a purely contemporary sense, may not necessarily prove an advantage and occasionally even turn out to be a disadvantage, can, historically speaking, be turned into something extremely valuable; for if names can function quite adequately as meaningless units in later linguistic strata or in

12

later stages of the language which coined them, then the languages spoken in these islands during the last 20 or 30 centuries must have left behind them traces of their existence in such names, as it is unlikely that all names belonging to a particular language have been obliterated or replaced in the course of linguistic change. It should therefore be possible to reconstruct a relative chronological stratification of the languages spoken in this country in the last three thousand years and, as place-names are attached to pieces of ground, to add to this vertical distribution in time the horizontal distribution in space, the geographical scatter, so that the proper investigation of place-names should provide a fairly accurate answer to the double question: 'Which language was spoken when and where in the British Isles?' This answer could only be supplied by names and not by ordinary words since the latter only become available in the earliest phase of surviving written inscriptions and are non-existent as evidence before that time. However, even names, however precise they may be in the delineation of the settlement area of a given linguistic people, can only provide a *relative* chronological stratification since *absolute* dates are hardly ever referred to in names and since even the earliest recorded spelling does not necessarily indicate for how long before this record the name has been in existence. The time of earliest documentation and the time of coining are not usually the same.

The names of towns and cities are, of course, also linguistic fossils which can be placed into the framework of chronological stratification, and it is to be expected that most strata are represented within the covers of this volume. A quick check will establish whether this is a reasonable expectation. *English* names are, of course, to be found everywhere and for this linguistic category it is more a question of establishing strata within the stratum by proving, for instance, that names in -*ing* (Barking GTL, Hastings SSX), -*ingham* (Gillingham KNT, Altrincham CHE), and -*ington* (Addington GTL, Bridlington YOE) belong to the earliest English names in Britain, that Belper DRB, Bridgwater SOM, Melton Mowbray LEI, and Montgomery MTG show Norman influence, and that Coalville LEI and Clydebank DNB are nineteenth-century creations. These are only very crude distinctions and

13

English onomasticians are able to separate the various strata in a much more delicate fashion than this. The *Scandinavians* left their traces in Corby NTP, Derby DRB, Scunthorpe LIN, Kirkwall ORK, Lerwick SHE, and Swansea GLA, and again the trained scholar has the ability to isolate within this broad group of *Scandinavian* names those of Danish, Norse, Irish-Norse, and English-Norse origin as well as chronologically significant types and sub-groupings. Names of *Gaelic* origin are not only found in areas where Gaelic is still spoken to-day (Inverness INV, Dornoch SUT) but also where the language has been dead for many centuries (Kilmarnock AYR, Greenock RNF, Inverurie ABD, and Dundee ANG). *Welsh* names naturally abound in Wales (Llanfairfechan CRN, Pontarddulais GLA, Tredegar MON) but are not always easily distinguished from names belonging to earlier stages of that language. Here the earliest recorded names are those of Celtic tribes like the *Demetae* in south-west Wales (*Dyfed*), and the Silures. Between the fifth and tenth centuries some regions received their names from an eponymous ancestor to which a territorial suffix was added, the whole signifying 'the descendants of so-and-so' or 'the territory of so-and-so', as in Cedweli CRM and Cardigan CRD. Early settlements are those of fortified places of Iron Age forts preceded by the elements *din* and *caer*. What for Wales are chronological subdivisions of a fairly homogeneous history of the language still spoken to-day are, in England and Scotland, pointers to a pre-English and pre-Gaelic linguistic stratum. Bathgate WLO, Lanark LAN, Renfrew RNF, Carlisle CMB, and Dover KNT are relevant examples of that layer. *Cornish* has left us names like Penzance and Truro, both in Cornwall, and perhaps one might be allowed to claim Aberdeen ABD and Arbroath ANG as *Pictish* for, although the element *Aber-* is also extremely common in Wales, it largely has what might be described as a Pictish distribution in Scotland. Unfortunately, none of the typically Pictish names beginning with *Pit-* (like Pitlochry PER and Pittenweem FIF) has made the grade of this dictionary by any of the criteria applied. There are, however, some names of Roman origin, or with Roman associations, in our list, such as Gloucester GLO, Leicester LEI, Lincoln LIN, etc. This proportion, incidentally, is much higher amongst the names of towns and cities than in general naming.

14

Naturally, these strata are not always represented by their best examples, as these sometimes attach to fairly minor settlements, and the proportions of names associated with the various linguistic groups may also not always be right, but there appears to be a sprinkling of everything, and readers will get a good idea of what English, Norman, Norse, Danish, Gaelic, Welsh, Cornish, Pictish, Brittonic, and Roman names were like and in what forms they have survived to the present day. In this respect, the large number of early names, connected with the earliest English settlements, with the Romans, with pre-English settlers in England and Scotland, with early territorial ascriptions in Wales, etc. demonstrate a remarkable cultural continuity and often 1,500 to 2,000 years of settlement history on the same spot for our towns and cities.

As far as the geographical extent of the individual linguistic contributions to Britain's past is concerned, our names give only a very patchy picture as no category is completely represented in the dictionary. No attempt has therefore been made at the sketching of such geographical distributions, apart from hints under individual names as to their distributional, as well as chronological context. Reliable accounts of such areas are available in recent publications, such as Cameron's and Reaney's volumes on *English Place-Names,* and the nature of our own venture precludes adequate treatment of this subject. Readers are therefore referred to these two books and to the place-name feature in the *Reader's Digest Atlas of the British Isles* which contains maps of all pre-English place-name regions.

III

We have already hinted that the reasons behind the choice of names to be included have not been linguistic ones, and yet some linguistic factors are so intricately linked with what is primarily an extra-linguistic category of names that a number of valuable points emerge which are worth discussing in detail. In the following some of these points are therefore taken up so that they will only need a brief cross-reference under the individual names concerned. The items selected for discussion do not, of course, cover all the important aspects which might have been worthy of such treatment. They should only be regarded as illustrations of what the name of a town or city might convey to those who are prepared to look.

(a) Names of the type Barking GTL or Hastings SSX in which -ingas added to a personal name is thought to denote a group of people dependent on a leader, have long been considered to reflect the earliest English settlements in the country, and statements to this effect will be found in most standard history books dealing with the period. The groups of people to which they referred must have varied greatly in size. Sometimes examples occur so close together that the names can only have referred to the inhabitants of a single settlement (see Lancing and Worthing SSX), whereas in the case of Hastings the group was either very large, or it succeeded in imposing its leadership on a great many other groups of settlers. Clusters of them are to be found in the west and south of Sussex, part of central Kent between Chatham and Maidstone, east Kent inland from Dover, and a small district of south-west Surrey. They are common, but more evenly distributed, in Essex, Norfolk, and Suffolk. Apart from this, they occur sporadically over most of the eastern half of England, but are very rare in the western half.

The theory which associates these place-names with the earliest Anglo-Saxon settlements has always appeared more satisfactory to philologists than to archaeologists. The archaeological evidence for early settlement consists mainly of pagan burials, and there are very serious discrepancies between the distribution of the known burials and that of names of the Barking type and of the -ingahām type which is discussed under (b). It is probable that in the next few years place-name scholars will revise their estimate of the historical role of both types of place-name. Nevertheless, names in -ingas will retain their special significance in so far as they are primarily names of people and not of settlements and preserve for us the flavour of the age of migration.

(b) The natural sequel to the type discussed under (a) are names like Altrincham CHE, Birmingham WAR, and Gillingham KNT in which Old English -hām is linked with the genitive plural of the folk-name in -ingas implying occupation by a group of people

16

dependent on a named leader, rather than association with a single person, as denoted by a personal name in the genitive singular (see under (*d*)). It has long been assumed that these names, together with the type represented by Barking and Hastings, reflect the conditions of the earliest English settlements in Britain when groups of settlers were arriving from the Continent, each with its own leader. In the light of new archaeological evidence, this theory may require revision, and for the time being it cannot be regarded as certain that names in *-ingahām* go back to the earliest arrival of the English in England, although they are the earliest in Scotland about 200 years later. In England this type of name occurs notably in Norfolk and Suffolk and parts of Lincolnshire, and sporadically in Northumberland (linking with south-east Scotland), the north-west and south.

Altrincham, Birmingham, and a substantial number of other names with Middle English spellings in *-ingeham* exhibit, either in the modern spelling or in the modern pronunciation, a development of *-ing-* to *-inch-* or *-indge-*. In some names, this development is indicated by the spelling but ignored by the pronunciation, as in the case of Altrincham, which is pronounced as if it were spelt Altringham. In others it is not apparent from the modern spelling but is firmly preserved in the local pronunciation, as in Ovingham NTB, pronounced as if it were spelt Ovindgeham. In others, such as Atcham SHR (Atingeham 1086), it has transformed the whole appearance of the name, or given rise to a significant local variant, like Brummagem for Birmingham. This phenomenon (sometimes called palatalisation and sometimes assibilation) and its occurrence in some but not others of these names, has long been regarded as presenting a difficult philological problem, and different scholars have explained it in different ways. It has recently been suggested that names in which this development occurs are of different origin from those of the type Gillingham, and are not formed by the addition of *-hām* to the genitive plural of a folk-name. The suggestion is that in the case of Altrincham there was an original place-name *Aldheringi* (locative case), formed by the addition of *-ing* to a man's name. Such a name would mean 'thing (i.e. place or settlement) associated with Aldhere', and the addition of *-hām* would give a compound which meant 'village at

17

Aldheringi'. Since *-hām* was added to the locative of the earlier name, the case ending *-i* would cause the development of *-ing-* to *-inch-*. This means that it would not be necessary to explain the peculiar development of *-ing-* as due to some modification of the genitive plural inflection.

At the time of writing this important new suggestion has not yet been fully assessed and both types of name (Gillingham and Altrincham) have therefore in the context of this dictionary been regarded as belonging to the same category.

(*c*) In connection with the theory referred to under (*b*) place-names of the type Addington GTL may also take on a new significance, for instead of treating the connecting particle *-ing* as corresponding to the possessive *-s-* of the Brighton type (*Beorh-thelmes tūn*), which is discussed in (*d*), a new division *Eadding* 'place associated with Eadda' plus *tūn* 'estate' may have to be envisaged.

Because of the enormous number of these *-ingtūn* names, acceptance of this theory would mean that there was an early name-giving period in which it was extremely common to designate a settlement by adding *-ing* to a man's name. It would also be necessary to assume that there was something about these early place-names which in the course of time made them seem unsatisfactory without the addition of a word for a settlement, since they only survive as the first part of a compound such as Addington. It is easy to find surviving names in which *-ing* has been added to a noun, such as Clavering ESX 'clover place', or Guiting GLO, which is a stream-name formed by adding *-ing* to *gyte* 'flood'. But similar formations in which the first element is a personal name are certainly rare and possibly non-existent among surviving place-names, although some are on record in Old English sources. This does not prove that such formations were never more widely current, but it is a bold assumption that they were common enough to lie behind all the *-ington* names and a number of those in *-ingham*.

It is therefore an open question whether names of the *-ingtūn* type should be regarded as having a radically different significance from that attached to Brighton, which can simply be translated as 'Beorhthelm's estate'. It is noteworthy that there do not appear to

18

be as many names of the Addington type as of the Brighton type in which the personal name can be connected with a person mentioned in a surviving record. Most known examples of this, some of which are quoted under (*d*), are certainly formations in which the word for a settlement is added to the genitive of the personal name. This suggests that the Addington type may be on the whole earlier than the Brighton type. A possible exception is Tredington WAR. This place is the subject of a charter of 757, in which the estate is given by a local ruler to the church of Worcester 'with the same boundaries by which the king's companion Tyrrda formerly held it'. It seems probable that in Tredington we have an -*ingtūn* formation based on the name of a nobleman who held the estate in the first half of the eighth century. We have, however, no evidence that this type of name was still being formed in the ninth and tenth centuries.

(*d*) The whole subject of the relationship between names of the Addington and Brighton type needs re-examination. Place-names in which a personal name is associated with one of the common words for a settlement, such as *hām*, *tūn*, *worð*, *burh*, present an interesting historical problem which has not yet received the consideration it deserves. Some history books imply that the man or woman whose name is the first element of such a place-name is to be regarded as the founder of the settlement. In areas for which there are early written records, however, the personal name can sometimes be identified as that of a person who is granted the estate by a charter from a king or bishop. In these instances, the man or woman derived income from the estate, and may or may not have had a house there; but he (or she) was neither the founder of the settlement nor one of the farmers who worked the land. This phenomenon is best observed in Gloucestershire and Worcestershire, where the survival of some early charters belonging to the monastery of Worcester provides the necessary written evidence. Perhaps the clearest instance is Bibury GLO. There is a charter of 718–45 by which the Bishop of Worcester leases land here to a nobleman called *Leppa*, for his lifetime and for that of his daughter *Beage*. The estate is not named in the charter, but is identified as 'by the river called Coln', and has a set of boundaries which clearly go round the modern parish. The name Bibury,

19

which means 'Beage's manor-house', is first recorded in a later charter of 899. It seems clear that the estate acquired its modern name about 750, when the lady Beage, having inherited the lease of it from her father, built a new manor-house. In the boundaries of the same charter of 718–45 there is a boundary-mark *Leppan crundlas* 'Leppa's chalk-pits', which presumably means 'chalk-pits on the boundary of Leppa's estate', and is an interesting parallel to names like Boston and Braintree. The main point is that both Leppa and Beage appear in place-names, but neither was in any sense a farmer. It could be asserted that at an earlier date than this villages were actually founded by men and women of noble rank who had led followers over from the Continent, but it seems easier to imagine such men and women being given manorial rights over settlements already in existence, which had been established and were being farmed by people of humbler rank.

¯ This type of place-name was still being formed in the later Old English period, and even after the Norman Conquest, and in these late names the 'manorial' significance is beyond doubt. Woolston BRK can be proved to derive its name from a thegn named Wulfric, who obtained the estate in the mid-tenth century, East Garston BRK (earlier *Esgareston*) is named from Esgar who owned land there in 1066, and Chanston HRE has as first element the Norman family-name Cheney.

The problem is whether this evidence, which can only be expected to survive for a small number of place-names, justifies an assumption that all the numerous names which mean 'x's settlement' are the result of an estate being assigned by some political or ecclesiastical authority to an owner who was of higher status than that of the peasant farmers. It is in accordance with this possibility that 'estate' has been used instead of 'farm' in etymologies given in this dictionary for English names of this type. This would accord well with the relatively high proportion of feminine personal names in these place-names, but such an origin would mean that none of them can date from the earliest period of the settlement, and that in most cases they replaced an earlier name.

(e) In his investigations, the place-name scholar cannot be content with ascertaining the likely meaning of a name in general terms only. He must be precise and specific, and to this end he has frequently to combine with the local historian or an expert in another related field of research, if he does not feel competent or able to achieve this precision. Simply to state that Bristol GLO is the 'assembly place by the bridge' is not enough; one has at least to speculate on the possibility that the bridge in question 'was perhaps the forerunner of Bristol Bridge, which carried the main road south across the Floating Harbour, and is mentioned in records of the twelfth century' (see p. 54). If one paraphrases the meaning of Carshalton GTL as 'farm by the river-source, noted for watercress' then it is also essential that one should search the appropriate local records until one comes across the requisite thirteenth-century grant of property which mentions a *kersenaria*, i.e. a watercress-bed, and that one should investigate the present-day situation finding that 'there are still watercress-beds by the River Wandle, which rises at Carshalton' (see p. 194). Chorley LNC undoubtedly means something like 'meadow-land of the peasant farmers', but were these the people really who were called *ceorls* in Old English? Here a comparison with Charlton helps (see p. 67). The potential interpretation of Faversham HNT as 'village of the smith', ultimately from Latin *faber*, receives support from the fact that 'Faversham is adjacent to a small Romano-British settlement . . .' and that grave-goods in Anglo-Saxon burials nearby 'suggest that there was a centre of fine metal-working here during the pagan Anglo-Saxon period' (see p. 88).

One particularly instructive name of this kind is Croydon GTL which has a linguistically convincing etymology in 'saffron valley' from Old English *croh*, derived from Latin *crocus* (see p. 195). But the name presents other problems: the Autumnal Crocus, *Crocus sativus*, the stigmas of which yield saffron dye, is a native of southern and central Europe, the Levant, and western Asia. If the Old English word for it really occurs as the first element of Croydon, it is necessary to inquire how the plant reached this country, and how a name derived from Latin came to be used by the Anglo-Saxon country-people among whom the place-name arose. The dye was in common use among the Romans, and one interesting possibility is that they introduced the plant to this country. A plant grown in the Roman period could have con-

21

tinued to flourish for a while afterwards: and as it has an attractive flower, it would naturally be noticed by English settlers. The British people of the neighbourhood could have passed on to them the Latin name *crocus*, in the same way as they appear to have passed on the Celtic name for the hill at Caterham, a few miles to the south, and the Celtic name Penge, a few miles north. There is archaeological and place-name evidence from the area which would lend some support to a hypothesis requiring continuity of occupation from Roman to Anglo-Saxon times. There is known to have been a Roman building in Beddington, the adjacent parish to the west; the adjacent parish to the east, West Wickham in Kent, has a name which points to early Saxon occupation; and Anglo-Saxon finds from Croydon now in the Public Library include some pieces of equipment which belonged to Germanic mercenary soldiers employed by the Romans in the fourth century.

If the Autumnal Crocus and the word *croh* were in fact to be found in the Surrey countryside before the year 809 (when Croydon is first recorded), both the plant and the word appear to have disappeared at some date after that. The plant is stated in the *Encyclopædia Britannica* to have been reintroduced to western Europe by the Crusaders. The English no longer had the native word *croh* for it in the medieval period, but used instead the foreign word *saffron*, which they transferred from the dye to the plant. The modern word *crocus* is a new coinage from the Latin. It was not known to herbalists writing in the sixteenth century.

An example of the complex problems which a single place-name sometimes presents is Ilkley YOW, for which no satisfactory explanation has ever been suggested; in particular the claim has to be examined whether the Roman fort here is the place referred to in Ptolemy's Geography as *Olicana*, and if so whether *Ilk-* is derived from the Romano-British name. The most recent discussion accepts the identification and endeavours to dispose of the difficult philological problems raised by the assumption that a name which appears about A.D. 150 as *Olicana* could become Old English *hillic-* or *yllic-*.

The position of Ptolemy's *Olicana* cannot be ascertained precisely. The same Roman site is believed to be indicated by the name *Alicuna* in the list of Roman places known as the Ravenna

Cosmography, but as all that is known of *Alicuna* is that it was on a Roman travel-route which went from Manchester to a fort in Ambleside WML, it cannot be said that this was certainly the fort at Ilkley.

When a Roman site can be identified quite certainly with an English settlement (as in Dover, Cirencester, Dorchester, etc.), and the English name bears a rough resemblance to the Romano-British one, it is probable that the later name is based upon the earlier, and this probability sometimes outweighs linguistic difficulties in reconciling the two. When the identity of the sites is possible but not proven, however, the argument can easily become circular, the assumption being that as *Olicana* was somewhere in the general region of Ilkley, and as the names are similar, therefore Ilkley is *Olicana*. Neither Ptolemy nor the Ravenna Cosmography provide such precise evidence of location as the Antonine Itinerary, on which many such identifications are based, and it might be better to regard this identification as incapable of proof, and to try to explain Ilkley without reference to *Olicana*.

If Ilkley is an English place-name, it is probably a compound of *lēah*, 'clearing' or 'pasture', with a noun. The first element is not likely to be a personal name, as the two pre-Conquest spellings show no sign of a genitival inflection. There is no Old English word on record which is suitable. There is a group of related words, comprising *halc* 'cavity', *holc* 'hollow', and *hylc* 'bend, tortuous way, inequality of surface, roughness of land'. In view of the dramatic nature of the topography round Ilkley these are tempting; but the idea that Ilkley contains a word belonging to this group should probably be rejected on the grounds that the first element of Ilkley had *-ll-*, not *-l-*, as can be seen from the spellings *hillicleg*, *yllic-leage*. Confusion between *-l-* and *-ll-* in the writing of Old English is extremely rare, and this *-ll-* is one of the major difficulties in reconciling Ilkley with *Olicana*, unless Ptolemy's form is emended to *Ollicana*. The first element of Ilkley is an unsolved mystery, but the absence of a recorded Old English word which suits the spellings is yet another factor telling against identification with *Olicana*. Irregular philological developments in English names containing Romano-British names can sometimes be explained, as in Gloucester, as due to the substitution of a known word for a meaningless element. But if no Old English word can be found which would explain Ilkley if it were an English name, then it follows that popular etymology cannot be held responsible for its irregular development if it is regarded as containing the Romano-British name. There is no question of a categorical statement that Ilkley is not *Olicana*. Obviously the two could be identical. But the names can only be equated by linguistic adjustments (such as emending Ptolemy's spelling) which depart from the evidence as we have it; and it is doubtful whether such expedients should be resorted to except when the identification is certain on geographical grounds.

IV

Of the special problems and aspects discussed in the last section perhaps the one concerning the relationship between personal names and other elements in settlement names is of the most general significance. It is not necessary to reiterate the difficulties encountered in determining the exact nature of that relationship but it may perhaps be worth mentioning that in a large number of such place-names we feel quite lucky if we can say with a degree of certainty that the first (or explanatory) element is a personal name and not a common noun or adjective, used attributively; and even if it is clear that a personal name is involved it is frequently impossible to know what the exact form of that name was. Sometimes we happen to encounter names which have been recorded in connection with the place-name concerned but more often than not the person involved, even if we can establish his or her name, has to remain anonymous as a personality without proper place in space or time. Because of the difficulties encountered in this respect the tendency of many place-name scholars has been to resort to the expedient of the personal name as an explanation when no other derivation seemed to be forthcoming, and it is more than likely that quite a number of these personal names only existed in the scholars' imagination, especially when there was no record of them elsewhere. The tag 'unrecorded personal name' is one which should be regarded with suspicion, although there are naturally some which, although they did exist, for some reason or other are not preserved for us in the surviving records. The whole problem is so important because this dictionary contains so many names which contain a personal name plus another element, a fact worth noting from the point of view of settlement history, whether such naming implies private ownership or not.

In addition to this rather striking association with the names of individual persons, the special collection of names made for the purposes of this book brings out another rather interesting feature and that is the close connection of city and town names with the names of watercourses. Most common perhaps are names which indicate that the settlement in question was formed at the mouth of a particular river, like Aberdeen ABD 'mouth of the Don', Inverness INV 'mouth of the Ness', and Tynemouth NTB. In other cases, an element signifying 'farm' or 'village' may have been added to a river-name without pin-pointing any particular spot, only its course; examples would be Dovercourt ESX, Burnham BUC, Colchester ESX, Doncaster YOW, and Exeter DEV. Favourite places for important settlements to develop are river-crossings, such as fords and bridges, and there is a fair crop of such names in our list, such as Ashford MDX, Bideford DEV, Crayford KNT, Dartford KNT, and Ilford GTL; Cambridge CAM, Stourbridge WOR, and Weybridge SUR. Sometimes such an association with rivers is implied rather than expressed, as in Ashford KNT, Brighouse YOW, Bristol GLO, Chelmsford ESX, Crewe CHE, Gosforth NTB, Guildford SUR, and others. In these instances the actual name of the watercourse is not mentioned and the place of crossing is characterised in some other way. In contrast to this group of names there are those which in their modern form, and usually also historically, are identical with the river-name itself, without any further addition. To illustrate this point it is only necessary to list names such as Andover HMP, Blackburn LNC, Blaydon DRH, Blyth NTB, Colne LNC, Darwen LNC, Douglas IOM, Frome SOM, Louth LIN. These are usually rendered in the dictionary as '(place by) the River X', and normally the linguistic phenomenon called ellipsis has been assumed to have operated here, although in the majority of cases this can no longer be proved. Exceptions are, for instance, such Scottish names as Nairn NAI and Ayr AYR in which a word

25

for 'river-mouth' (Gaelic *inbhir*) is known to have dropped out a few hundred years ago. Most of the names in this group apply to the most important settlements by the watercourses in question.

Similar lists could be provided for names indicating other favourite locations such as river-meadows (*hamm*) and forest-clearings (*lēah*), but it is not the aim of this Introduction to analyse all the possibilities, especially when so much depends on a detailed knowledge of local history. It is therefore left to the reader familiar with such knowledge to complete the picture or work out the local implications. These problems more than any other give an indication of the involvement of the local historian in place-name studies. Only field-work on the spot by someone conversant with local records, etc. can ultimately produce a satisfactory answer and put the flesh on the linguistic skeleton. It is with such a hope in mind that this book has been planned and devised, and nothing would please the writers more than the knowledge that it might serve as an encouragement to those interested in these matters to proceed with their own local investigations, and to stimulate others who maybe have never given much thought to such problems into trying their hand on a local place-name problem for the first time. There is nothing like the name of the place in which you live, to start off with, and we can only hope that the reader will find the name of his town or city in this book to give a good start.

(Discussions of English place names on pp. 16–24 are adapted from Dr Gelling's articles on the names in question.)

County Abbreviations

In order to conform with Scottish and Welsh practice, the names of English counties have been abbreviated by a three-letter system. Practically all of them differ therefore from the abbreviations used by the English Place-Name Society and by Ekwall.

ABD	Aberdeenshire	DRH	Durham
AGL	Anglesey	ELO	East Lothian
ANG	Angus	ESX	Essex
ARG	Argyllshire	FIF	Fife
AYR	Ayrshire	FLI	Flintshire
BDF	Bedfordshire	GLA	Glamorgan
BNF	Banffshire	GLO	Gloucestershire
BRE	Brecknockshire	GTL	Greater London
BRK	Berkshire	HMP	Hampshire
BTE	Bute	HNT	Huntingdonshire
BUC	Buckinghamshire	HRE	Herefordshire
BWK	Berwickshire	HRT	Hertfordshire
CAI	Caithness	INV	Inverness-shire
CAM	Cambridgeshire	IOM	Isle of Man
CHE	Cheshire	IOW	Isle of Wight
CLA	Clackmannanshire	KCB	Kirkcudbrightshire
CMB	Cumberland	KCD	Kincardineshire
CNW	Cornwall	KNR	Kinross-shire
CRD	Cardiganshire	KNT	Kent
CRM	Carmarthenshire	LAN	Lanarkshire
CRN	Caernarvonshire	LEI	Leicestershire
DEN	Denbighshire	LIN	Lincolnshire
DEV	Devon	LNC	Lancashire
DMF	Dumfriesshire	MDX	Middlesex
DNB	Dunbartonshire	MER	Merionethshire
DOR	Dorsetshire	MLO	Midlothian
DRB	Derbyshire	MON	Monmouthshire

COUNTY ABBREVIATIONS

MOR	Morayshire	SHR	Shropshire
MTG	Montgomeryshire	SLK	Selkirkshire
NAI	Nairnshire	SOM	Somerset
NFK	Norfolk	SSX	Sussex
NTB	Northumberland	STF	Staffordshire
NTP	Northamptonshire	STL	Stirlingshire
NTT	Nottinghamshire	SUR	Surrey
ORK	Orkney	SUT	Sutherland
OXF	Oxfordshire	WAR	Warwickshire
PEB	Peebles-shire	WIG	Wigtownshire
PEM	Pembrokeshire	WLO	West Lothian
PER	Perthshire	WLT	Wiltshire
RAD	Radnorshire	WML	Westmorland
RNF	Renfrewshire	WOR	Worcestershire
ROS	Ross and Cromarty	YOE	Yorkshire (East Riding)
ROX	Roxburghshire	YON	Yorkshire (North Riding)
RUT	Rutland		
SFK	Suffolk	YOW	Yorkshire (West Riding)
SHE	Shetland		

A

Aberaeron (CRD, Wales): mouth of the River Aeron (*ad ostium Ayron* 1184, *aber aeron* 15th cent., *Aber Ayron* 1536–9, *Aberayron* 1565–6). A compound of *aber* 'mouth' and a Welsh river-name *Aeron* 'goddess of battle' from Welsh *aer* 'battle', and a suffix *-on* which frequently has a mythological significance in river-names. The earlier references are to the actual estuary. *Ayron* represents a medieval Welsh spelling. The present town dates its importance from 1807 when the Rev. Alban Thomas Jones Gwynne built break-waters to form a harbour.

Aberafan (Aberavon) (GLA, Wales): mouth of the River Afan (r. *Auan*, *Auen* c. 1150, *Aveninae fluvium* c. 1200, *Avennae fluvius* c. 1200, *Avan* 1455–85, *Ecclesia de Avene* c. 1291, 'vill' *Aven* 1208, *Aber*[a]*uyn* c. 1400, *Aber Avon* 1536–9, *Aberavan* 1548, *Aber Afan* 1606). The river-name *Afan* was also used for the commote of the same name, and the vill at the mouth of the River Afan was called *Aberafan*. *Afan*, *Afen* is probably a personal name. The change of *Afan*, *Afen* to *Avon* is fairly early [cf. *Ecclesia de Abbona* 1348], and may be due to confusion with English river-name *Avon*. Welsh speakers use *Aberafan* (dialect. *Byrafan*). The docks which were built at Aberavon

Harbour in 1836 to deal with exports of coal and iron were named *Port Talbot* in honour of the Talbot family of Margam, important landowners.

Aberavon (GLA, Wales), see *Aberafan*.

Aberayron (CRD, Wales), see *Aberaeron*.

Aberconwy (CRN, Wales), see *Conway*.

Aber-dâr (Aberdare) (GLA, Wales): mouth of the Dâr (*Aberdar* 1203, *Aberdar* 1253, *Aberdaer* 1348, *Aberdare* 1528, *Aberdayer* 1536–9, *Aberdaer* 1578, *Aberdare* 1610). Welsh *aber* 'mouth' + *dâr*, *daer* which is obscure. *Dâr* could be Welsh 'oak', or the element in *cynddaredd* 'rage'. *Daer* could represent dialect pronunciation of a narrow *a*. The confusion of forms makes an etymology uncertain. The 'anglicised' form *Aberdare* approximates to the local pronunciation. The town is at the confluence of the Rivers *Dâr* and *Cynon* (*Canan* 1253, *Kenon* 1536–9, *Kynon* 1638). *Cynon* may represent the name of the 'hound-goddess' or the personal name, British **kunon-*.

Aberdare (GLA, Wales), see *Aber-dâr*.

Aberdaugleddau (PEM, Wales), see *Milford Haven*.

Aberdeen (ABD, Scotland): the mouth of the Don (*Aberdon* c. 1187;

Aberden c. 1214; *Apardion, Apardjon* 13th cent. Orkneyinga Saga; latinised adjective *Abbirdonensis* 1136, *Aberdensis, Aberdonensis* 1292, *Abbyrdonensis* 1489). A compound of Brythonic *aber* 'mouth, confluence', still well known in Wales but in Scotland chiefly in former Pictish territory, and a Celtic river-name *Don* from **Devona* 'goddess (river)'. Historically the name first applied to the ecclesiastical settlement on the Don, the present Old Aberdeen, although it must have originated as a geographical name referring to the mouth or estuary of the Don. Compare Arbroath, Aberaeron, etc.

Aberdovey (MER, Wales), see *Aberdyfi.*

Aberdyfi (MER, Wales): the mouth of the River Dyfi (*Aberdewi, Aberdiwy* 12th cent., *aber dyfi* 14th cent., *Aberdeui* 1536–9, *Aberdivy* 1592). A compound of Welsh *aber* 'mouth' and the river-name *Dyfi* (*Deui* 12th cent., *Devi c.* 1200, *Dyui* 1281, *Dyvi* 1428), from Welsh *du* (earlier **duf*) 'black, dark'. The earlier references are to the actual estuary. The present place owes its importance to its development as a watering-place in the nineteenth century. The anglicised spelling *Aberdovey* is an approximation of the pronunciation.

Abergafenni (Abergavenny, Y Fenni) (MON, Wales): the mouth of the River Gafenni (*Gobannio(n)* Roman period, r. *Geuenni c.* 1150, *Abergavenni* 12th cent., *Abergevenni* 1191, *Bergeveny* 1255, [district] *Bro Venni* 15th cent., *y Venny* 15th cent.). A compound of Welsh *aber* 'confluence' and the river-name *Gafenni.* The Romano-British *Gobannion* is cognate with Welsh *gofan* 'smith',

and may be a proper name which was given to the river. *Gefenni* shows vowel affection over two syllables. The usual form in Welsh is *Y Fenni* (with loss of first syllable).

The town, which stands at the confluence of the Rivers Gafenni and Usk, was the centre of the Norman lordship of Abergafenni.

Abergavenny (MON, Wales), see *Abergafenni.*

Abergele (DEN, Wales): mouth of the Gele (*Opergelei* 9th cent., *Abergele* 1257, *Abergelou* 1290, *Abergeleu* 1310, *abergeleu* 14th cent., *Abergelow, Abergell'* 1334). Welsh *aber* 'mouth' and the river-name *Gelau, Gele* from *gelau* 'blade, spear'. *Gele* is a dialect form from *gelau.* Words like *cyllell* 'knife' and *cleddau* 'sword' are common in river-names, referring either to their straight course or to the flashing of the water.

The town became part of the possessions of the Lordship of Denbigh after the Norman Conquest, and was the centre of the commote of Is Dulas, part of the cantref of Rhos. The duality of Norman towns is illustrated by the terms *Abergele Anglicana* and *Abergele Wallicana* in a document of 1554.

Aber-gwaun (PEM, Wales), see *Fishguard.*

Aberhonddu (BRE, Wales), see *Brecon.*

Aberpennar (GLA, Wales), see *Mountain Ash.*

Aber-porth (CRD, Wales): mouth of the port of Hoddni (Hoddnant) (*Aberporth* 1284, 1299, *Aberporth* 1502). Welsh *aber* 'mouth' and *porth* 'port'. The 'port' is *Porth Hodni c.*

30

1200, *Porthotny* 1331, *Blaen Porth Hodnant c.* 1300. The brook-name varies between *Hoddni* and *Hoddnant* (*Hownant*) which are derivatives of *hawdd* 'quiet, pleasant', cf. *Aberhonddu*; *nant* may here be 'valley' rather than 'brook'.

Abertawe (GLA, Wales), see *Swansea*.

Aberteifi (CRD, Wales), see *Cardigan*.

Aberteleri (MON, Wales): mouth of the Teleri (*Teleri* 1332, *Aber-Tilery* 1779, *Abertillery* 1856). Welsh *aber* 'mouth' + pers. name *Teleri* (< prefix *ty* + *Eleri*). The brook Teleri runs into the River Ebwy Fach at Aberteleri. The local pronunciation is *Abertyleri*. *Abertillery* is a poor anglicised spelling. This is a nineteenth-century industrial town. The church was established in 1856 under the parish church of Aberystruth. See further *Blaenau*.

Abertillery (MON, Wales), see *Aberteleri*.

Aberystwyth (CRD, Wales): mouth of the River Ystwyth (*Aberestuuth* 1232–3, *aber ystwyth* 14th cent., *Aberustuyth* 1402, *Aberustwith* 1438, *Abbrustwyth* 1485). A compound of Welsh *aber* 'mouth' and a Welsh river-name *Ystwyth* 'very curved, winding river'. For *Ystwyth* cf. *-stuccia* [read *estuctia*] 2nd cent., *Ustwith River* 1536 9, *Ystwyth* 1684–5. The original Norman castle was built in 1110 on a site about a mile and a half south of the present town in the Ystwyth valley. The second castle was built in 1211 on the present site which is near the mouth of the River Rheidol and the name Aberystwyth continued to be used although 'Aber Rheidol' would have

been a more correct geographical form. In the earlier examples of the name Aberystwyth refers to the castle. The earlier ecclesiastical settlement was at *Llanbadarn* church of St Padarn.

Abingdon (BRK, England): Ebba's hill (*Abbandune* 968, Charter of King Edgar to Abingdon Abbey). The monastery of Abingdon stood on flat ground by the Thames. The thirteenth-century monks who compiled the Abbey's cartulary probably felt that *dūn* ('hill') was an unsuitable word for this site, and it may have been to explain the discrepancy that they wrote down a story about the original foundation being near the Boar's Hill, and the name having been transferred with the monastery to the later site by the river. This story of an earlier foundation near Boar's Hill is of doubtful authenticity. Probably *Æbbandūn* was originally the name of the block of high ground north of Abingdon (in the same way as *Æscesdūn* was applied by the Anglo-Saxons to the whole of the Berkshire Downs).

Accrington (LNC, England): acorn farm (*Akarinton* 12th cent.). This does not seem to be an *-ingtūn* name (like Addington), as there is no personal name which could be the first element. *æcern* 'acorn', has not been noted in any other place-name besides this one, but the etymology is convincing. Accrington was on the edge of Rossendale Forest, and acorns were of economic importance for feeding pigs.

Airdrie (LAN, Scotland): this has never been satisfactorily explained. Neither the modern form nor the earlier spellings warrant derivation from Gaelic *airigh* 'a shieling', and whereas a Gaelic *Ardruigh* 'high reach' or 'high slope' is possible from the point of view of the anglicisation of Gaelic sounds, there is still the problem of stress, although there seems to be a parallel in another Airdrie in Nairn. There are also farms called Airdrie in Fife and Kirkcudbrightshire. The absence of really early spellings does not help, for the name is not recorded until 1584 and then immediately in the modern spelling. It is *Ardrie* in 1633. The lateness of these spellings possibly points to a late transfer of the name of a geographical feature to a new settlement. Airdrie did not become a burgh of barony until 1821.

Aldershot (HMP, England): projecting piece of woodland where alders grow (*Alreshete* 1248). The second element, Old English *scēat*, means 'that which projects', and there are good grounds for thinking that in place-names it usually refers to woodland. There is an area in west Surrey and the adjacent part of Hampshire where names in -shot are fairly common, including (besides Aldershot) Grayshott, Bagshot, Bramshott, and Mytchett. The term occurs sporadically elsewhere, but is only common in this area east and south of Windsor Forest.

Aldridge (STF, England): dwelling among alders (*Alrewic* 1086). *wic* is a place-name element which has several different meanings. The most recent study gives these as 'town, port, harbour, salt-works, street, dwelling, dependent farm', including under the last 'dairy-farm, grange'. The variants of the modern form can be divided into two main categories, those with palatalisation (e.g. Aldridge, Bromwich) and those without (e.g. Smethwick). The palatalised examples are more likely to contain *wic* in the singular, and the unpalatalised to be plural, but this distinction cannot be rigidly applied. The precise meaning in each case must be inferred from the nature of the place and its relationship to surrounding places. Aldridge was an independent estate at the time of the Domesday Survey, so 'dwelling' seems a more suitable translation than 'dependent farm'. As for the alders, a history of Aldridge says that there is frequent mention of alder groves in medieval documents. The name may have been interpreted as 'alder ridge' in modern times.

Alexandria (DNB, Scotland): named about 1760 after Alexander Smollett, M.P., of Bonhill.

Alfreton (DRB, England): Ælfhere's estate (*Elstretune* 1086, *Alferton* 1202). This name is similar in significance to Brighton and Ulverston but the formation is different, as the personal name does not show the possessive form. This omission of the genitive is more common in the northern half of England than in the south. Alfreton is at the southern edge of a dense concentration of names ending in -ton.

Alloa (CLA, Scotland): rock-plain (*Alveth* 1357, *Alwey, Aluethe, Alloway* in notes of charters). Underlying this name is an old Gaelic compound *allmhagh*, also seen in such names as Alva in the same county (*Alweth* 1489, *Alloway* 1508), Alloway in Ayrshire (*Auleway* 1324) and Alvah in Banffshire (*Alveth* 1308, *Alueth* 1329–32), and others.

Altrincham (CHE, England): village of the family or followers of Aldhere (*Aldringeham* 1290). For a full discussion of this type of name see *Introduction*, pp. 16–18.

Amersham (BUC, England): Ealhmund's village (*Agmodesham* 1066, *Amundesham* 1227, *Hakmersham* 1483, *Hamersham* 1536, *Agmondesham vulgo Amersham* 1675).

The element *hām* is usually translated 'village', as there is literary evidence to suggest that it meant a bigger settlement than *tūn*, which is usually rendered 'farm'. The distribution of names in *-hām* is more limited than of those in *-tūn*. Its frequency is greatest in the southeast, in the Thames valley, and in parts of East Anglia; it is fairly common in the north-east, but rare in the north-west, the Midlands, the West Midlands, and the south-west. This distribution, together with other evidence suggests that names in *-hām* belong to the earlier period of the English settlement. A noteworthy feature of *hām* and *tūn* is that they never appear in place-names without a distinguishing first element, unlike other words for a settlement, such as *stoc* and *wīc*, which are sometimes used alone.

The main unsolved problem of English place-name studies is the nature of the relationship which men like the Ealhmund of Amersham bore to the settlements named after them. This problem is discussed in some detail in the *Introduction*, p. 19.

Amlwch (AGL, Wales): near the pool (*Anulc* 1254, *Amelogh* 1352, *Amlogh* 1413, *Amloch* 1547, *Amlwch* 1590).

Welsh *am* 'near, about' and Welsh *llwch* 'pool, swamp, mud'. *Llwch* may here refer to the cove which was later improved into a harbour when the copper mines of nearby Mynydd Parys were in full production. *Llwch* may also be any muddy, swampy ground.

Ammanford (CRM, Wales): ford on the River Aman (r. *Amman* 1541, *Amman* 1575, *Aman* 1610, *Aman c.* 1700). A compound of Welsh *Aman(w)*, a river-name based on Welsh *banw* 'pig, pigling', cf. Irish *banb*, and used for a river rooting through the ground, and English *ford*. The name is a late nineteenth-century formation for the town which grew around the public-house called *Cross Inn*. *Rhydaman* is a literal Welsh translation of *Ammanford*.

Andover (HMP, England): ash-tree river (*Andeferas* 955, *Andovere* 1086). This was originally the name of the River Anton, on which the town stands, which was called *Andever* until the late sixteenth century. It is a Celtic river-name, the second element of which is identical with Dover. For comments on settlements named from rivers see *Introduction* pp. 25–6. Andover was probably first understood as 'place by the River Andever'. The Anton is a short river, and Andover may have been the only noteworthy settlement by it at the time when the name gained currency.

Annan (DMF, Scotland): (the) river or water (*Anava* 7th cent., *Anand* 1304, *Estrahanent* 1124, *Stratanant* 1152, *vallum de Anant* 1147–53, *Annandesdale* 1179, *Valle Anand* 1187). Quite clearly the name is first recorded as a river-name and then as part of the name of the valley through which the river which flows into the Solway Firth not far from Annan, runs. Derived from the valley-name is the district name Annandale which provides most of our early evidence. In *Estrahanent* the first element is Welsh *ystrad* 'river-valley', in *Stratanant* it is either the Gaelic cognate *strath* or a shortened form of *ystrad*. In *Annandesdale* of 1179 and many later examples, Norse *dalr* or Old English *dæl* has been added to the river-name. The name of the river is one of the oldest in Scotland. If it is an early Celtic name, it is possibly from a root **pen-/pon-* 'water, mire'. There are some rivers called *Anava* on the Continent, as well as a tribal name *Anauni*. In form and meaning the Scottish river-name and its Continental parallels may, however, well be pre-Celtic although Indo-European. The present form Annan appears to derive from the genitive *Anann* of a Cumbric *Anan*.

Arbroath (ANG, Scotland): the mouth of the Brothock [Burn] (*Aberbrudoc* 1189–98, *Abirbrothoc* 1199, *Abberbrodoch* 1187–1203, *Aberbrothic c.* 1200, *Abbirbrothe* 1240, *Aberbroth* 1266, *Arbroth* 1290). For *aber* see under Aberdeen; the stream-name is probably based on Gaelic *bruth* 'heat' and as *Brothag* must mean 'the little boiling one'. In Modern Gaelic the name is still *Obar Brotháig*. The gradual reduction of the second element from *-brudoc* or *-brothoc* to *-broth* (or *-broath*) and the shortening of *Aber-* to *Ar-*, most likely under the influence of the second *-b-*, are clearly demonstrated

by the spellings quoted which are only a selection from the many early forms recorded for this particularly well documented name. It is noticeable that the modern shorter form of the name must have been current in local speech by the end of the thirteenth century at the latest.

The parallel name Inverbrothock, now the name of part of Arbroath, is apparently a late creation, possibly dating only from the year 1827. The Brothock Burn flows into the sea at Arbroath.

Ardrossan (AYR, Scotland): the point of the little promontory (*Ardrossane* 1315–21, 1375, 1528–9, 1576; *Ardrosse* 1374–5). In this name, Gaelic *ros* and *aird* are practically identical in meaning, and it looks as if *aird* was added at a later stage pleonastically, possibly when *ros* was no longer understood.

Armadale (WLO, Scotland): thus on a map of 1818. This is a transplanted name and originally belongs to the parish of Farr in Sutherland. William Honeyman, Lord Armadale, bought land in the parish of Bathgate, and the burgh which was built thereon was named after property he had inherited from his mother. In its original location the name is Scandinavian and seems to mean something like 'arm valley'. Armadale cannot be construed as reflecting Norse influence in West Lothian.

Arnold (NTT, England): eagles' valley (*Ernehale* 1086, *Arnold* 1474). A small stream with a well-defined valley runs through this suburb of Nottingham, and 'valley' seems in this instance a suitable translation for the final element, Old English *halh*. The general meaning of the word is 'nook or corner of land', and the precise meaning has to be estimated in each case from the topography. Other meanings are discussed under Bracknell and Bramhall. The development to -*old* has disguised the origin of Arnold; *halh* is much more commonly represented by -*hale*, -*hall*, -*ale*, or -*all* in modern names.

Ashford (KNT, England): ford of the ash-wood (*Essetesford* 1046). The first part of the name is either **æscet* 'clump of ash-trees', or **æscscēat* 'projecting wood where ash-trees grow', the latter being a compound similar to that found in Aldershot. *Ford* occurs very commonly in place-names in all parts of England, as settlements frequently arose at river-crossings. Ashford is on the road from Maidstone to Hythe, at the junction of the East Stour and Great Stour Rivers.

Ashford (MDX, England): (?) ford on a river called Ecels (*Ecelesford* 969, *Echelesford* about 1050, *Exforde* 1062, *Assheford* 1488). The River Ash, on which Ashford is situated, is called *eclesbroc* in a document of 962. There are phonetic difficulties which make it dangerous to associate this name with the word discussed under Eccles, and the origin of the stream-name must be left unsolved. Both these Ashfords have been interpreted as 'ash-tree ford'; there are places called Ashford which really do have that meaning in Devon and Shropshire.

Ashington (NTB, England): valley where ash-trees grow (*Essenden* 1205). Both *denu* 'valley' and *dūn* 'hill' are often confused with *tūn*, which is the most common of all place-name suffixes. The modern town of Ashington has grown up near the mining establishment. It is possible that the original settlement is represented by Ashington Farm, south-west of the town and near the River Wansbeck which runs in a well-marked valley.

Ashtead (SUR, England): ash-tree place (*Stede* 1086, *Estede* c. 1150, *Ashsted* 1235). The word *stede* is compounded in place-names most frequently with a word denoting vegetation. It is an ancient place-name element, very common in the south-east of the country. Ashtead is the western outlier of a cluster of names in -*stead*, one of which is Banstead.

Ashton-in-Makerfield (LNC, England): ash-tree farm (*Eston* 1212, *Ashton* 1255). Ashton is a very common name, and the need to distinguish between the various places so called led to many of them acquiring distinctive additions in the Middle Ages. Most of these additions refer either to medieval owners, or to the district in which the place lies. The district called Makerfield extended for about six miles south of Wigan. The name consists of Old English *feld* 'open land', added to a Celtic name meaning 'wall, ruin'. Perhaps the Roman fort at Wigan became known as 'the ruin' to the British population, and this name was taken over from them by the English. Round Makerfield there is one of the densest concentrations of Celtic names in the country.

35

Ashton-under-Lyne (LNC, England): ash-tree farm (*Haistune c.* 1160, *Asshton under Lyme* 1305). The addition in this case is a British name meaning 'elm wood', which appears to have applied to a large forest district which included Macclesfield Forest and stretched from near Manchester (where Ashton-under-Lyne is situated) to near Market Drayton in Shropshire (where Betton in Hales was earlier Betton-under-Lyme), a distance of about 40 miles. Although it has become Lyne in this name, the more usual form is Lyme, as in Newcastle-under-Lyme. With forest names, 'under' appears to mean 'near', and the places called *-under-Lyne* or *-under-Lyme* seem to have been near the northern and southern edges of this great forest.

Atherton (LNC, England): Æðelhere's estate (*Aderton* 1212, *Atherton* 1322). The genitival inflection indicating the possessive is omitted in this name, as in Alfreton.

Auchinleck (AYR, Scotland): field of the flat stones (*Auchinlec c.* 1239), from Gaelic *Achadh nan leac*. Names beginning with *Auch-* (from Gaelic *achadh*) are important pointers as far as Gaelic settlement in Southern Scotland (and elsewhere) is concerned, particularly after the breakdown of the Cumbric kingdom of Strathclyde.

Audenshaw (LNC, England): Aldwine's copse (*Aldwynshawe c.* 1200). Names in *-shaw* occur sporadically in all parts of England, but are most common in Lancashire and the West Riding of Yorkshire. It is comparatively rare for the first element to be a personal name, as in Audenshaw, more typical compounds having tree-names (as in Aldershaw STF), animal and bird-names (as in Cronkshaw LNC 'crane copse', Evershaw BUC 'boar copse'), or other significant words. The distribution of names in *-shaw* has not been studied in Lancashire; in the West Riding of Yorkshire, where it has been examined in detail, it has been found that clusters of such names often occur on the periphery of the main woodland areas.

Aylesbury (BUC, England): Ægel's fortified place (*Ægelesburg c.* 900 Anglo-Saxon Chronicle). The element *burh* denotes a fortification, which may be of several different kinds. It was the term applied by the Anglo-Saxons to Iron Age hill-forts, most of which have names in *-bury*, and it was occasionally applied to a Roman fort. In examples where the name is certainly pre-Conquest and there are no archaeological remains, it is likely to refer either to an Anglo-Saxon fortification against a national enemy, or to a manor-house defended by a ditch and palisade. The earliest reference to Aylesbury occurs in the Anglo-Saxon Chronicle under the year 571, where it is stated that the West Saxons captured Limbury, Aylesbury, Bensington, and Eynsham after a battle with the Britons. This can hardly mean that Aylesbury and the other places were known by these English names in the year 571. Even if, as some authorities consider, this was a reconquest of lands which had at an earlier date been in English hands, the surviving English names of the places seem likely to date from after the final annexation. But evidently a

West Saxon tradition connected these places with the conquest of 571, and it may be significant that two of the four, Aylesbury and Limbury, have names in *-bury*. Perhaps they were places at which the British had fortifications before 571, or perhaps the West Saxons built forts there soon after the battle. The meaning of *burh* is different in late names such as Newbury.

Ayr (AYR, Scotland): the river (*Ar c.* 1177, *Are* 1197, *Air c.* 1230, *Ayre* 1237, *Aare c.* 1400). To-day the settlement name is identical with that of the river on whose banks it stands, but the Modern Gaelic *Inbhir-àir* 'Ayr-mouth' and the earlier *Inber-air* of 1490 indicate that originally the name was of the Inverness type (q.v.)

but that subsequently the first element was dropped. The underlying river-name is one of the most interesting in Scotland, indeed in Britain. Not only is it identical with the Oare Water in Somerset and the Ore in Suffolk but also with the Ahr, a tributary of the Rhine, the Ahre, a tributary of the Nuhne near Arnsberg, and other European rivers such as Aar and Are in West Flanders, Aar in Holland, and Ara in Spain. For various reasons, mainly of a phonological nature, it is likely that Ayr together with the other names in question belongs to an early pre-Celtic Indo-European stratum of river-names in Great Britain and that it has come down to us from something like 1500 B.C.

Bacup (LNC, England): valley by a ridge (*Fulebachope c.* 1200). Old English *hop* usually means 'valley' in place-names in the Midlands and the North, and in this name it can be more precisely defined as 'smaller opening branching out from the main dale'. The main dale is the valley of the upper Irwell, and the smaller valley in which Bacup lies is formed by the head-water of the river, running at right angles to the main part of the stream. The 'ridge' may be the high ground to the west of the town. The spelling of about 1200 has *fūl* 'foul, muddy' prefixed.

Baildon (YOW, England): circle hill (*Bægeltune, Bældune c.* 1030). Baildon Hill is roughly circular in shape, and the name probably refers to this. Alternatively, the first element may refer to ancient circles of standing stones, or to 'Cup and Ring' marks carved on rocks.

Bala (MER, Wales): the outlet from a lake (*Bala* 1278, *la Bala* 1331, [*kastell*] *y bala* 14th cent., *the Bala* 1582, *o vala Lhyn Tegid c.* 1700). Welsh *bala* 'outlet' is a common noun used as a place-name, and therefore requires to be preceded by the definite article (*Y Bala*). The town is at the outfall of the River Dee from Bala Lake (*Pemmelesmere* 1191, *Thlintegit = Pemblemere* 1285, *Llyn Teget* 1523, *Llyn Tegyd* 1592, *a stagno Pymblemere* 1592, *Llyn Tygidd alias Pemble meer* 1698). The English form may be for Middle English *pimble, pimble* 'pebble' with *mere* 'lake'. *Llyn Tegid* is Welsh *llyn* 'lake' and the personal name *Tegid* (either from Latin *Tacitus* or a derivative of Welsh *teg* 'fair'). The English *Pimblemere* is obsolete. A bardic name for the lake is *Llyn Aerfen* 'lake of Aerfen' ([*i*] *lynn Aerfen* 15th cent.). Welsh *llyn* + *Aerfen* 'goddess of war' [< Welsh *aer* 'battle']. *Aerfen* was also an alias for *Dyfrdwy* 'River Dee', < Welsh *dwfr* 'water, stream' + *dwy(w)* 'goddess'.

Banbury (OXF, England): Banna's fortified place (*Banesberie* 1086, *Banneberia* 1109). This is an area in which Iron Age hill-forts are common, and although no such remains can now be traced at Banbury, the second element may refer to one which has disappeared. Grimsbury, immediately to the north-east of Banbury, is a name applied elsewhere to Iron-Age camps.

Banff (BNF, Scotland): (?) young pig (*Banb c.* 1150, *Banef c.* 1136, *Bamphe* 1290, *Banffe* 1291). Frequently taken to be identical with *Banba* (later *Banbha*) a poetic name for Ireland which is said to have been used as a district name in this part of Scotland. Its situation at the mouth of the River Deveron may indicate, however, that *Banbh* 'young pig' was another name for that river and that both the town and the county derive their names from it. Animal names are quite frequently used as river-names (see Ammanford).

Bangor (CRN, Wales): cross-bar in a wattled fence (*Benchoer moer in Britannia* 634, *Bangor* 1191, *Bangor* 1291, *Bangor* 14th cent., *Bangor fawr yng-Wynedd* 1612). Welsh *bangor* 'strong plaited rod in a fence' refers either to the wattled construction of the original monastic cell, or to the fence which surrounded it. The verb *bangori* is still used for 'plaiting'. *Bangor* early achieved an ecclesiastical or monastic significance, and the Caernarvonshire Bangor was the example for other names, such as Bangor in Ulster and Bangor in Flintshire (q.v.). Bangor was founded by Deiniol in the sixth century, near the passage to Anglesey from the mainland, and at the junction of the two cantrefs Arllechwedd and Arfon. For this reason it is often known as *Bangor Fawr yn Arfon*. It became the diocesan centre of the kingdom of Gwynedd (north-west Wales).

Bangor (FLI, Wales), see Bangor CRN: (*Bancor, Bancornaburg* 'stronghold of the men of Bangor' 8th cent., *Bangor* 1277, *Bankeburw* 1291, *Bangor* 1344, *Bangor monachorum* 1607). For the meaning see Bangor CRN. This monastery was probably founded by the same Deiniol as in the case of Bangor CRN. The monks were massacred by Æthelfrith of

Northumbria after the battle of Chester in 615. The place has various aliases, e.g. Bangor Is-coed (it was later part of the parish of Is-coed), and Bangor-on-Dee.

Banstead (SUR, England): bean place (*Benestede* 1086). Names of this type are discussed under Ashtead. Certain 'earlier' spellings for this name have not been considered here as they have turned out to be from forged charters.

Barmouth (MER, Wales): mouth of the River Mawddach (*Abermau* 1284, *Abermowth* 1410, [river] *Maudhu* 1209, *Mawddv* 1356, *Mauhach* 1356, *Abermowdhach* c. 1700, *Maviae* c. 1200). This is Welsh *aber* 'mouth' and river-name *Mawdd[ach]*. The original river name seems to have been *Mawdd* [? a personal name] and *Mawddwy* 'territory of Maw(dd)'. *Mawddach* was a tributary name of the original river *Maw(dd)*, a diminutive in *-ach*. The English form *Barmouth* has dropped the first syllable, and has assimilated English *mouth* from *Mawdd*. Welsh *Abermawdd* became successively *Abermaw*, *Abermo*, and *Y Bermo* by wrongly dividing the first syllable, as though it contained the definite article *y*. Unstressed final syllables in *-aw* became *-o* in Modern Welsh.

Barnsley (YOW, England): Beorn's forest-clearing (*Berneslai* 1086). Names in *-ley* usually contain *lēah*, a very common place-name element, possibly the commonest English one apart from *tūn*. It is especially frequent in forest areas. Barnsley is on the western edge of a fairly dense cluster of such names, but most of the other settlements in this cluster have remained small. For most names in *-ley* the appropriate meaning is 'forest-clearing', but in some (e.g. Cheadle, Bexley) it means 'wood', and in others (e.g. Shipley) it means 'pasture'. These meanings are discussed under the appropriate names. The word can occur without a first element, as in Leigh.

Barnstaple (DEV, England): bearded post (*Beardastapol, Bardanstapol* 979–1016, *Barnestaple* 1086). There are three other examples of this name, one of the places being Barnstaple Hall in Basildon ESX, which was the site of a 'hundred' meeting-place. Probably the posts had something resembling a beard attached to them, perhaps a besom, in which case they would resemble the posts which mark a navigation channel in the sea outside Malmö in Sweden. The purpose may have been similar in the tidal estuary at Barnstaple, but as the other examples are inland, this type of post could evidently be used for other purposes, such as the marking of a meeting-place. Posts are also referred to in Dunstable and Whitstable.

Barrhead (RNF, Scotland): founded about 1773. Barr is presumably Gaelic *barr* 'the top of something'.

Barrow-in-Furness (LNC, England): promontory island (*Barrai* 1190, *Oldebarrey* 1537). Barrow was originally the name of a small island, later called Old Barrow, and joined with the mainland in modern times. The second element is Old Norse *ey*, 'island', which has been added to a Celtic name from *barro-*, which normally means 'hill', but in this instance seems more likely to mean 'point of a promontory'. Barra in the Hebrides contains the same

elements, but there the meaning 'hill' is appropriate for *barro-*. The addition 'in-Furness' seems to have come into use in modern times, probably to distinguish this Barrow from other places which have the same modern name, though none has the same etymology. Furness, the peninsula on the end of which Barrow is situated, has an interesting name. It is *Fuththernessa* about 1150, which is to be explained as follows: Peel Island, which lies off the most southerly tip of the peninsula, was in the early Middle Ages called *Futh*, an Old Norse anatomical term which could be applied to the human posterior. This is considered an allusion to the shape of the island, which has a long, fairly deep depression running from south to north. The headland opposite Peel Island was called *Futharnoss*, an Old Norse compound which means 'headland of *Futh*', and this name spread to the whole peninsula.

Although Barrow has a Celtic first element, both Barrow and Furness testify to the presence of Norse speaking people, and there are many other names of Norse origin in Furness.

Barry (GLA, Wales): hill brook (*Barry* 1176–98, *Barri* 1186–92, *Barren* 13th cent., *Barrenam insulam* 13th cent., *Isle or Warren of Barre* 1510, *Barrye Island* 1610, *Aberbarrey* 1536–9, *Barry Island* 1666–7). Welsh *barren* is probably a derivative of *barr* 'rise, summit', descriptive of the site of Barry, and used for the brook name. The narrow channel between the island and the mainland was probably called *Aberbarri* (Welsh *aber* 'mouth' and river-name

Barri). The town is on hilly ground rising from the channel, and owes its importance to the docks which were built as a result of industrial expansion in the hinterland. The current Welsh forms are *Y Barri* for the town, and *Ynys y Barri* for the island. Both forms contain the definite article *y*, presumably by analogy with such names as *Y Bala*, *Y Bermo*, q.v.

Basildon (ESX, England): Beorhtel's hill (*Berlesdune* 1086, *Berdlesdon* 1176, *Bartelisdon* 1247, *Bastelden* 1510, *Basseldon* 1594). The 100-foot contour surrounds the place, and the land inside this was doubtless regarded as a hill in this marshy region by the Thames estuary. A number of other places in the vicinity, such as Horndon, Ockendon and Laindon, occupy similar sites and also have names in *-dūn*. The identity of Beorhtel is a problem similar to those discussed in the *Introduction*, p. 19.

The form of the name has undergone a great deal of alteration. The change of *-e-* to *-a-* is a normal feature of Essex dialect. In addition to this, the *-r-* has been lost and it looks as if a process akin to metathesis (see Birmingham) has caused the *-s-* to change its position, then *Bastelden* has become *Basseldon* by assimilation of *-t-* to *-s-*.

Basingstoke (HMP, England): outlying hamlet belonging to Basing (*Basingastoc* 990). Basing, about two miles east of Basingstoke, is a name of the same type as Barking (see *Introduction*, p. 16), and means 'Basa's people'. Old English *stoc*, meaning 'place', which has been added to the genitive of *Basingas*, is

probably the most colourless habitation term in the place-name-forming vocabulary. It may originally have meant 'secondary settlement, component part of a large estate'. Basingstoke perhaps started as a hamlet dependent on Basing, but in spite of this humble beginning it had developed into an independent place by 1086, the date of the Domesday survey. It was by that time the meeting-place of the Hundred of Basingstoke, in which both places were situated, and the survey states that 'it was always a royal manor'.

Bath (SOM, England): the baths (*Bathum* 796). The name refers to the Roman baths, the ruins of which made a great impression on the Anglo-Saxons, who obtained possession of the city in the year 577. There is an Anglo-Saxon poem known as *The Ruin*, which almost certainly refers to Bath, since it includes the statements 'stone courts stood here; the stream with its great gush sprang forth hotly; the wall enclosed all within its bright bosom; there the baths were hot in its centre.' Bath is called *Hat Bathu* 'hot baths' in a charter which purports to date from 676, but which may be a later forgery.

Bathgate (WLO, Scotland): Boar wood (*Batket* 1153–65, *Batchet* 1163–73, *Bathcat* 1164, *Bathgat* 1369–70). A pre-Gaelic Celtic name, presumably of Cumbric origin. The closest cognates of the two elements involved are Welsh *baedd* 'boar' and *coed* 'wood'; an earlier form of the latter would have been **cēto-n*. See *Betws-y-coed*, Wales.

Batley (YOW, England): Bata's forest-clearing (*Bathelie* 1086). This is a name of the same type as Barnsley. Names in *-ley* and *-wood* are very frequent in this district south of Leeds, which must have been heavily forested.

Beaconsfield (BUC, England): open land of the beacon (*Bekenesfelde* 1184). There is a Beacon Hill in Penn which, although it is three miles away, could be the site of the signal-fire from which Beaconsfield is named. The town is overlooked by higher ground to the north and west, so is not itself a likely position for a beacon. The ending *-field* denotes a stretch of uncultivated country, and this may have extended westward as far as the higher ground at Penn.

Bearsden (DNB, Scotland): this name has so far eluded all satisfactory explanation.

Beaufort (MON, Wales): this industrial town dates from about 1780 when a lease was granted to an iron-master called Edward Kendall. The settlement was at first known as *Cendl* (a Welsh spelling of *Kendall*), until it was superseded by *Beaufort*, the family name of the landowner, the Duke of Beaufort. The place was originally in the parish of Llangatwg in Breconshire, but was transferred to Monmouthshire in 1894.

Beaumaris (AGL, Wales): beautiful marsh (*Bello Marisco* 1284, *Beaumaris* 1296, *Beaumareys* 1301, *Beaumarres* 1370, *Bewemarras* 1489, *Bewmaris* 1610, *Duwmares* 16th cent., *duw Mares* 16th cent., *Bewmares* 1612). Norman French *beau marais* 'fair marsh', from its low-lying situation on the banks of the Menai Straits. The town received its charter in 1296

when the castle was completed. Local Welsh pronunciation is *Biwmaris*. The sixteenth-century forms show a substitution of *Duw* (Welsh 'God') for *Biw*.

The older Welsh name may have been *Carreg* or *Cerrig y Gwyddyl* 'The rock(s) of the Irishmen' (*Carrikuthel* 1352, *carrek Wythell* 1449, *kerryk gwythell* 1479, *Cerrig y gwyddel* 1562, *Kerrig gwythyl* 1590).

Bebington (CHE, England): estate associated with someone named Bebbe (*Bebington c.* 1100). This is a name of the same type as Addington (see *Introduction*, p. 18). Names in which *tūn* is associated with a personal name are particularly common in the Wirral.

Beddgelert (CRN, Wales): grave of Celert (Cilart) (*Bekelert* 1258, *Bedkelerd* 1269, *Bedkelert* 1281, *Bethkelert* 1286, *Berthkelert* 1487, *Bethkilhart* 1561, *bedd kelert* 1566, *Bethgelert* 16th cent., *Bethgelert* 1688, *Bethgelert* 1778, *Beddgelert* 1791). Welsh *bedd* 'grave' and the (?) Irish personal name *Celert*, *Cilert*. Forms in *Gelert* do not appear until the sixteenth century, and they are obviously influenced by the legend of Gelert, the hound of Llywelyn, Prince of Wales. This is an international folk tale which relates how a prince leaves his baby son in charge of a hound. On his return the prince finds an empty bloody cradle, and slays the hound. The baby is then found alive and well together with the body of a wolf (or snake) which the hound had killed in defending the baby. It is said that David Prichard, the landlord of the Royal Goat Hotel, towards the end of the eighteenth century caused a

43

stone to be raised commemorating the story of Gelert. This reinforced the popular notion that Gelert was connected with Beddcelert (Beddgelert).

Bedford (BDF, England): Bīeda's ford (*Bedanford* 880, *Bydanford c.* 1000). Roads from all directions converge on Bedford, where the river-crossing must have been an important one. The association of such a river-crossing with a personal name is surprising; possibly a settlement which might have been known as *Bedantūn* or *Bedanhām* became *Bedanford* because the ford was so well-known a feature.

The battle in 571 between the West Saxons and the British (see Aylesbury) was fought at a place called *Bedcanforda*. The tempting identification of *Bedcanforda* with Bedford was made by an Anglo-Saxon historian in the tenth century, and has been followed by many modern writers. This identification has not been, and cannot be, accepted by philologists, and the refusal of some archaeologists to abandon it illustrates the unfortunate estrangement between linguistic and archaeological studies of the Dark Ages which characterised the post-war period.

Beeston (NTT, England): bent-grass farm (*Bestune* 1086). Beeston is one of the thick fringe of names in *-ton* which borders the River Trent in Nottinghamshire, Derbyshire, and east Staffordshire. Bent-grass is referred to in a considerable number of place-names, more commonly by the word *beonet* (modern *bent*) than by *bēos*, as in Beeston. *bēos* is fairly common, however, and there

are four examples of Beeston in Norfolk and one in Staffordshire, as well as the present one. Bent-grass is good thatching material, and this is probably why its presence seemed a noteworthy feature.

Belper (DRB, England): beautiful retreat (*Beurepeir* 1231). This is a French name, of the same type as Belasis, Bellasis, Bellasize, Belsize ('beautiful seat'), and Beaulieu ('beautiful place'). Beaurepaire HMP is identical with Belper. These names were given after the Norman Conquest by the members of the new Norman aristocracy to their new estates. They resemble modern house-names, and are quite different from most pre-Conquest names, which became current among the inhabitants of the countryside by some process of mutual agreement about the distinguishing feature of a place. The French names are mostly boastful. Occasionally, as in Montgomery, the name of a Continental place is used, the parallel with modern house-naming being here very apparent.

Bellshill (LAN, Scotland): unexplained. The forerunner appears to be a farm *Belziehill* or *Balzie Hill*. For the first element, development from Gaelic *baile* 'settlement' has been claimed but this is not easily substantiated.

Berkhamsted (HRT, England): homestead on or near a hill (*Beorhðanstædæ c.* 975, *Beorhhamstede* 1066). The modern town of Berkhamsted is in a river-valley between hills. Names in *-hāmstede* are rather common in Hertfordshire.

Bermo, Y (MER, Wales), see *Barmouth*.

Berwick-upon-Tweed (NTB, England): grange on the River Tweed (*Berwic* 1095, *Berewic* 1130–3, *Berewyc* 1153–9, *Berewich* 1167, *Berewicum super Twedam* 1229). Berwick is a common place-name, but unusual as the name of a place which became a town. Literally it means 'barley farm', and in the Domesday Survey it is used as a common noun to denote small settlements dependent on a larger one. The name implies that a place was once organised so as to contribute to the upkeep of a larger unit, but in spite of this implied humble origin Berwick had become an important borough by the middle of the twelfth century. Tweed is a pre-English river-name.

Bethesda (CRN, Wales): chapel name —*Bethesda* 1838. This is the Biblical name of the Calvinistic Methodist Chapel established in 1820, on a site formerly known as *Y Wern Uchaf* 'upper marshland'. The progress of Welsh Nonconformity, particularly in the nineteenth century, led to the establishment of many chapels which gave their names to the hamlets and villages which developed around them. Thus we find such names as *Saron, Cesarea, Nebo, Carmel*, etc.

Betws-y-coed (CRN, Wales): prayer house in the wood (*Betus* 1254, *Betws* 1284, *Bettus* 1352, *o vetws y koed* 1545, *Ll.V'el y bettws* 1566, *Bettus Seyrion Ython* [= Betws Wyrion Iddon] 17th cent., *Bettws y Coed* 1727, *Llanvihangell Bettus* 1722). Welsh *betws* from Middle English *bed-hūs* 'oratory'. The distinguishing elements are Welsh *y Coed* 'the wood', *Llanfihangel* (Welsh *llan*

'church' and *Mihangel* 'Michael'), and *Wyrion Iddon* 'descendants of Iddon'. In 1352 three 'stocks' or family groupings are given under Betws. The legal term for these in Welsh was *gwely*, literally 'bed', metaphorically 'stock'. The three *gwely* in question were *Gwely Iorwerth ab Iddon, Gwely Griffri ab Iddon*, and *Gwely Cynwrig ab Iddon* 'stock of Iorwerth son of Iddon, Griffri son of Iddon, and Cynwrig son of Iddon'. The descendants from the common ancestor Iddon were called *wyrion* (literally 'grandsons'), and these held certain rights in the church. A similar name is seen in *Betws Wyrion Gwgon*, an alias of Betws-yn-Rhos in Denbighshire.

Beverley (YOE, England): beaver stream (*Beferlic* c. 1000, *Beoferlic* c. 1150, *Beuerlea* 1190). The final element, which is a word for a stream only recorded in this place-name, has been confused with the common ending *lēah*. The name is presumed to have referred originally to Beverley Beck.

Bexhill-on-Sea (SSX, England): box-tree wood (*bexleu* 772, *Bixel* 1278, *Byxhell* 1496). The second element is *lēah*, which has been confused with -*hill*. Bexley has the same origin. The early meaning of *lēah* is 'wood', and although there are many names in which it means 'clearing', and some in which it means 'pasture', 'wood' seems the best translation when it is combined with a tree-name. It is thought that the common box may be native in the chalk hills of the south of England.

Biddulph (STF, England): (place) by the digging (*Bidulf* 1086). The reference may be to early stone quarries. The use of a preposition (*by* in this instance) as first element of a place-name is well-evidenced, though not very common. A similar formation is found in *Twynham*, the earlier name of Christchurch.

Bideford (DEV, England): (?) ford by the stream called *Byd* (*Bediford* 1086, *Budiford* 1232). There was a river-name *Bȳd*, possibly of Celtic origin, surviving in the form Boyd in Gloucestershire. In the first element of Bideford we may have another instance of this river-name, to which was added Old English *ie*, dative of *ēa* 'river'. The resulting compound (*Bȳdīe*) would be the name of the stream which joins the Torridge at Bideford. Bidford on Avon WAR has similar early spellings.

Billericay (ESX, England): a medieval Latin term for a dyehouse or tan-house (*Byllyrica* 1291, *Billerica* 1342). There are two other examples besides the Essex name: a lost *Billerica* in Lympne KNT and Bellerica Farm in Witham Friary SOM.

Billingham (DRH, England): (?) village at the place called Billing (*Billingham c.* 1050, *Billingaham* 1085, *Billingeham* 1203). A first element *Billing* occurs in a number of place-names, including Billington LNC, Billingsley HRE, Billingshurst SSX. There are hills called Billing Hill in the West Riding of Yorkshire, Billinge Hill in Cheshire and Lancashire; and an Old English hill-name *Billing*, containing *bill* 'sword', has been inferred from these. Billingham is not on or near a prominent hill, but it is on the edge of a large

tract of marsh, and the site may have been thought of as a promontory of firm ground, and so have been given a name normally applied to hills. The alternative would be to consider Billingham a name of the same type as Altrincham, with a personal name *Billa* as first element. This would give an etymology 'village of the followers of Billa' (see Introduction, pp. 16–18), but without the special development of *-ing-* seen in Altrincham and Birmingham.

Bingley (YOW, England): forest-clearing of the people of Bynna (*Bingelei* 1086) see *Introduction*, pp. 16 and 26. Place-names with a personal name followed by *-inga-* most frequently have *hām* as the final element, but the type occurs sporadically with other suffixes. Bingley is one of a cluster of names in *-ley*, which includes Keighley and Shipley.

Birkenhead (CHE, England): headland overgrown with birch-trees (*Birkened c.* 1150). The headland may have been Bidston Hill. *Birken-* (instead of *Birchen-*) is due to Old Norse influence; there are a number of Norse names in the Wirral.

Birmingham (WAR, England): village of the family or followers of Beorma (*Bermingeham* 1086, *Brumingeham* 1189, *Bermincham* 1245, *Brymedgham* 1537, *Birmingham vulgo Bromwichham* 1675). This is a name of the same type as Altrincham, and the local pronunciation (Brummagem) preserves the significant soft *-g-* which distinguishes these names from those of the type Gillingham (see *Introduction*, p. 17). The form Brummagem also displays the linguistic phenomenon known as metathesis, which has caused *Burm-* to become *Brum-*. In the sixteenth and seventeenth centuries the name was sometimes written *Bromwicham*, from association with the neighbouring place-name Bromwich.

Bishop Auckland (DRH, England): (?) the cliff on the river *Clyde* (*Alclit c.* 1050, *Aucland* 1254). The earliest spellings suggest that this name is identical with *Al-clut*, an earlier name of Dumbarton in Scotland, which is a British place-name, meaning 'the rock on the Clyde'. The Durham name applies not only to Bishop Auckland, but to Auckland St Andrew and St Helen, and West Auckland, about two miles away. All the places are on a river now called Gaunless; this is an Old Norse name, meaning 'useless', which cannot be older than the Norse invasions of the late ninth century, and may have replaced an earlier British river-name, Clyde. This seems to be more reasonable than the suggestion that *Alclit* was transferred from Scotland. See Dumbarton.

The change from *Alclit* to *Aucland* is due to association of the name with Old Norse *aukland* 'additional land'. The Bishop is the Bishop of Durham, whose Castle is a notable feature of the town.

Bishopbriggs (LAN, Scotland): (?) The bishop's bridge (*Bishop Bridge* 1665, *Bishop brigs* 1666). It is thought by some that the second element is not Scots *brig* 'bridge' but *rigg(s)* 'a field, etc.'. More detailed local information and better documentation is required to come to a definite conclusion.

Bishop's Stortford (HRT, England): ford of the tongues of land (*Storteford* 1086, *Sterteford* 1198). The river-name Stort is technically known as a 'back-formation', which means that it arose from a feeling that Stortford should be on a river called Stort; see Cambridge. The word *steort*, which means 'tail', occurs fairly frequently in place-names, and study of the topography of some of the places so named suggests that the meaning varied, but was sometimes 'tongue of land between two streams' or (as in the case of Start Point DEV) 'narrow promontory'. Streams from all directions flow into the Stort in the vicinity of Bishop's Stortford, and a number of 'tails' are thus formed, so that the genitive plural of the first element is quite appropriate. *Bishop's* records ownership by the Bishop of London.

Blackburn (LNC, England): (place by the) black brook (*Blacheburne* 1086). The stream in question, a tributary of the Darwen, is now called the Blackwater. A reference to dark-coloured water is quite frequent in river-names, see Douglas. Old English *burna* is fairly common in the south and north of England, but rare in much of the Midlands. It is frequently qualified, as here, by a word describing the stream.

Blackpool (LNC, England): black pool (*Pul c.* 1260, *Lepoole, commonly called Black-poole* 1637). The small settlement which preceded the town was named from a peaty-coloured pool of water about half a mile from the sea, which had been turned into meadowland by 1788. The stream into which the pool discharged now forms the main sewer.

Blaenau (MON, Wales): uplands (*Blayne Gwent* 1594, *Blaeneu Gwent c.* 1700). Welsh *blaenau*, pl. of *blaen* 'source, upper reaches, uplands', and *Gwent*, a cantref name approximating to the modern Monmouthshire. The tribal centre of the British tribe of the Silures was at *Venta Silurum*, where *Venta* is a Romano-British form for the later Welsh *gwent* 'field' > 'market-place'. *Gwent* became the name for a native Welsh kingdom, divided into *Gwent Is Coed* 'Gwent on this side of the forest' and *Gwent Uwch Coed* 'Gwent the other side of the forest'. The name survives in *Caer-went* and *Cas-gwent* (Chepstow), q.v. *Blaenau* is used in Welsh for 'uplands' as distinct from 'lowlands' (*bro*), cf. *Blaenau Morgannwg* 'uplands of Glamorgan' and *Bro Morgannwg* 'Vale of Glamorgan'. *Blaina* is a poor spelling for the dialect *Blaenau*.

Blaenau, like Nant-y-glo (q.v.) grew as a result of industrial development in the nineteenth century out of the old parish of *Aberystruth* 'mouth of the brook Ystrwyth' (*Aberstrewyth* 1391, *Aberystrwyth Blaeney Gwent* 1590, *Aberustuth* 1558, *Aberustroithe* 1581, *Aberystroyth* 1619, *Aberustruth* 1705). Welsh *aber* 'mouth, confluence' + *Ystrwyth* (pers. name < Latin *instructus*). The *Ystrwyth* brook flows into the River Ebwy Fach at Aberystruth. Documentary forms often show confusion with *Aberystwyth* CRD.

Blaenau Ffestiniog (MER, Wales): uplands of Ffestiniog (*Festynyok* 1419–20, *Ffestiniok* 1479, *Ffestiniog* 1508, *Ffestiniog* 1590). Blaenau Ffestiniog is some two miles higher up than Ffestiniog and owes its growth to the slate-quarrying industry of the nineteenth century. Welsh *blaenau* 'headwaters, uplands' (see *Blaenau* MON) + *ffestiniog* 'defensive position, stronghold' < *ffestin* 'defence' + adjective suffix *-iog*, or possibly 'territory of Ffestin (pers. name). Cf., Gaulish *Festiniacum* > *Festigny* (France).

Blaina (MON, Wales): see *Blaenau*.

Blairgowrie (PER, Scotland): the plain in Gowrie (*parva* and *magna Blar* 1235, *Blare* 13th cent., *Blair in Gowrie* 1604). Locally just known as *Blair*, its official designation distinguishes it from Blair Atholl, which is sufficiently close to be confused with it. Gaelic *blàr* means 'a field or plain', and Gowrie (*Gouerin* 1165, *Goverine* 1306) reflects an old territorial name derived from the sixth-century Gaelic king of Dal Riata, Gabran, who in Welsh genealogies appears as *Gafran*. In a poem by Taliesin this is the name given to a district in Scotland, undoubtedly our Gowrie. Parallels in this respect would be Kyle, Cowal, Lorne, and Angus which all derive from personal names of similar antiquity.

Blantyre (LAN, Scotland): unexplained (*Blantir* 1289, *Blanntyre* 1368–9, *Blantire* 1426). There is a possibility that the second element is Gaelic *tir* 'land'.

Blaydon (DRH, England): (?) (place by) the River *Bladon* (*Bladon* 1340). Usually rendered 'black hill', from Old Norse *blár* and Old English *dūn*; but this hybrid formation is not altogether convincing in an area where Norse names are very rare. If the second element is *dūn*, the reference is to the hill south-west of Blaydon, on which the town of Winlaton stands. Possibly, however, Blaydon is a river-name, identical with Bladon in Oxfordshire. There is a small tributary of the Tyne here, now called Barlow Burn from a place named Barlow higher up its course. On this, at a distance of one and a half miles from the town of Blaydon, is a hamlet called Blaydon Burn, and it is possible that the name originally denoted this stream. The river-name is unexplained.

Bletchley (BUC, England): Blecca's forest-clearing (*Blechelai c.* 1108). This is a name of the same type as Barnsley. Bletchley is near Whaddon Chase, which was a heavily wooded area.

Blyth (NTB, England): the gentle one (*Blida* 1130). This is a river-name, of Old English origin, other examples of which occur elsewhere in England. The Northumberland River Blyth is about 11 miles long, and the town is situated at its mouth. In 1236 and 1250 it was called *Blithmuth, Blithemuth,* '(place at) the mouth of the Blyth'. Compare the relationship between Nairn and Invernairn NAI.

Bognor Regis (SSX, England): coast belonging to a woman named Bucge (*Bucgan ora c.* 975). Regis was added in 1929, to commemorate the residence of George V, while convalescing after a serious illness.

Old English *ōra* is an element only found in the southern half of England. It is cognate with Latin *os,* 'mouth'; and the Germanic stem shares with the Latin one the semantic development which results in a meaning 'shore' (Latin *ora*). Some Scandinavian cognates mean 'estuary'. The sense 'river-bank' is well evidenced in English place-names (see Windsor); and the English word also developed a meaning 'hill-slope' (possibly arising from the idea of land sloping down to a coast or river), in which sense it is used in place-names which have no connection with rivers or the sea, as, for instance, in the Chilterns, where it is the final element of the Oxfordshire names Stonor, Chinnor, Lewknor.

Although 'coast' may be one of its earliest meanings, *ōra* is not common in coastal names. Bognor is one of a small group in West Sussex, the adjacent part of Hampshire, and the Isle of Wight. Other examples in this area are Ower HMP, Bouldnor IOW, Itchenor SSX, and the lost *Cymenes ōra* where, according to the Anglo-Saxon Chronicle, the South Saxons landed in 477. It is difficult to say why the shore seemed a definitive feature of these settlements, as their situations appear similar to those of neighbouring coastal settlements, in whose names *ōra* is not used. Perhaps the reference was to a settlement where boats habitually put in, so that the shore seemed the most important aspect of the place to the people of the surrounding countryside. Some special circumstance of this kind might mean that the personality of the land-owner was temporarily important, so that a personal name became the first element of the place-name. Ekwall postulates a meaning 'firm foreshore or gravelly landing-place', possibly on account of the names

Cymenes ora and *Cerdices ora,* where the ancestors of the South Saxon and West Saxon royal families are said to have landed. Following this train of thought, it might be argued that Itchenor was the landing-place of the followers of a chieftain called Icca; but the historical records of the settlement give no grounds for thinking that a woman could have played a leading part in the first landings, and such an explanation is not therefore satisfactory for Bognor, which contains a feminine personal name. It seems necessary to think of Bucge as a landowner.

Bolton (LNC, England): settlement with a special building (*Boelton* 1185, *Bothelton* 1212). This name occurs in the English counties of LNC(4), YOW(5), YOE, YON(4), WML, CMB(2) and NTB, and there is one Scottish example, in ELO. It seems clear that *bōthl-tūn* was a place-name-forming compound only in use north of a line from the Mersey to the Humber. Old English *bōthl*, which is the first part of the compound, is discussed under Bootle.

Bo'ness (WLO, Scotland): the point of Borrowstoun. This was originally called Ness (*Nes* 1494) and later Borrowstounness (*Burnstounnes* 1532) after the nearby farm of Borrowstoun (*Berwardeston* 1335–6) which means either 'Beornweard's farm' or 'bearkeeper's farm'. To-day the shortened version Bo'ness is always used in everyday speech.

Bonnybridge (STL, Scotland): bridge on the River Bonny (which is *aquae de Boine* in 1682). This appears to be a fairly late name, not more than 200 years old, connected with the rise of industry in the area. The meaning is clearly a literal one.

Bonnyrigg (MLO, Scotland): the ridge or field shaped like a *bannock* (*Bannockrig* 1773). This is a geographical name or field-name which gave rise to a settlement name at a fairly late date, probably when a name for a colliery village was required. However, even the late eighteenth-century form shows that the first element is not *bonny* as in so many other Scottish place-names but *bannock* 'a thick, round, flat cake' (usually of oatmeal). As a small burgh, Bonnyrigg and Lasswade were united in 1929; Lasswade (*Laswade* 1148, *Lesswade c.* 1150) is a compound of *lǣswe*, genitive of Old English *lǣs* 'pasture' and (*ge*)*wǣd* 'ford', the whole name meaning 'pasture ford', with reference to its situation on the river North Esk.

Bootle (LNC, England): special building (*Boltelai* 1086, *Botle* 1212). This is an uncompounded use of the word which is the first element of Bolton. There are three variants: *bōthl* (as in Bolton and in Bothel CMB), *bōtl* (as in Bootle and in Newbottle DRH etc.) and *bold* (as in Bold LNC, SHR, Newbold CHE, etc.). Study of the whole corpus of names containing the various forms of this term suggests that it denoted a building of exceptional size and importance; and the large number of examples in England and Scotland in which *bōtl* and *bold* are qualified by 'new' suggests that such buildings belong to the later part of the Anglo-Saxon period. One of the Scottish examples of this compound has the modern form Newbattle.

Boston (LIN, England): Botwulf's stone (*Botuluestan* 1130). This name has been considered to refer to St Botulf, who, in the mid-seventh century, built a monastery at a lost place in East Anglia called *Icanho*. *Icanho* is sometimes said to be an earlier name of Boston, but this is not possible as *Icanho* was in East Anglia, and Boston is in the territory occupied by the Middle Angles. In fact there is no firm reason why the Botwulf whose name occurs in Boston should be identical with the East Anglian saint; for discussion of a similar problem see Oswestry. *stān* is combined with a personal name in a number of place-names, including Allerston YON, Axton KNT, Aylstone HRE, Brixton SUR, Cuddlestone STF, Keston KNT, Keystone HRE, Tilston CHE, so this is not an exceptional type of name. In the present instance, and in Guthlaxton LEI, the personal name has been considered to be that of a saint, the implication being that this was a stone at which the saint once preached. The Botwulf and Guthlac of these names could well be ordinary landowners, however, and the reference may have been to a stone marking the boundary of an estate belonging to the individual mentioned. A number of these names (Axton, Brixton, Cuddlestone, and Guthlaxton) are the names of hundredal divisions, and here it seems possible that the stone was used to mark the meeting-place of the 'hundred'.

Bournemouth (HMP, England): mouth of the stream (*La Bournemowthe* 1407). The small stream can be seen on the one-inch map, running through the centre of the town. The first recorded mention of Bournemouth does not occur until 1407, but place-names containing *burna* are usually regarded as dating from an early stage of the Anglo-Saxon settlement (see Burnham RUC).

Bracknell (BRK, England): Bracca's corner of land (*braccan heal* 942). The second element is *healh*, the Kentish and West Saxon form of *halh*, which is discussed under Arnold, where it is translated 'valley'. Bracknell, however, is not in a valley, but on a raised spur of land. A distinctive feature of its situation is that it occupies the south-west corner of the parish of Warfield, and it may be one of a group of names in which *healh* refers to land in a projecting corner of a parish. This meaning is well evidenced in the neighbouring part of Surrey, instances being Broom Hall near Bagshot, Portnall south of Egham, and Michen Hall, which occupies a projecting corner of the parish of Godalming.

Bradford (YOW, England): broad ford (*Bradeford* 1086). The ford was presumably a crossing-place on Bradford Beck, in the centre of the present town. The place-name is a fairly common one.

Braintree (ESX, England): Branca's tree (*Branchetreu* 1086, *Brantre* 1472, *Braintree c.* 1490). Braintree belongs to a class of place-names in which the word 'tree' is associated with a personal name in the genitive (possessive) case. Other examples in this volume are Coventry, Elstree, and Oswestry. This type of name presents problems similar to those discussed under Boston, in which a personal

51

name is combined with the word 'stone'. As with four of the names in that category, some names of the same type as Braintree refer to 'hundred' meeting-places; these include Culliford Tree DOR, Doddingtree WOR, Toltingtrough KNT, Wixamtree BDF. The reference is probably in most cases to a prominent tree, and the personal name that of the owner of the estate on which it grew; but *trēow* is also used in Old English of the cross, and these names could refer to a cross erected by the man whose name is the first part of the place-name. Interpretation is especially difficult when the personal name could be᾽ that of a saint, as in Oswestry.

The development to *Brain-* is abnormal, and may have been influenced by the alternative name, *Magna Reines*, by which Braintree was sometimes known from 1202 till 1441. *Magna* was for distinction from the other settlements still known as Rayne, two miles west. The etymology of this is uncertain. The name of the River Brain is a 'back formation' (see Bishop's Stortford).

Bramhall (CHE, England): rivermeadow where broom grows (*Bramale* 1086). Old English *brōm* often becomes Bram- or Bramp- in placenames. In this area *halh* (which is discussed under Arnold) frequently refers to a piece of low-lying land by a river, as does its modern derivative *haugh*. This meaning probably arose from the sense 'a piece of land almost enclosed by the bend of a river', which was one aspect of the original meaning 'nook or corner of land'. The sense-development is

similar to that of *hamm*, discussed under Buckingham.

Brechin (ANG, Scotland): from an early Celtic personal name *Brychan*, as seen in Brecon (Wales), q.v. A genitive *Brec(h)ini* occurs in the Book of Deer, and is *Brechne* in the Pictish Chronicle. In the Book of Taliesin, the district is called *Brecheiniawc* which again parallels the Welsh name.

Brecon (BRE, Wales): land of Brychan (*Brecheniauc* 1100, *Brechennio* 1230, *Brechonie* 1276, *Brecknock* 1321, *Bregnok* 1322, *Breghnoc* 1409, *Brecon* 1412, *Brecheinyawc*, *Brychein(n)yawc* 14th cent., *Brycheinioc* 15th cent., *Brecknock* 1547). Welsh personal name *Brychan* + territorial suffix *-iog*. Brychan was the ruler of a district in the mid-fifth century, and the kingdom was later called *Brycheiniog* after him. This name gradually became *Brecknock* in English. The name of the town of *Brecon* seems to be an anglicisation of *Brychan*.

The Welsh name of the town is Aberhonddu—'mouth of the River Honddu'—(*Aberhotheni* 1191, *Aberhodni* 14th cent., *Aber Hoddni* 15th cent., *Aberhodni* 1566, *Aberhonddi* c. 1700. The river is *Hotheni* 1191, *Hodni* 1350–1450, *The Hotheney* 1387, *Hothny* 1465, *Honddye* 1536–9, *Honddi* c. 1700). Welsh *aber* 'mouth, confluence' + *Honddu* from an earlier *Hoddni*, a derivative from *hawdd* 'pleasant, quiet'. In the later form Honddu there has been metathesis of *-ddn-* > *-ndd-* (cf. *Rhondda* s.n.), and *-ddu* has replaced *-ddi* under the influence of Welsh *du* 'black'. The River Honddu flows into Usk at Brecon.

52

Brentwood (ESX, England): burnt wood (*Bosco arso* 1176, *Boisars* 1226, *Brendewode* 1254). This is probably a name which arose after the Norman Conquest. The translation of the vernacular form into Latin (*Boscus ursus*) and French (*Boisars*) suggests that it was a meaningful name in the twelfth and thirteenth centuries, and may indicate that the remains of the conflagration were visible for a long time near the road from London to Chelmsford on which Brentwood is situated. Such translations would be made by government clerks, who would be unable to attach a meaning to most of the place-names they had to write down in the government records, so their ability to translate this one correctly may be significant.

Bridgend (GLA, Wales): end of the bridge (*Byrge End* 1535, *Brygend* 1542, *Brigend* 1578). Old English *brycg* 'bridge' + *ende* 'end'. The Welsh form is Pen-y-bont (ar Ogwr) —'end of the bridge over the River Ogwr'—(*Pennebont* 1536–9, *Pen y bont* 1612). Welsh *pen* 'end' + definite article *y* 'the' + *pont* 'bridge' + *ar* 'over' + river-name *Ogwr*. Ogwr is *Ocmur, ocuur* c. 1150, *Hoggemora* c. 1148, *Ugemor'* 1207, *Uggemore* c. 1250, *Ogemor* 1314, *Ogomore* 1406, *Ogor* 1476–7, *Ogmor* 1578, *Ogmour* 1631). Welsh *og-* 'sharp, keen' + obscure element *-mur*. The *-m-* remained in anglicised forms to give *Ogmore*, but Welsh forms developed as *Ogfwr > Ogwr*.

Bridgwater (SOM, England): bridge belonging to Walter (de Dowai) (*Brugie* 1086, *Brigewaltier* 1194). Roads from all directions converge on this crossing of the River Parret.

Bridgwater is one of several places in England which were originally called 'the bridge', but acquired distinctive additions after the Norman Conquest. The post-Conquest addition of an owner's name to distinguish a place from others of the same name is a common feature. In the case of Bridgwater, the addition is a Christian name; more commonly, it is a surname, see Melton Mowbray.

Bridlington (YOE, England): estate associated with Berhtel (*Bretlinton* 1086, *Bridelington* c. 1135, *Bridlington* 1197). This is a name of the same type as Addington.

Brierley Hill (STF, England): clearing where briars grow (*Brereley* 14th cent.). Brierley is one of a cluster of names in *-ley*, which bear witness to the forested nature of the country west of Birmingham when the English settled there. Dudley is another name in this group.

Brighouse (YOW, England): houses by the bridge (*Brighuses* 1240). This is an ancient crossing of the River Calder. The name probably dates from after the Norse settlements. *Brycg* is an English word, but is here pronounced in the Norse way. *hūs* is both English and Norse, but its use as a place-name element is largely Scandinavian.

Brighton (SSX, England): Beorhthelm's estate (*Bristelmestune* 1086, *Bricthelmeston* 1301, *Bryghteston* 1437, *Brighthelmston* 1816). The abbreviation Brighton did not come into common use until the early nineteenth century. For a full discussion of place-names of this type see the *Introduction*, p. 18.

53

Bristol (GLO, England): assembly place by the bridge (*Brycg stowe* late 11th cent., *Bristou* 1086, *Brestol* 1290). The change from *Bristow* to Bristol is due to Norman French influence. *stōw* means 'place', but in place-names it has been shown to have two main senses, 'place where people assembled' and 'religious place'. It is not possible to say with any certainty which meaning applies to Bristol, but 'assembly place' is perhaps more likely, because in connection with a 'religious place' the defining element is usually a saint's name (as in Bridestow DEV), a reference to God (as in Godstow OXF), the adjective 'holy' (as in Halstow DEV, KNT), or the word 'church' (as in Cheristow, Churchstow DEV).

The bridge was perhaps a forerunner of Bristol Bridge, which carried the main road south across the Floating Harbour, and is mentioned in records of the twelfth century.

Brixham (DEV, England): (?) Brioc's village (*Briseham* 1086, *Brisehamme* 1088, *Brixaham*, *Brixeham* 1143, *Brixham* 1242). The personal name Brioc is a Celtic one, found also in Brixton DEV.

It is impossible to say whether Brixham contains *hām* (see Amersham) or *hamm* (see Buckingham). *Hām* is not likely to occur in many names in Devon, on account of the relatively late date of the English settlement, but it cannot be ruled out, especially for Domesday manors like Brixham, and the single spelling with *-hamme* is not conclusive evidence against it. The site of Brixham does not fall with absolute precision within any of the topographical meanings which can be demonstrated to belong to *hamm*. A case could be made for *hamm* meaning 'promontory', on the grounds that the name might originally have applied to the promontory of Berry Head; or the stream which flows out through the town could have river-meadows, and the name contain *hamm* in that sense. A final decision is not possible in this case.

Broadstairs (KNT, England): broad stair (*Brodsteyr Lynch* 1434–5, *Brodestyr* 1479, *Brodestayer* 1505). The plural *stairs* was in use by the fourteenth century, so the absence of -s in the fifteenth-century spellings for Broadstairs may mean that only one stair was referred to, not a flight of them. It is impossible to say with certainty whether this was a natural or an artificial feature. The first reference has *hlinc* 'bank', added to the name, and it is perhaps possible that there was a natural bank here which bore an exceptional resemblance to a stair; but as *stæger* does not seem to be recorded in any other place-name in this sense, a man-made stair seems more likely. It is known that a gateway to the sea was built here in 1440, and the 'broad stair' may have been a slightly earlier work, connected with the development of the shore.

Bromborough (CHE, England): Bruna's fortified place (*Brunburg* 12th cent., *Brumburh* 1155, *Brunburh* 1214–22, *Broneburgh* 1260). This is a name of the same type as Aylesbury. Bromborough may be the site of the battle of *Brunanburh*, in A.D. 937, at which the English under King

54

Æthelstan defeated an invading army of Norsemen from Ireland, allied with the kings of Scotland and Strathclyde. The change from *Brun-* to *Brum-* was due to assimilation of *n* to *m* before *b*, and the development to Bromborough was doubtless helped by association with *brōm*, 'broom'; see Bromsgrove.

Bromsgrove (WOR, England): grove or thicket of a man named Brēme (*Bremesgrefan* 804, *Bremesgrave* 1086, *Bromesgrava* 1167). There was originally no connection between this name and Birmingham, though the proximity of Birmingham (earlier *Brumingeham*) and West Bromwich may have assisted the development to Bromsgrove, instead of the more normal *Brimsgrove* or *Bremsgrove*. The main cause, however, was probably association with the word *brōm* 'broom'. A lost place *Bremesburh*, which was fortified in 909 during the wars against the Danes, had the same first element, and may possibly have been near Bromsgrove.

Broxburn (WLO, Scotland): badger's stream (*Broxburne* 1638), from Old English *brocc* 'badger' and *burna* 'stream'. The older name is Easter Strathbrock, i.e. the eastern half of the barony of Strathbrock 'Badger's valley' (*Strathbroc* 1226), from Gaelic *srath* 'valley' and *broc* 'badger'.

Brynbuga (MON, Wales), see *Usk*.

Bryn-mawr (BRE, Wales): great hill (*Bryn-mawr* 1832). Welsh *bryn* 'hill', *mawr* 'big, great'. This is one of the industrial towns which mushroomed in the nineteenth century. The alternative name at first was Gwaun-helygen 'moorland of the willow-tree' (*Gwaun-helygen* 1832). Welsh *gwaun* 'moor' + *helygen* 'willow-tree'. But the ecclesiastical parish of Bryn-mawr was created within the parish of Llangatwg in 1872.

Buckhaven (FIF, Scotland): founded about 1555 (*Buckheven* 1605, *Buckhevin* 1618). The meaning seems to be literal.

Buckhurst Hill (ESX, England): wooded hill covered with beeches (*Bocherst* c. 1135, *Buckhurst alias Goldhurst* 1485). 'Wooded hill' seems the best translation of *hyrst* in this name, as there is a well-defined hill, and the alternative name, *Goldhurst* (which probably refers to the autumn colouring), suggests that the beech-trees were dense. In other names *hyrst* can mean simply 'hill' (see Chislehurst GTL) or 'wood'.

Buckie (BNF, Scotland): the Buck [River] (*Buky*, 1362, *Bukkie* 1580). Presumably from the name of the stream on which it stands, now called the Burn of Buckie. If this is correct, the underlying name would be *Bocaidh* from Gaelic *boc* 'buck'. There are quite a few rivers of this formation, based on Gaelic animal names.

Buckingham (BUC, England): land in a river-bend belonging to the family or followers of Bucca (*Buccingahamme* 918 Anglo-Saxon Chronicle). This is a name similar to Gillingham, but with *hamm* as a final element, instead of *hām*. Old English *hamm* is a word of which the significance is usually topographical. One of its commonest senses is 'land hemmed in by water or marsh' and in some place-names it refers to land enclosed by a loop in a river.

Buckingham and Evesham are excellent examples of this. In other names it means 'river-meadow', and this sense has survived in dialect. It is only found in the southern half of the country, and may have been a Saxon and Jutish word, not used by Anglian settlers.

It is not always possible to distinguish *hām* from *hamm*, and a certain amount of confusion between the two place-name endings is evidenced even in Old English texts. In the case of Buckingham, however, the earliest spelling and the nature of the site tell very strongly in favour of *hamm*. Unlike *hām*, *hamm* could be used without a defining element, and there are many instances of places called Ham, or Ham Farm, from this source.

Builth Wells (BRE, Wales): cowpasture (*Buelt* 10th cent., *Bueld* 1191, *Buelth* 1241, *Buheld* 1251, *Buelld* 1271, *Buelth* 1330, *Buellt* 1425, *Builte* 1603). Welsh *buellt* from British **bow-gelt*, i.e. Welsh *bu* 'cow' + Welsh *gellt*, later *gwellt* 'grass, pasture'. *Buellt* was originally a cantref name. The spelling *Builth* is a poor English pronunciation of *Buellt*. *Wells* was added in the nineteenth century when the town became famous for its chalybeate springs. The parish church was Welsh *Llanfair-ym-muallt*, and is now the Welsh name for the town (*Lanveyr* 1254, *Llanveir in Bueld* 1271, *Lanueir in Buelth* 1279, *Lanveyr'* 1291, *Lanveir in Buelt* 1317, *Llanvaire in Beelt* 1542, *Ll. fair y byellt* 1566. Welsh *llan* 'church' + *Mair* (Mary) + *yn* 'in' + *Buell*). The late form *Buallt* may have been influenced by Welsh *allt* 'hill'.

56

Burgess Hill (SSX, England): hill associated with a family named Burgeys (*Burges Hill* 1597). This is a medieval name, which did not originally refer to a settlement. The modern town grew up after the opening of the Brighton railway in 1846. A family surnamed *Burgeys* is known to have lived in Clayton in the late thirteenth and early fourteenth centuries, as John Burgeys appears in tax-lists in 1296, 1327, and 1332; and it is likely, though by no means certain, that Burgess Hill is named from this family.

Burnham (BUC, England): village by the stream (*Burneham* 1086, *Burnham* 1175). This compound, which occurs also in Essex and Norfolk, probably dates from an early stage of the Anglo-Saxon settlement, as both *burna* and *hām* went out of use before the settlement was complete. Burnham is on rising ground overlooking a flat area through which several small streams meander into the Thames. None of these streams passes near Burnham Church (which may be near the centre of the original settlement); but it is an area where the drainage is likely to have changed. The contours on the one-inch map suggest that a stream may once have flowed immediately to the west of the church and down to the Thames past Burnham Abbey. This is a more likely explanation than derivation from a personal name, as has been suggested.

Burnham-on-Sea (SOM, England): river-meadow near the stream (*Burnhamm c.* 880 King Alfred's Will). The *burna* is the River Brue, which flows into the estuary just south of the town. See Buckingham for a discussion of the final element. Names in *hamm* are common near Burnham, and for over 35 miles north, along the bank of the Severn estuary, as far as Ham in Berkeley GLO. In much of this strip the flat land by the Severn seems to consist entirely of river-meadows, and it is possible that in such districts, where a word for a river-meadow would hardly distinguish a site from neighbouring sites, a more specialised use of *hamm* is to be reckoned with. The word may have developed a meaning 'dry ground in a marsh'. This would be similar to the sense-development of Old Norse *holmr*, for which see Durham. The site of such a settlement as Burnham may have been determined by the presence of comparatively dry ground.

Burnley (LNC, England): forest clearing by the River Brun (*Brunlaia* 1124, *Brunley* 1154, *Burneley alias Brunley* 1533). The river-name is probably derived from Old English *brūn* 'brown'. Brownside and Brunshaw, near Burnley, are named from the same river.

Burntisland (FIF, Scotland): Burnt (is)land (*Bruntisland* 1530, *Brunteland* 1543, *Bruntiland* 1619, *Bruntyland* 1653). The first element must be the metathesised Scottish form *brunt* of the past participle *burnt*, and the other part of the compound is possibly the word *island*. It has been said that the name arose when fishers' huts were burnt on an islet east of the present harbour, but it is doubtful whether we know the precise event and the exact point in time which caused the name to be given. If *Brunteland* is any guide, the second element may simply be the word *land*, and reference might be intended to a way of clearing land for cultivation.

Burton-upon-Trent (STF, England): farm of the fortified place (*Byrtun* 1002, *Bertone* 1086, *Burton super Trente* 1234). Burton is a very common place-name, which in most cases derives from Old English *burh-tūn*. In a few cases, of which Burton-upon-Trent is one, it derives from *byrh-tūn*, *byrh* being the genitive of *burh*. For both compounds a number of translations are possible, and the meaning may not be the same in all cases. Study of the whole corpus has suggested, however, that all the 'fort settlements' referred to in places called Burton and Bourton (and in some instances of Broughton) might have been part of an early Anglo-Saxon defensive system. For a discussion of *burh* see Aylesbury.

Trent is a Celtic river-name which may mean 'the trespasser'. This would refer to flooding.

Bury (LNC, England): at the fortified place (*Biri* 1194, *Bury* c. 1190). This is the dative of the word *burh*, discussed under Aylesbury. In this case the date and nature of the fortification are entirely unknown.

Bury St Edmunds (SFK, England): town associated with St Edmund (*Sancte Eadmundes Byrig* 1038). St Edmund was a king of East Anglia who was killed in 869 by heathen Danish invaders, and who quickly became revered as a martyr. His relics were taken to a place called *Beadriceswyrth* ('Beaduric's enclosure') early in the tenth century, and a small monastic community established there to guard them. A charter of 945 granting land to this establishment describes the place as 'Bædricesworth, where St Edmund king and martyr rests in the body'. In the eleventh century, when the great Benedictine monastery had been founded, and the place had become an important ecclesiastical centre, the old name was replaced by *Byrig* or *Seynt Eadmundes biri*, *Sancte Eadmundes Byrig*, etc. Bury is from the dative of *burh*, used in the late sense 'town' which is discussed under Newbury. Peterborough has a similar history.

Bushey (HRT, England): (?) box enclosure (*Bissei* 1086, *Bisshe* 1199, *Bisheye* 1230, *Bussheye* 1330). This etymology assumes that the first element is **byxe* 'box-tree' (which is good fencing material), and that the Normans found *byx-gehæg* difficult to pronounce, and modified it to *Bissei*. Alternatively, the first element could be **bysc* 'bush, thicket', but this does not give such good sense with *gehæg* 'enclosure'. *gehæg* is fairly common in Hertfordshire, and occurs also in the name of the neighbouring settlement of Oxhey.

Bushey was alternatively known as *Hertesheved* ('hart's head') from 1291 to 1428, and sometimes by both names, as *Bissheyehertesheved* 1346, *Bissheye Herteshede* 1349. For this alternative name, see Gateshead.

Buxton (DRB, England): rocking stones (*Buchestanes* before 1108, *Buckstones* 1251). The name Buckstone occurs in Gloucestershire and Monmouthshire and in both these instances refers to a rocking stone. Such stones have not been located at Buxton, and no record of any has been found; but this is a likely region for such a feature. The source is an Old English **būg-stān* 'bowing stone'.

C

Caerdydd (GLA, Wales): see *Cardiff.*

Caerffili (Caerphilly) (GLA, Wales): fort of Ffili (*Kaerfili* 1271, *Kaerfilly* 1281, *Kaerphilly* 1314, *kaerffili* 14th cent.). Welsh *caer* 'fort' and the personal name *Ffili* of whom nothing is known. The town was the centre of the Welsh cantref of Senghennydd, and became a Norman stronghold. *Caerphilly* is a poor anglicised spelling.

Caerfyrddin (CRM, Wales), see *Carmarthen.*

Caergybi (AGL, Wales), see *Holyhead.*

Caerleon (MON, Wales): fort of the legions (*Cair Legeion guar Usic* (l. *Uisc*) *c*. 800, *Cairlion, civitas legionum c*. 1150, *Kaerleun* 1191, *Carliun* 1222, *Carleon* 1234, *Karliun* 1254, *Kerlyun* 1282, *Kaerlion* 1322, *kaer llion ar wysc* 14th cent., *kaer llion* 1566, *Caer-lleon ar wysc* 1612). Welsh *caer* 'fort' and *llion* (from Latin *legionum* 'of the legions'). This was the Roman fort of *Isca*, headquarters of the second Augustan Legion. *Caerleon* represents a stereotyped English pronunciation. The Welsh form is *Caerllïon-ar-Wysg. Ar Wysg* 'on Usk'. For *Isca* and *Wysg* see *Usk.*

Caernarfon (CRN, Wales): the fort in Arfon (*Kairarvon* 1191, *Kaer yn Arv58, Con 12aer in Aruon* 1269,

Kaerinaruon 1272, *Kaer in Arvon* 1284, *a chaer enarvon* 14th cent.). Welsh *caer* 'fort' + *yn* 'in' + *Arfon.* Arfon was the cantref which extended from Bangor to Yr Eifl and lay opposite Anglesey (Môn). Arfon = 'facing Anglesey' (*Aruon* 1269, *Aruan* 1284, *Aruon* 1304–5, *Arvon* 14th cent.).

Caernarfon was the site of the Roman station of Segontium (*Segontio* Roman period). The name of the station was taken from that of the river which developed in Welsh as *Saint* (*Seynt* 1284, *aquam Seynte* 1321, *Seynte* 1342, *Seiont flu* 1570, *Avon y Saint* 1584, *Seiont called now Avon y Sant* 1719). British **Segont-* < **sego-* 'strong, powerful' [the strong river']. *Caer* 'fort' was prefixed to this (*Caer Segcint* 9th cent., *Kaer Seint yn Aruon* 14th cent., *Kaer Seint* = *Kaer yn aruon* 1346). The forms *Seiont* are an incorrect 'antiquarian' restoration.

Caerphilly (GLA, Wales), see *Caerffili.*

Camberley (SUR, England): this is not an old place-name. A settlement which grew up by the military camp was called Cambridge Town after the Duke of Cambridge, who built the Staff College in 1862. This name was found to lead to confusion in the postal services, and was arbitrarily changed to Camberley.

Camborne (CRN, England): curved hill-slope (*Camberon* 1181, *Cambron* 1294, *Camborne* 1431). This is a Cornish name, referring to the hill called Camborne Beacon south of the town, which was called *Carne Camborne* in 1592, *Carn Camborne* in 1884.

Cambridge (CAM, England): bridge on the River Granta (*Grontabricc c.* 745, *Grantanbrycge c.* 925, *Cantebrigie* 1086, *Caumbrigge* 1348, *Cambrugge* 1378). The meaning of the river-name Granta is uncertain.

The change from *Grantanbrycg* to Cambridge is due partly to Norman difficulty in pronouncing *Gr-*. This became *Cr-*, then was further simplified to *C-*. The consonant group *-ntbr-* in *Cantbrige* was simplified to *-nbr-*, then *n* was assimilated to *m* before *b* (as happened in Bromborough). The river has been renamed Cam by the process of 'back-formation' (see Bishop's Stortford).

Some Old English sources, including the Venerable Bede, call the town *Grantacaestir*, *Granteceaster* 'Roman town on the River Granta'. This name was still used by some writers in the twelfth century.

Cambuslang (LAN, Scotland): bay of ships *Camboslanc* 1296, *Cameslong* 1319). From Gaelic *camas long*, i.e. *camas* 'bay, bend' and *long* 'ship'. The highest point to which the tide on the Clyde flows is approximately opposite Cambuslang.

Campbeltown (ARG, Scotland): under the date of 15 October 1667, the Register of the Great Seal records in a charter to Archibald, Earl of Argyle, Lord Kintyre, Campbell, and Lorne, a grant: 'erecting the said town of Lochead into a free burgh of barony, to be called the burgh of Campbeltown.' The Gaelic name for Campbeltown is still *Ceannloch* 'Lochend', or in full, *Ceann Loch Chille Chiarain* to-day, after the loch on which it stands (in English now also Campbeltown Loch).

Cannock (STF, England): small hill (*Chenet* 1086, *Chnoc c.* 1130, *Cnot* 1156, *Canot* 1157, *Canoc* 1198). The name may refer to Shoal Hill, north-west of the town. Cannock is usually said to be a Celtic name, on the basis of a form *Canuc*, which occurs in the boundaries of an Anglo-Saxon charter of A.D. 956. It is very doubtful, however, whether this charter can refer to land in Staffordshire. It is a grant of a small estate at an unidentified place called *Wudetun* (modern Wootton). The boundary marks include a chalk-pit, and from this, and the fact that the charter is preserved in the cartulary of Winchester Cathedral, it seems likely that the land in question was in the south, perhaps in Wiltshire or Hampshire. So the Old English spelling *Canuc* is not relevant to the etymology of Cannock. Cannock is probably Old English *cnocc* 'hillock', modified by Norman pronunciation. The Normans sometimes inserted a vowel between two consonants (see Shrewsbury), and the development of *Cnoc* to *Canoc* would be parallel to that of the name of King *Cnut*, which became *Canute*.

Canterbury (KNT, England): the town of the people of Kent (*Cantwaraburg c.* 900 Anglo-Saxon Chronicle). *Cantware* 'people of Kent', is formed from the name

Kent (which is Celtic, and probably means 'coastal district') and the Old English suffix *-ware* 'dwellers'. The Romano-British settlement here was called *Durovernum*, which is a Celtic name meaning 'alder swamp by the walled town'. This pre-English name was used by the Anglo-Saxons at least until the end of the ninth century, at which date it appears that *Dorubernia* and *Cantwaraburg* were interchangeable. The later name may be of comparatively late origin, and 'town' is a reasonable translation of *burh*.

Cardenden (FIF, Scotland): the hollow of (or near) Carden (*Cardenane*, *Cardenenie* 14th cent., *Cardwane* 1516). Nearby Cardenbarns has been formed similarly from the name Carden, still surviving in Carden Towers. Carden is the same as Welsh *Cardden* 'thicket' and occurs as a place-name element in Scotland almost exclusively north of the Forth-Clyde line, with an easterly distribution. *Den* is Old English *denu* 'hollow'.

Cardiff (GLA, Wales): fort on the River Taf (*Kairdif* 1106, *Kaerdif* 1191, *Kerdif* 1263, *Kaerdif* 1290, *Kerdyf* 1322, *kaerdyf* 14th cent., (*o*) *gaer dydd* 1566, *Caer Didd* 1698). Welsh *caer* 'fort' + genitive singular of *Taf* (river-name). In official documents and in English speech *Caerdyf* became *Cardiff* with the usual hardening of Welsh *f* (*v*) to *ff* (cf. *Taf* > *Taff*). In Welsh there was the common alternation of *f* (*v*) with *dd*, which resulted in *Caerdydd* (accent on second syllable).

The River Taf (*Taf* c. 1102, *Taf* c. 1170, *Taph* 1191, *Taaf* 1281, *Taaf* 1314, *Taphe River* 1536–9, *Taff*

1578). Welsh *taf* 'water, stream' < British **Tamos*, cf. *Tawe*.

The cathedral church of St Teilo is *Llandaf* 'church on the River Taf' (*Lanntaf* c. 1150, *Landaph* 1191, *Landath* 1254, *Llanndaf* 14th cent., *Ll.Daf* 1566). Welsh *llan* 'church' + *Taf* as above. The final *-f* had been hardened by the twelfth century in English speech, so that there is a doublet *Llandaf* (Welsh pronunciation), and *Landaff* (English pronunciation). *Llandaf* is probably a later compound than *Caerdyf*, *Caerdydd*, otherwise one might have expected **Llandyf* as a parallel form. The alternation of *-th* (= *dd*) and *-f* (= *v*) can be seen in 1254 (*Landath*).

Cardigan (CRD, Wales): land of Ceredig (*cereticiaun* 12th cent., 1191, *Kereticam regionem* 1191, *Kerdigan* 1194, *Keredigiawn* 1283, *Keredigyawn* 14th cent., *Kyredigiawn* 15th cent.). These earlier references are to the province of Ceredigion, i.e. the personal name Ceredig (5th cent.) with a territorial suffix *-ion*. During the thirteenth century the small commote of Is Coed Is Hirwern including the town of 'Cardigan' and the land to the east was known as Cardigan(shire) (*Cardegan* 1229, *Kardigan* 1230, *Kardigansyre* 1244, *Cardigan* 1250, *Kardiganshire* 1282). *Cardigan* as an anglicised form referred to this small portion of Ceredigion. In 1284 the larger 'shire' of Cardigan was established, containing most of the old Ceredigion (*Cardigan* 1285, *Cardygan* 1320). Cardigan was retained as the 'English' name of the town.

The Welsh name for the town is *Abertcifi* 'mouth of the River Teifi', originally applied to the estuary (*Aberteivi* 1191, *Aber Teifi* 14th cent., *Aberteiui* 14th cent., *Cardigan alias Abertive* 1448, *Aber teifi* 1566, *Aberteifi* 1612). The River Teifi (τονερόβιος [l. τονεγόβιος] 2nd cent., *Tebi c.* 1100, *Teibi* 11th cent., *Teiwi* 12th cent., *Teivi* 1301–2, *Teiui* 14th cent., *Teifi* 1460, *Tyue* 1536–9). Welsh origin obscure.

Carlisle (CMB, England): fortress called Luguvalio (*Luguvallo, Luguvalio* 4th cent. Antonine Itinerary, *Luel* 9th cent., *Luel, quod nunc Carleol apellatur c.* 1106, *Karlisle* 1318). The Romano-British name, *Luguvalio*, meant '(place) belonging to a man named Luguvallos'; see London. After the Roman period, Welsh *caer* 'fortified place' was prefixed to the old name, probably with reference to the walls round the Roman town.

Carluke (LAN, Scotland): fortification of (?) (*Carneluk* 1315, *Carluk* 1359). If the earliest spelling is anything to go by, the first element appears to be Gaelic *carn* 'cairn', rather than Welsh *caer* 'fortified house'. However, all other spellings have consistently *car-*, and thus it might be a pre-Gaelic name after all. The second element is obscure.

Carmarthen (CRM, Wales): fort near the sea (*Maridunum* Roman period, *kaer wyrtin* 12th cent., *Lann Toulidauc ig Cair Mirdin* 1130, *Kairmerdin urbs Merlini* 1191, *Caermerdin* 1229, *Kaermerden* 1234, *Carmarthen* 1309, *kaeruyrdin* 14th cent., *Kermerthyn* 1280, *kaer ferddin* 15th cent., *Kaer fyrddin* 1566, *Caer Firdhin* 1586). The Romano-British *Mari-dunum* 'sea-

fort' (Welsh *môr* 'sea', *din* 'fort') would produce *Myrddin* in Welsh. To this name was added tautologically the Welsh *caer* 'fort'. By the twelfth century the compound name had been wrongly analysed as *caer*+the personal name *Myrddin*, and identified with a warrior of the sixth century, who later became a legendary figure to whom were ascribed prophetic poems. Geoffrey of Monmouth latinised his name as *Merlinus* and drew him into the Arthurian Legend.

The original dedication of the church was to Teulyddog, cf. the form quoted under 1130 above. The parish church is now St Peters.

Carnoustie (ANG, Scotland): unexplained (*Donaldus Carnusy* 1493, *Carnowis* 1510, *Carneustie, Carnuysty* 1595, *Carnowstye* 1600). The first element could be Gaelic *cathair* or *carr*, or conceivably *carn*, in spite of the modern pronunciation. The second element is completely obscure.

Cas-gwent (MON, Wales), see *Chepstow*.

Casnewydd (MON, Wales), see *Newport*.

Castell-nedd (GLA, Wales), see *Neath*.

Castellnewydd Emlyn (CRM, Wales), see *Newcastle Emlyn*.

Castleford (YOW, England): ford by the Roman fort (*Ceaster forda* 948 Anglo-Saxon Chronicle, *Casterford c.* 1130, *Castleford* 1290). There is known to have been a Roman fort where the road called Roman Ridge crosses the River Aire. In spite of the spelling in the Chronicle, the local form of the name was probably *cæster-ford*, *cæster* being the northern form of Old English *ceaster* (discussed under Chester). The development to *C-* instead of *Ch-* may have been partly due to Norse influence. Later, *Caster-* was confused with Old French *castel* 'castle'.

Castletown (IOM): town round the castle (*villa castelli c.* 1370, *Castletown* 1511). The ancient castle here is called Castle Rushen. It was used as their headquarters by the Stanleys, who ruled the island in the fifteenth century; this would bring a large English-speaking element into the population, and the English name Castletown probably came into use at that period. It is impossible to say what vernacular name was Latinised to *villa castelli* in the bounds of monastic lands dating from about 1370; it could have been Norse or Gaelic.

Caterham (SUR, England): village by the hill called *Cadeir* (*Catheham* 1179, *Katerham* 1200). *Cadeir* is a Celtic place-name, from a word meaning 'chair'. This word is used in Welsh mountain-names, such as Cader Idris, perhaps to denote an eminence with a commanding view. In Caterham it presumably refers to the high ground south of the town. The British name must have been fairly widely known at the time of the English settlement, in order to be adopted by the newcomers. For names which are partly British and partly English, see Chatham and Cheadle.

Cedweli (CRM, Wales): land of Cadwal (*Cetgueli* 10th cent., *Chedveli* 1130, *Cedgueli c.* 1150, *Kedwely* 1191, *Kedwely* 1221, *Kedweli* 1250, *Kedwely* 1278, 1291, *Ketweli* 14th cent., *Kydwelly* 1458, *kydweli* 1566, *Cedwelli* 1612). Welsh personal name *Cadwal* + territorial suffix *-i*. This suffix *-i*, with others, was used to denote the territory inhabited by the descendants of the person named. The name was first applied to that area which became the commote of Cedweli, and then to the town of Cedweli. Popular etymology has incorrectly analysed the form as *-gwely* (Welsh *gwely* 'bed'), c.f. Leland's *Kidwely o. Cathgweli i.e. Cattilectus* 1536–9 [i.e. 'cat's bed']. Other speculations offer *cyd-wely* 'common bed', referring to the two rivers Gwendraeth Fawr and Gwendraeth Fechan which reach the sea near Cedweli. *Kidwelly* is a poor anglicised spelling.

Chadderton (LNC, England): farm by the hill called *Cadeir* (*Chaderton c.* 1200, *Chaterton* 1224, *Kaderton c.* 1250). The first element is the Celtic hill-name discussed under Caterham. There is a place called Hanging Chadder in the adjacent township of Royton, and this doubtless refers to the same hill.

Chalfont St Peter (BUC, England): spring frequented by calves (*Celfunte* 1086, *Chelhunte* 1185, *Chaufhunte* 1195, *Chafhunte* 1196, *Chalfhunte* 1227, *Chalfunt* 1235). Previous reference books give an Old English spelling *Ceadeles funtan* under Chalfont, but this is much more likely to refer to Chadshunt WAR, which means 'Ceadela's spring'. The second element of both names is *funta* 'spring', an Old English loan-word from Latin *fons*, accusative *fontem*.

63

The spelling -*hunte*, which is frequent in medieval references to Chalfont, is not inconsistent with derivation from *funta*, as an interchange of -*f*- and -*h*- in this element is very well evidenced in a number of names, such as Boarhunt and Mottisfont HMP, Teffont WLT; see also Cheshunt and Havant. The use of a loan-word from Latin instead of the Germanic word (Old English *welle*) may indicate that there were Roman building-works at the spring.

Chalfont is the name of two settlements, Chalfont St Peter and Chalfont St Giles, which are two miles apart, and have been distinguished from each other since the thirteenth century by the addition of their church dedications to the place-name. One is probably a daughter settlement of the other. If the 'calf-spring' could be located, it would be possible to say which was the earlier.

Chatham (KNT, England): village by the forest (*Cætham* 10th cent., *Ceteham* 1086, *Chatham* 1195). The country south of Chatham is still well wooded. This name is a hybrid, with one element Celtic and one English. *Chat-* is from the British equivalent of modern Welsh *coed* 'wood'. It is impossible to say exactly how such names arose, but they seem to imply that the two languages co-existed for a time. Possibly British people referred to the wooded area south of Chatham as 'the forest', and English settlers did not realise that this was a common noun, but took it for the name of the district. (See Cheadle.) In such a name as Caterham, where the

British element is a true place-name, not a common noun denoting a feature of the countryside, the phenomenon is slightly different.

Cheadle (CHE, England): wood called *Cēd* (*Chedle c.* 1165). This, like Caterham and Chatham, is a hybrid name, but of a special kind, in which a Celtic word has been combined with an English word of the same meaning. Another example of this process is provided by the names Bredon WOR and Breedon LEI, in which English *dūn* 'hill' has been added to British *brigā*, also meaning 'hill'. This looks very much like a linguistic misunderstanding on the part of the English settlers. They may have heard British people talking of *the* wood or *the* hill, and taken the common noun for a place-name.

Cheadle STF has the same etymology as Cheadle CHE.

Chelmsford (ESX, England): Ceolmǣr's ford (*Celmeresfort* 1086, *Chelmaresford* 1200). Roads from all directions converge on this crossing of the River Chelmer. Chelmer is a 'back-formation', which must have come into use before the name had been abbreviated from Chelmersford to Chelmsford. The river was earlier called *Beaduwan*, from which are derived Great and Little Baddow; the etymology of this is uncertain.

Cheltenham Spa (GLO, England): (?) Celta's river-meadow (*Celtanhomme* 803, *Ciltan ham* 11th cent.). The final element in this name is undoubtedly *hamm* in the sense 'river-meadow', but although much has been written about English place-names in *Chelt-* or *Chilt-*, no certain conclusions have been reached. The main suggestions have been for a hill-name (probably Old English), a river-name (possibly pre-English) and an Anglo-Saxon personal name. For Cheltenham, the personal name seems to offer the simplest solution. The river-name Chelt is a 'back-formation'.

Chepstow (MON, Wales): market-place (*Chepstowe* 1308, *Chapestowe* 1338, *Chappestowe* 1399). Old English *cēapstōw*. The place had more than one name. *Strigull* [origin obscure] (*Strigoielg, Estrighoel* 1086, *Strugull* 1150, *Strigull* 1224). An early Welsh name was *Emrygorfa* (*Emricorua* c. 1150) from Welsh *amrygyr* 'busy' + *-ma* 'place'. Another was *Castell-gwent* 'castle in Gwent' (*castell guent* c. 1150, *Kastell gwent* 1566, *Castle Went* 1586, *Kaswent* or *Castelh Gwent* 1722). The modern Welsh name is *Cas-gwent* (*Cas-gwent* 1612), where *cas* is an abbreviation of *castell*. For *Gwent* see *Blaenau*.

Chertsey (SUR, England): island belonging to a man named Cerot (*Cerotaesei* c. 730 Bede's Ecclesiastical History, *Ceortesige* 964). This is an interesting name because the personal name is Celtic, not Germanic, and the combination of a Celtic personal name with an English topographical term seems to imply a Celtic strain in the English population of the area. The town occupies an island site between streams flowing into the Thames.

Chesham (BUC, England): river-meadow near a heap of stones (*Cæstæleshamme* 1012, *Cestreham* 1086, *Cestresham* 1199, *Chesham*

1247). The meadowland would be on the banks of the River Chess, the name of which is a 'back-formation' from Chesham. The *ceastel*, or 'heap of stones', is a circle of boulders on which the church is built.

Cheshunt (HRT, England): (?) spring by the Roman town (*Cestrehunt* 1086, *Cesterhunte* 1198, *Chesthunte* 1292, *Chessehunt* 1561). Although there are no early spellings with -*f*-, the second element of Cheshunt is probably *funta* 'spring', discussed under Chalfont. The first element may be *ceaster*, for which see Chester. There is no record of a Roman settlement at Cheshunt, but the Roman road later called Ermine Street runs immediately to the west of the town, and it is possible that Roman building remains were visible by the road here at the time of the English invasions. It is unusual, though, for anything big enough to be called a *ceaster* to disappear completely, and the first element might be *ceastel*, as in Chesham.

Chester (CHE, England): Roman town (*Ceaster* 1094 Anglo-Saxon Chronicle). The Venerable Bede calls Chester *ciuitas Legionum* or *Legacaestir* 'city of the legions'. It was in fact a legionary fortress in Roman times, known as *Deva* from its situation on the River Dee; but it is not certain whether the English name refers to the remains of the military fort or to the civil settlement which was also there. The English seem to have used *ceaster* (which is a loan-word from Latin *castra*) for any Roman site where the building remains were impressive,

65

without distinguishing between military forts and civil settlements. In the Anglo-Saxon Chronicle under the year 577 it is recorded that the English captured from the Britons the three *ceastra* of Gloucester, Cirencester, and Bath. Gloucester had been a legionary fortress and a *colonia*, but the other two were only towns.

Chesterfield (DRB, England): open land by the Roman town (*Cesterfelda* 955). (See Chester.) The Ordnance Survey Map of Roman Britain marks Chesterfield as the site of a 'minor settlement'. Possibly it looked a little more impressive than this to the Anglo-Saxons, since *ceaster* seemed the appropriate term for it.

Chester-le-Street (DRH, England): Roman fort on a Roman road (*Cestra c.* 1160, *Cestria in Strata* 1400). (See Chester.) In this case the reference seems more likely to be to the Roman fort of *Concangium* than to the civil settlement which was also here, but which does not seem to have been very impressive. In a narrative of about A.D. 1050, this place is referred to as *Cuncaceastre, Cunceceastre*. The first part of this is a survival of the Romano-British name *Concangium*; see Cirencester for this type of formation. The addition of -le-Street is to distinguish this place from Chester CHE. The French definite article is fairly frequently used in Middle English place-names instead of English *the*. Such names as Chester-le-Street, Thornton-le-Street YON (on the same Roman road), Bolton-le-Sands LNC were at first distinguished as *-on-le-Street* or *-in-le-Sands*, but the preposition was dropped, and *le*

was then felt to be a sort of connective particle.

Chichester (SSX, England): Roman town belonging to Cissa (*Cisseceastre* 895, *Cycester* 988, *Cicestre* 1086). The remains of the Romano-British town here are still impressive, and must have been much more so in the second half of the fifth century when the English name came into use. It is generally assumed that Chichester was named from Cissa, who appears in some early annals of the Anglo-Saxon Chronicle (477, 491) as one of the sons of Ælle, the first king of the South Saxons. This compound would be Old English *Cissanceaster*, and it seems necessary to assume that this had been shortened to *Cisseceastre* by 895, when the place-name is first recorded.

Chilwell (NTT, England): spring where young people assemble (*Chideuuelle* 1086, *Childewell* 1194). Another instance of this name is Childwall, east of Liverpool. The first element is the genitive plural of Old English *cild*, modern *child*, probably used of teenagers as well as children. Several small streams rise near Chilwell.

Chippenham (WLT, England): (?) land in a river-bend belonging to Cippa (*Cippanhamme c.* 900 Anglo-Saxon Chronicle). The final element is *hamm*, probably in the sense 'land in a river-bend', referring to the part of the town enclosed by a sharp loop of the Avon; see Buckingham. The first element is usually stated to be a personal name *Cippa*. Doubt about this etymology arises from the occurrence of four more names, one of them certainly, and the others probably, identical with Chippenham WLT. The other certain example of Old English *Cippanhamm* occurs in some eighth-century boundaries of an estate near Bishop's Cleeve GLO. The three probable ones are Chippenham CAM, Cippenham in Burnham BUC, and Sydenham GTL (*Cyppenham* 1319). The early spellings for the last three names end in -*ham*, which may mean that they contain *hām* rather than *hamm*, but, as explained under Brixham and Buckingham, it is seldom possible in the south of England to be certain that medieval -*ham* does not represent *hamm*. The sites of all three places are appropriate to *hamm* in the sense 'river-meadow'. If all five names end in *hamm* (which is possible, but not certain), then we are faced with the apparent phenomenon of five land-owners named Cippa all owning the same sort of land; this type of problem is discussed under Wellington. *Cippa* is not on independent record as an Old English personal name, and it would be preferable to have a significant word which was likely to be compounded five times with *hamm*. No such word is on record, but research in the Germanic languages might produce a likely stem for one. The same first element, whether word or personal name, occurs in Chipley SOM (*Cyppan leage c.* 854) and a lost place called *Cippenhale* near Chippenham CAM. Other names in Chip- (such as Chipley SFK, Chipnall SHR, Chipchase NTB) can be derived from the genitive plural (*cippa*) of *cipp* 'log'. This is not possible for Chippenham, as the first element is *cippan*, which cannot be an inflected case of *cipp*.

Chirk (DEN, Wales): River Ceiriog (*Chirk(e)* 1295, *Cheyrk* 1309, *Churk* 1540). The town and district (Chirkland) are anglicised forms of the Welsh *Ceiriog*, a river-name probably from a personal name *Ceiriog* (a derivative of *car*- 'love'). The River Cciriog rises on the Berwyn mountains and runs through Glyn Ceiriog past Chirk. Chirk was the centre of the Norman lordship of Chirkland (Welsh *Swydd y Waun*). The Welsh name is *Y Waun* 'the moorland' from Welsh *gwaun* (*Ewevn* 1291, *Y Waun* 1368, *Waen* 1562, *Y Waun* 1566).

Chorley (LNC, England): (?) meadowland of the peasant farmers (*Cherleg* 1246, *Cherle* 1252, *Chorley* 1257). This is a fairly common place-name, which should probably be considered together with the even more common name Charlton, Chorlton, Carlton, and the fairly common Charlcote, all of which have as first element the genitive plural of Old English *ceorl*. It has been pointed out that a name meaning 'farm of the peasants' is not a good way of distinguishing one village from another at a time when all settlements were farmed mainly by men of the social class known as *ceorls*. There is clear evidence that Charlton is not an early place-name, and the suggestion made is therefore that it arose at a comparatively late date to describe a settlement inhabited by men whose labour was essential to the cultivation of a large estate, and that it was intended to distinguish one hamlet from others on such an estate.

This is a satisfactory explanation for Charlton or Chorlton, but it is, of course, not necessary to regard

Chorley as having a similar significance. Some places called Chorley may have been in the first instance clearings made in woodland by the communal efforts of a group of *ceorls*. The distribution of the name, however, with examples in Cheshire, Hertfordshire, Lancashire, Shropshire, and Staffordshire, suggests a rather late origin, and the probability is that it refers to settlements of the same type as those called Charlton, situated in country where *lēah* seemed a more appropriate word than *tūn*. It is possible that in Chorley LNC the meaning of *lēah* is 'meadowland', not 'forest-clearing'. Chorley is between two rivers, and there are a number of names in *-ley* in this part of Lancashire for which the meaning 'meadow-land' seems the most appropriate.

Christchurch (HMP, England): church of Christ (*Cristescherche* 1177, *Cristechurch Twynham* 1242). The name belonged originally to the Priory, which was re-constituted in the mid-twelfth century as a house of Augustinian Canons and at the same time given the name Christchurch, which subsequently ousted the old name of the settlement, which was *Twynham*.

Twynham, the earlier name of the settlement, appears as *æt Tweoxneam* 901 Anglo-Saxon Chronicle. This means '(place) between the rivers' (from *betweoxn* 'between', and *ēam*, dative plural of *ēa* 'river'), an obviously appropriate description of the site, which is between the Rivers Stour and Avon. It is interesting that in 901, when the complete Old English phrase *betweoxn ēam* would still be intelligible, *be-* was dropped

and the remainder considered as a proper name, so that the redundant preposition 'at' could be prefixed. *betwēonan*, which also means 'between', is more common in place-names than *betweoxn*, and has replaced *betweoxn* in the later spellings for *Twinham*. Both words occur in the phrase *betwixt and between*. Twineham SSX and Twinyeo DEV also mean 'between the rivers'.

Chryston (LAN, Scotland): unexplained (*Crystoune* 1605, *Chrystoun* 1615, *Carystoune* 1700). The first element looks like a personal name but it is difficult to decide which name is involved.

Cirencester (GLO, England): Roman town called Corinion (*Korinion c.* 150 Ptolemy, *Cironium c.* 650 Ravenna Cosmography, *Cirenceaster c.* 900 Anglo-Saxon Chronicle, *Cycestre* 1276, *Cisetur* 1453). The Roman town here was called *Corinion*; the etymology of this British name is unresolved. Anglo-Saxon settlers added *ceaster* to the Romano-British name as they heard it from Celtic speakers in the sixth century, but philologists are not in complete agreement about how this became *Ciren* (pronounced *Chiren*) in Old English speech. The present form is due to Norman French inability to pronounce Ch-. The name of the R. Churn preserves the Old English pronunciation. For other examples of this type of name see Dorchester, Gloucester, Manchester. The pronunciation represented by the spelling *Cisetur* is not used locally now, though it was common in the fifteenth, sixteenth and seventeenth centuries.

The River Churn and North and South Cerney (both originally *Cyrnea* 'Churn river') are derived from the same British root as the first element of Cirencester. The meaning of the British name is uncertain.

Clacton-on-Sea (ESX, England): estate associated with a man named Clacc (*Claccingtune c.* 1000, *Clachintune* 1086, *Claketon* 1204, *Clacton c.* 1330). This is a name of the same type as Addington. (See *Introduction*, p. 18.)

Clas-ar-Wy (RAD, Wales), see *Glasbury*.

Cleethorpes (LIN, England): hamlets attached to Clee. Clee (an ancient settlement a short distance inland) is *Cleia* 1086, and derives from Old English *clæg* 'clay', referring to the soil. The ancient hamlets of Hole and Itterby were grouped together for administrative purposes, and the amalgamated unit was called Cleethorpes. It appears that the name Cleethorpes was in use in the seventeenth century.

Clevedon (SOM, England): hill of the cliffs (*Clivedone* 1086). Only close acquaintance with the place could enable firm suggestions to be made about the precise application of this name. *Clif* often means 'steep slope of a hill-side, escarpment', and it may be the position of Clevedon at the junction of two escarpments which suggested the genitive plural 'of the cliffs', rather than any feature of the sea-coast. Cleeve, a few miles south-east of Clevedon, is presumably called 'at the cliff' because it is situated at the bottom of an escarpment. Clevedon may have referred originally to Dial Hill,

which overlooks two escarpments stretching north-east, with a deep valley between them. The stretch of coast north of the town, however, appears to have a fairly steep cliff, and the name could obviously refer to this.

Clitheroe (LNC, England): hill with loose stones (*Cliderhou* 1102, *Clitherow* 1124). The second element, Old English *hōh* or Old Norse *haugr*, refers to the hill made of loose, crumbling limestone on which Clitheroe Castle is built. The first element, which has only been noted in this name and in Clitherbeck in Danby in the North Riding, is not on record in Old English, but is assumed to be the ancestor of the Devon dialect word *clider*, *clither*, 'a pile of loose stones or granite debris'.

Clydebank (DNB, Scotland): (village on the) banks of the Clyde. A comparatively recent name. Grew as a town in the nineteenth century when housing was required for the workmen employed in shipbuilding.

Coalville (LEI, England): this is a name invented in the first half of the nineteenth century for an entirely new settlement which grew up round Whitwick Colliery, established in 1824. Except for fanciful nineteenth-century formations of this type (of which other examples are Charterville OXF, founded by the Chartists in 1847, Ironville DRB) the French word *ville* does not occur in English place-names. When -*ville* occurs as the modern ending of an ancient place-name, as in Morville SHR, Wyville LIN, it is a corruption of -*field* or -*well*.

Coatbridge (LAN, Scotland): bridge on the land called Coats (*Coittis* 1584, *terran de Coats, Coatburn* 1617, *Cotts* 1676). Coatbridge rose to prominence in connection with the development of mining in the nineteenth century. It appears that the bridge in question was not built until about 1800. *Coats* is the same as the second element in Saltcoats (Old English *cot* 'cottage').

Colchester (ESX, England): Roman town on the River Colne (*Colneceaster* 921 Anglo-Saxon Chronicle, *Colecestra* 1086). Colne is a pre-English river-name of uncertain meaning, which occurs also in Clun NTT, SHR, and Clowne DRB. A Welsh historian writing about A.D. 800 calls Colchester *Cair Colun*, which is the exact Welsh equivalent of English *Colneceaster*.

In Romano-British times the settlement of Roman army veterans here was called *Colonia Camulodunum*, or sometimes simply *Colonia*, which was the technical term for such a settlement. It has been suggested that the *Colne-* of *Colneceaster* is the word *colonia*, but this is not likely, and there seems to be no doubt that it is the name of the River Colne. It would be surprising, however, for the Romano-British names to have been forgotten in the fifth century, when the English name arose. Possibly there was already some confusion in late Roman times between the three names *Camulodunum, Colonia*, and the river-name *Colun*, and the river-name was accepted as the name of the town before the English settlement.

In the thirteenth century, when the -*n*- had disappeared, Colchester was believed to derive its name from the legendary King Cole.

Colne (LNC, England): (place by) the River Colne (*Calna* 1124, *Caune* 1251, *Colne* 1296). The river-name occurs also in the West Riding of Yorkshire (with the modern form Colne, but Middle English spellings *Calne*) and is the source of the town-name Calne WLT. It is not identical with the River Colne in Essex, from which Colchester is derived, but is another pre-English river-name of uncertain meaning.

Colne Water, the river from which Colne is named, is a fairly short tributary of Pendle Water, and Colne is still the only settlement of any size beside it.

Colwyn Bay (DEN, Wales): whelp, young animal (the brook-name is *Avon Colloine* 1638, *Avon Golwyn* alias *Avon Benmen* 1684–5). The township which took its name from the brook is (*Coloyne* 1334, *Colwyn* 1578, *Colwyn* 1587, *Colwyn* 1669, *Kolwyn c.* 1700, *Colewyn* 1738). Welsh *colwyn* 'young of any animal' (frequently used as a brook-name). The growth of the town as a seaside resort in the nineteenth century resulted in the addition of 'Bay'. The Welsh form is *Bae Colwyn*. The older township is now known as *Hen Golwyn* in Welsh, or translated into English as *Old Colwyn*.

Congleton (CHE, England): unexplained (*Cogeltone* 1086, *Congelton* 1282). No convincing etymology has yet been suggested for this name. The final element is *tūn* 'farm'.

Conisbrough (YOW, England): the king's fort (*Cunugesburh c.* 1003, *Coningesburg, Cuningesburg* 1086,

Cunesburc 1201). This is apparently a hybrid Old Norse and Old English name, from Old Norse *konungr* and Old English *burh* (for which see Aylesbury); but *konungr* may have replaced English *cyning* after the Norwegian settlements of the first half of the tenth century. English place-names were sometimes partly translated into Danish or Norse.

Conisbrough is one of a group of names in *burh*, the others being Sprotbrough, Mexborough, Masbrough, Worsborough, Stainborough, and Kexbrough. It has been suggested that these names represent an organised system of defence, but there are no historical references to such a system, and the date of the forts is unknown.

Consett (DRH, England): (?) headland of the hill called *Cunuc* (*Covekesheued* 1183, *Conekesheued* 1228). This name and three names in Wiltshire (Knook, Conock in Chirton, and Conkwell in Winsley) are usually derived from a hill-name *Cunāco*, sometimes said to be Celtic, though its origins are actually obscure. The topography of Consett is quite suitable for this etymology.

Conway (CRN, Wales): glorious river (*Canubio, Kanovio, Conovio* (Roman period), *Conguoy* 12th cent., *Cunewe flumen* 1191, *Conewey* 1290, *Coneway* 1394, *Conway als Aberconway* 1698). The Latin forms refer to the Roman station at Caerhun, on the river Conwy, and are probably based on British **Cān-*, cf. Welsh *go-gon-* 'fame, glory'. The form *Conway* is an anglicised spelling. The Welsh name of the town is *Aberconwy*, originally referring to the mouth (*aber*) of the River Conwy (*Aber-*

conuy 12th cent., *Aberkonuy* 1247, *Aberconnewy* 1258, *Aberconwy* 1272, *Aberkonwy* 14th cent., *Aberconway* 1591–2). The River Conwy formed the boundary between the two territories of the kingdom of Gwynedd—Gwynedd Is Conwy ('G. this side of Conwy') to the east, and Gwynedd Uwch Conwy ('G. the other side of Conwy') to the west. The Norman castle and town became the administrative centre of the cantref of Arllechwedd (Welsh *ar* 'on, near' + *llechwedd* 'slope', i.e. the eastern portion of the Snowdonian range). The River Conwy rises in *Llyn Conwy* (Welsh *llyn* 'lake') (*Llin Conwey* 1536–9, *Lhyn Konwy* c. 1700, *Llyn Conwey* 1710, *Llyn Conwy* 1795). The valley of the Conwy was called *Nant Conwy*, and gave its name to the commote of *Nantconwy, Nanconwy*—(*Nant Convy* 12th cent., *Nanconewey* 1371, *Nanconwy* 1350). Welsh *nant* 'valley', then 'brook'.

Corby (NTP, England): Kóri's village (*Corbei, Corbi* 1086, *Corebi* 1166). This is a Danish name. It dates from the period after the Danish wars of A.D. 865 to 886, when the Danish armies took large areas of north-east England and the East Midlands for settlement by themselves and other Danish immigrants who came to join them. As a result of these settlements, this part of England was known as the Danelaw, and it contains many Danish place-names, a large number of which have the characteristic endings *-by* and *-thorp*. Much work has been done on the historical implications of these names. Environmental studies have suggested that many of them represent new Danish settlements in land uncultivated in the ninth century, but others may result from the fragmentation of large English estates. Some (see Derby) are ancient English settlements renamed by Danish speakers. (There must have been considerable Danish immigration to produce such a quantity of names.) Two-thirds of the names in -by in England have a personal name as first element. This is in striking contrast to the use of the word in place-names in Scandinavia, and raises problems similar to those discussed in the Introduction, pp. 19ff. We do not at present know in what sense Corby was 'Kóri's village'. There is another Corby, of identical origin, in Lincolnshire.

Names in -by do not necessarily date from the late ninth century. The suffix was a living place-name element from then until the thirteenth or fourteenth century. Such a name as Corby, however, referring to a place which was an independent unit at the time of the Domesday Survey, probably goes back to an early stage in the Danish colonisation of the Danelaw.

Corwen (MER, Wales): (?) sanctuary stone (*Corvaen* 1254, *Corvaen* 1291, *Coruayn* 1309, *Korvaen* 14th cent., *Corwen* 1443, *Corwen* 1535, *Korwen* 1566, *Corwen* 1638). Welsh *côr* 'chancel, sanctuary' or Welsh *cor* 'small'+Welsh *maen* 'stone'. The early forms show conclusively that the second element is *maen*. In Welsh -*f*- may alternate with -*w*-, and -*ae*- in a final unaccented syllable may become -*e*-, thus *Corfaen>Corwen*. The popular etymology 'white choir' has no basis in fact.

Cosham (HMP, England): Cossa's village (*Cosham* 1015 Anglo-Saxon Chronicle, *Coseham, Cosseham* 1086). This is a name of the same type as Amersham.

Coventry (WAR, England): Cofa's tree (*Couentre* 1043, *Cofentreo, Cofantreo c.* 1060, *Couentreu* 1086). This is a name of the same type as Braintree.

Cowbridge (GLA, Wales): cow-bridge (*Coubrugge* 1263, *Couuebrugge* 1317, *Cowbridge* 1529, *Cowbrydge* 1560, *Cowbridge* 1570, *Cow-bridge* 1630) Old English *cū* 'cow' + *brycg* 'bridge'. The bridge had a Welsh alias (*Pont y Fywch* 1657–60, *Pont y Fuch* 1765). Welsh *pont* 'bridge'+ def. art. *y* 'the'+*buwch* 'cow'. Another bridge was called *y Bont Faen* 'the stone bridge' (*Bontvaen c.* 1500, *Pont Vayn* 1535–40, *Ponte Vain* 1536–9, (*y*) *Bont Faen* 1566, *Pont Vaen* 1600–7). During the eighteenth century a spurious form *Pont y Fôn* was invented as an alias for *Pont Faen*, and it was claimed that *Pont y Fôn* meant 'cow bridge' (*Pont-y-Fon* 1772, *Y Bont Faen or Pont Fôn* 1811). As early as the sixteenth century *Pont Faen* had been accepted as the Welsh name for Cowbridge: *Pontfain .i. pons lapidea, Angli falso Covvbrig, id est, pontem vacciniam vocant* 1571. There was also a Welsh version of English Cowbridge: *Cwbris* 15th cent.

Cowdenbeath (FIF, Scotland): (?) Cowden's place called Beith (*terris de Baithe—Moubray alias Cowdounes-baithe* 1626). The original name appears to have been Beith from Gaelic *beith* 'birch-tree'. To this other distinguishing elements were added. *Moubray* looks like a Norman family name as in Melton Mowbray LEI. If *Cowdounes* is English, it may mean cow-hill or cow-pasture; it could also be a surname Cowden derived from a similar place-name in Midlothian. Gaelic *calltuinn* 'hazel' is unlikely. Cowdenbeath grew rapidly in the second half of the nineteenth century because of the expansion of coal mining in the area. It is in the parish of Beath (*Beitht* 1521).

Cowes (IOW, England): (sandbanks called) The Cows (*Estcowe, Westcowe* 1413, *the Cowe* 1512, *one of the Kowes* 1545, *Cowes* 1622). The name belonged originally to sandbanks off the mouth of the River Medina, and was later transferred to the settlement on the coast. It is fairly common for hills or islands to have names like Cow or Calf. One of Speed's maps (1611) marks a sandbank called The Horse off Portsmouth.

Crawley (SSX, England): crows' wood (*Crauleia* 1203). The same name occurs in several other counties.

Crayford (KNT, England): ford over the River Cray (*Creiford'* 1199, *Craiford* 1202, *Crainford* 1322). Cray is a Celtic river-name, which occurs also in the West Riding of Yorkshire and is identical with Crai in Wales; it means 'fresh, clean'. The Roman road from London to Rochester crosses the river here. The Anglo-Saxon Chronicle records a great battle fought in 457 at *Crecganford* or *Creacanford*. This has usually been identified with Crayford, but the identification can only be accepted if the spelling in the Chronicle is regarded as corrupt. A similar problem is discussed under Bedford.

Crewe (CHE, England): fish weir (*Creu* 1086, *Cruue* 1288). This is a Celtic name, corresponding to the modern Welsh word *cryw*. The original meaning of the word was probably 'basket', but it was used of a wicker-work woven fence across a river to catch fish, and it also developed a sense 'stepping-stones', perhaps because a row of large stones was laid to reinforce a wicker-work weir.

Cricieth (CRN, Wales): mound of captives or bondmen (*Crukeith* 1273, *Cruketh* 1284, *Cruckeyth* 1350, *Krukeith* 14th cent., *Cruckeith* 1459, *Cryckieth* 1489, *Kruckieth* 1535, *Krikieth* 1566, *Criccieth o. Llansaint Catherine* 1756). Welsh *crug* 'mound' + Welsh *caith*, plural of *caeth* 'captive' or 'bondman'. The early references are to the Norman castle. The church is dedicated to St Catherine (*Llansaint y Kattring* 1565, *Sainct y Catherine* 1685, *Llan St y Catherine* 1700, *Llansaint y Catherine* 1708). The correct spelling is *Cricieth* rather than *Criccieth* since *-g-c-* > *-c-* in Welsh phonology.

Crickhowell (BRE, Wales), see *Crucywel.*

Crieff (PER, Scotland): (at the) tree (*Creffe* c. 1178, *Crefe* 1218). Gaelic *Craoibh*, from *craobh* 'a tree'. Reference is probably to a single tree of some importance, either because of its size and height, or for cult purposes, or perhaps as a conspicuous meeting-place.

Crucadarn (BRE, Wales): strong mound (*Kruc kadarn* 1550, *Kricadarn*

1555, *Kraig Kadarn* 1566, *Crucadarne* 1566–7, *Crickadarne* 1578, *Kerigkadarn* 1608, *Crigkadarn* 1623, *Crickadarn* 1727). Welsh *crug* 'mound'+*cadarn* 'strong, mighty, secure'. There was some uncertainty as to the first element, and such forms as *cerrig* 'stones' and *craig* 'rock' apparently result from popular etymology.

Crucywel (BRE, Wales): mound of Hywel (*Crikhoel* 1263, *Crukhowell* 1281, *Crukhowel* 1343, *Crughowell* 1405, *Cruc Hywel* 15th cent., *Crugehoel* 1508, *Krighwel* 1566, *Crickhowel* 1680, *Crickhowel* 1760). Welsh *crug* 'mound' + Welsh personal name *Hywel*. The spelling *Crickhowel* represents the usual anglicisation of Welsh *crug* to *crick*.

Cuckfield (SSX, England): Cuca's open land (*Kukefeld, Kukufeld c.* 1095, *Cucufeld c.* 1118, *Cukefeld* 1220). The early spellings *Kuku-, Cucu-* should probably be considered to indicate association with the word *cuckoo*, rather than derivation from it. The element *feld*, which refers in this instance to an unforested stretch in predominantly forested country, is fairly frequently compounded with a personal name. *Cuckoo* is a French word, and would probably not have been sufficiently widespread in the eleventh century to give rise to a place-name. People writing the name down would be likely to be familiar with it, however, and may have associated the two.

Cumbernauld (DNB, Scotland): confluence of streams (*Cumbrenald c.* 1300, *Cumrynald* 1417, *Combernald* 1427). Evidently Gaelic *comar nan allt*, from *comar* 'meeting, confluence', and *allt*, a typically Scottish-Gaelic term for a stream, originally meaning 'a cliff' and then a mountain-stream between high banks. Cumbernauld is one of the most prominent Scottish New Towns. A stream flows through the original village of C., joining another watercourse not far away. This may have been the 'confluence' from which the place derived its name.

Cumnock (AYR, Scotland): unexplained (*Comnocke* 1297, *Comenok* 1298, *Cumnock* 1300, *Cumnok* 1368–9). This name has never been explained satisfactorily.

Cupar (FIF, Scotland): unexplained (*Cupre* 1183, *Coper* 1294). Like Coupar Angus considered to be of pre-Gaelic Celtic origin. The Gaelic form is *Cùbar*.

Currie (MLO, Scotland): wet plain (*Curey* 1210, *Curry* 1213, *Curri* 1246). This name derives from the dative-locative of Gaelic *currach* 'bog, fen', an element quite common in Ireland.

Cwm-brân (MON, Wales): valley of the River Brân (*Cwmbran* 1707, *Cwmbrane* 1764, *Cwmbrane* 1803, *Cwm Brân* 1833). This is a New Town (under the New Towns Act of 1946), and designated as such in 1949. The site is at the junction of Nant Brân (< *nant* 'brook'+*brân* 'raven', probably as a personification. *Brân* is attested as a Welsh personal name) and *Afon Lwyd* (< *afon* 'river' and *llwyd* 'grey'). *Cwm*='valley, combe, glen'.

D

Dalkeith (MLO, Scotland): meadow or valley of the wood (*Dolchet* 1144, *Dalkied* 1142, *Dalketh* 1128-53). Compare Old Welsh *dol* 'meadow, valley' and *coet*, as in Bathgate. The Esk valley on which Dalkeith stands is still heavily wooded.

Dalry (AYR, Scotland): King's meadow (*Dalry* 1315-21), from Gaelic *Dail an Righ* 'meadow of the king'. Although this is the most likely explanation it could also be *Dail Fhraoigh* 'heather meadow'.

Dalton-in-Furness (LNC, England): farm in a valley (*Daltune* 1086, *Dalton in fournais* 1332). The town is in a broad valley among hills. Furness is discussed under Barrow-in-Furness.

Darlington (DRH, England): estate associated with Dēornōð (*Dearthingtun* c. 1009, *Dearningtun* c. 1130, *Derlinton* 1196, *Derlintone* 1228, *Derningtona* c. 1300, *Darlyngton* 1507, *Darnton* 1583, *Darneton* 1588). This is a name of the same type as Addington. Development to Darlington instead of Darnington is due to Norman French confusion between -*n*- and -*l*-.

Dartford (KNT, England): ford over the River Darent (*Tarentefort* 1086, *Derenteford, Derteford* 1194). The river-name, which is Celtic and derives from a word meaning 'oak-tree', has become Derwent in several other counties. The Roman road from London to Rochester crosses the Darent at Dartford.

Darwen (LNC, England): (place by) the River Darwen (*Derewent* 1208). The river-name is identical with Darent, which occurs in Dartford. The River Darwen is a short one, and Lower and Over Darwen are the only settlements on its course.

Deal (KNT, England): (?) low place (*Addelam* 1086, *Dela* 1158). The earliest spelling has the preposition *at* prefixed. Old English *dæl* (Kentish *del*) is a rather rare place-name element outside the areas of Norse settlement, and its precise meaning in such counties as Kent, Sussex, and Worcestershire is uncertain. The cognate Old Norse word *dalr* meant 'valley'. This gives many names in -*dale* in areas of Norse settlement, and probably influenced the use of Old English *dæl* in such north-country names as Dalton. In Old English literary sources, however, *dæl* is used chiefly of 'a pit', and this may be more relevant than 'valley' in areas where there is no question of Old Norse influence.

75

Denbigh (DEN, Wales), see *Dinbych*.

Denny (STL, Scotland): unexplained (*Litill Dany* 1510, *Denny* 1601, *Denne* 1622). Could this name be connected with Old English *denu* 'valley, hollow'?

Denton (LNC, near Manchester, England): valley farm (*Denton* 1255). A small brook rises close to the church and runs in a slight valley.

Derby (DRB, England): farm of the deer (*Deoraby* first half of 10th cent., *c.* 955, *c.* 1000). This is a Scandinavian name which occurs also in Lancashire (West Derby in Walton). The deer which frequented this part of Derbyshire are referred to again in the English name Darley ('deer wood or clearing'), less than two miles north of Derby.

An earlier, English, name for Derby is mentioned by a writer named Æthelweard, who translated the Anglo-Saxon Chronicle into Latin at the end of the tenth century. He refers to the burial of an ealdorman at 'the place which is called *Northworthige*, but *Deoraby* in the Danish tongue'. There is one more reference to this early name in a source dating from about 1020. It means 'north settlement', and may have been called that for distinction from Tamworth STF, which has the same final element. This type of name is discussed under Tamworth.

The earliest occurrence of the Danish name is on a coin of King Athelstan, who reigned from 927–939. The evidence suggests that both names were known from about 900 to about 1025, but that the Danish one prevailed after that. Other Danish names in eastern England may be replacements of earlier English ones, but Derby is one of the few instances in which the change of name is documented. Some of the problems connected with Danish place-names are discussed under Corby.

Devonport (DEV, England): a modern, artificial name which came into use in 1824. The district was earlier known as Plymouth Dock.

Dewsbury (YOW, England): Dewi's fortified place (*Deusberia* 1086, *Dewesbiri c.* 1095). This is a name of the same type as Aylesbury, but with an Old Welsh personal name instead of an Old English one. The combination of a Celtic personal name with an English final element is rare; another example is Chertsey.

Didcot (BRK, England): Duda's cottage (*Dudecota* 1206, *Didcot or Dudcot* 1657). Place-names ending in -*cot* are considered to date from the late Old English period.

Dinbych (DEN, Wales): little fort (*Dinbych* 1269, *Dinbey* 1282, *Dynebegh* 1311, *Dynbiegh* 1334, *Dinbych* 14th cent., *Dinbech* 1468, *Denbigh* 1536–9, *Denbigh Brit. Dimbech c.* 1700). Welsh *din* 'fort, stronghold' + Welsh *bych* 'small' (a variant form of *bach*). The local pronunciation *Dimbech* shows the normal development of -*nb*- > -*mb*-. The standard Welsh form is *Dinbych*. The anglicised form *Denbigh* (pronounced *Denby*) shows the representation of Welsh -*ch*- by -*gh*-, and its consequent loss.

The castle is known in antiquarian writings as *Castell Caledfryn*

76

yn Rhos (*Cled Brin en Ros* 1586, *Castelh Cledvryn yn Rhôs c.* 1700). Welsh *castell* 'castle', *Caledfryn* 'hard hill', *yn Rhos* 'in Rhos' (presumably referring to the cantref of Rhos, although Denbigh was in the cantref of Rhufoniog).

Dinbychypysgod (PEM, Wales), see *Tenby.*

Dingwall (ROS, Scotland): field of the 'Thing' (*Dingwell* 1227, *Dignewall* 1263, *Dingwal* 1308, *Dingwall* 1382). This is Norse *þing-vǫllr*, a compound of *þing*, the Norse general court of justice, and *vǫllr* 'meadow, field'. Even in Scandinavian times Dingwall, although situated at the very south end of the Norse sphere of influence, must have been an important centre. The Gaelic name for Dingwall is *Inbhir-pheofharan* 'Peffermouth'.

Dolgellau (MER, Wales): meadow of cells (*Dolkelew* 1254, *Dolgethleu* 1294, *Dolgethly* 1338, *Dolgelle* 1437, *Dolgellau* 15th cent., *Dolygelle* 1566, *Dolgelley* 1592, *Dolgella* 1769). Welsh *dôl* 'loop, bend' then 'lowlying land within loop of a river', 'meadow', 'dale' + Welsh *cellau*, plural of *cell* 'cell, booth'. The exact meaning of *cellau* in this name is uncertain. It may refer to monastic cells, or to merchants' booths or stalls. The anglicised spelling *Dolgelley* is a survival from medieval documents.

Doncaster (YOW, England): Roman fort on the River Don (*Doneceastre* 1002). In Roman times the fort was referred to simply by the river-name —it occurs as *Dano* in the Antonine Itinerary. This is a Celtic name,

from a root meaning 'water, moisture, river'.

Dorchester (DOR, England): Roman town called Durnovaria (*Dornuuarana ceaster* 847, *Dornwaraceaster* 864, *Dorecestre* 1086). The Roman cantonal capital here was called *Durnovaria*, a Celtic name, from *durn* 'fist', probably meaning 'fist-sized pebble', and an obscure second element. *Durnovaria* might have been the name of Maiden Castle. In borrowing this as *Dornwara-* the English settlers probably associated the second element with Old English *ware* 'dwellers', which occurs in Canterbury. Dorchester OXF has a different etymology. See also Dornoch SUT.

Dorking (SUR, England): Deorc's people (*Dorchinges* 1086, *Dorkingg* 1219). This is a name of the same type as Barking.

Dornoch (SUT, Scotland): place of pebbles (*Durnach c.* 1145, *Durnah* 1199, *Dornouch* 1456), from Gaelic *dornach* 'place of hand-stones, pebbly place', a derivative of *dorn* 'fist'. This is an element which we find as early as Gaulish *Durnomagos*, and Dornoch might in fact be interpreted as an older **Durnācon*.

Douglas (IOM): black stream (*Dufglas c.* 1257). This is a Celtic name, common in Ireland, Scotland, Wales, and England. In Ireland and Scotland it has the modern form Douglas, but in Wales it appears as Dulas or Dulais, and in England in various forms such as Dowles, Dowlish, Dawlish, Dalch. The Manx Douglas is noteworthy as one of a very small group of Manx names (comprising

77

only Douglas, Rushen, and Man itself) which can be confidently assumed to date from before the period of Norse rule. Most Celtic names in IOM probably originated in the fourteenth century or later, after the end of the Norse kingdom, when Gaelic was re-introduced from south-west Scotland.

Dover (KNT, England): the waters (*Dubris* 4th cent. and *c*. 425, *Dofras c*. 700, *Dobrum* 844, *Doferum c*. 1000). This is a Celtic name, from the plural of the British word which is the ancestor of Modern Welsh *dwfr* 'water'. It is well recorded in classical sources because of the Roman fort, and it is an interesting example of a Romano-British name which was adopted by the Anglo-Saxons without the addition of *ceaster*. There are a number of other streams in England with the same name, which appears in every case to be plural. Presumably 'waters' was felt to be synonymous with 'stream'. There is a small stream running into the sea at Dover, now called the Dour. This is referred to as *Doferware broc c*. 1040, 'the brook of the people of Dover', which suggests that the original naming of the settlement from the stream was forgotten, and the stream was re-named from the settlement after *Dofras* had been limited to the town.

Dovercourt (ESX, England): (?) farm-yard by the river called Dover (*Douorcortae c*. 1000 Anglo-Saxon Will). The first element is the Celtic word for a stream discussed under Dover, probably referring to the stream which flows past Wix, Great

Oakley, and Ramsey and into the sea north of Dovercourt. The final element is a rare word **cort(e)* or **curt(e)*, only noted in this name and in two names in Kent. It has been suggested that it is an Old English word meaning 'piece of land cut off', related to Old English *gecyrtan* 'to shorten', Latin *curtus* 'short'. Another possibility is that it is a British or Old English loan-word from Latin *cohors, cohortem*, which besides its more common meaning of 'multitude of people' is used by classical authors in an agricultural context to mean 'an enclosed yard'. This sense must have been current in late Latin, since it is the source of French *court*, from which is derived Modern English *court*. It is possible that the late Latin use was known in Essex and Kent at the very beginning of the Anglo-Saxon period. Roman buildings are recorded in Dover-court and near Little Oakley, about a mile away.

Drenewydd, Y (MTG, Wales), see *Newtown*.

Dudley (WOR, England): Dudda's forest-clearing (*Dudelei* 1086). This is a name of the same type as Barnsley. It is one of a group of names in *-ley* which characterises the Black Country, immediately west of Birmingham. This area must have been dense woodland at the time of the Anglo-Saxon settlement.

Dumbarton (DNB, Scotland): fortress of the Britons (*Dumbrethan, Dunbretan* 1290–91, *Dunbrettone* 1292, *Dumbarton c*. 1600), Gaelic *Dùn Breatann*. It was once the capital of the Strathclyde Britons. The development of *-n-* to *-m* before *b* is normal. Unfortunately, the county name was changed to Dunbarton, seemingly to avoid confusion between county and town but one cannot see where the confusion would have come in as dozens of counties in Britain are named after their county town. Another early name of Dumbarton was British *Alclut*, Gaelic *Ail Cluade* 'the rock of (the) Clyde'.

Dumfries (DMF, Scotland): fort of the copse(s) (*Dunfres* 1175, *Dunfrys*, *Dumfres* 1296). Gaelic *dùn* 'fort' and *preas* 'copse, thicket, covert'. There is a parallel series of spellings (*Dronfres*, *Drunffres* 1363, *Drumfreis* 1321, *Drumfres* 1384, etc.) with Gaelic *druim* 'ridge' as the first element and also Gaelic *dronn* 'hump'. These must originally have referred to another geographical feature—some kind of elevation— nearby, which appears to have been called 'copse ridge' or 'copse hump'. In all forms, the second part could be singular or plural, and Dumfries may therefore either derive from Gaelic *Dùn-phreas* 'fort of the copses' or *Dùn-phris* 'fort of the copse'.

Dundee (ANG, Scotland): fort of *Daig(h)* (*Donde* and *Dunde*, both in the second half of the 12th cent.). Gaelic *Dùn Dèagh*. Daig is possibly a personal name derived from *daig* 'fire'. This etymology is, however, speculative rather than certain.

Dunfermline (FIF, Scotland): fort of ? (*Dumfermelyn* 11th cent., *Dumferlin* 1124, *Dunfermlin* 1142, *Dunfermelin*, *Dunfermling* 1160, *Dunferlyne* 1375). The second element has never been explained properly. Some feel that

forms like -*fermelyn*, -*fermlin* etc., on the one hand, and -*ferlin*, -*ferlyne*, on the other, should be kept apart and that two different names have intermingled; this is, however, unlikely.

Dunoon (ARG, Scotland): fort of the river (*Dunnon* 1240, *Dunhoven* 1270, *Dunhon* 1300, *Dunnovane* 1476). Gaelic *Dùn Obhainn*.

Duns (BWK, Scotland): hills (*Duns c.* 1150, 1296, 1335). This is either Gaelic *dùn* 'hill, fort' with an English plural -*s* added (perhaps as a part-translation of a Gaelic plural *dùnan*, or the like), or Old English *dūn* 'hill' with the same plural. Although Gaelic names do occur in Berwickshire and the combination of Gaelic basic word with an English plural -*s* is not uncommon (compare *Largs*), perhaps complete English origin is more likely in this area.

Dunstable (BDF, England): Duna's post (*Dunestaple* 1123). The second element is the same as that of Barnstaple. The reference may be to a post on the boundary of an estate which belonged to a man named Duna; cf. Boston, Elstree.

Durham (DRH, England): island with a hill (*Dunholm c.* 1000, *Donelme* 1191, *Durealme c.* 1170, *Duram* 1297). This is a hybrid name, with first element English *dūn* 'hill', and second element Old Norse *holmr*. In this instance *holmr* refers to a high rock almost surrounded by the River Wear, but it is much more frequently used in place-names of low-lying ground by a river, or of an island of dry ground in a marsh; see Oldham. The prefixing of English *dūn* may have been due to consciousness that this was not a low, marshy site like most other places called *holmr*. The development from *Dunholm* to Durham is due mainly to Norman French influence which caused dissimilation of *n* to *r* in the first syllable because of the final *m*. The change in the second syllable is due to several influences, including association with the common English ending *-ham*.

E

Eastbourne (SSX, England): east stream (*Borne, Burne* 1086, *Estbourne* 1310). The stream rises near the parish church. 'East' was prefixed to distinguish this place from West-bourne, on the west boundary of the county, which was also known as *Borne* or *Burne* until the end of the thirteenth century. The two places are 50 miles apart. Both were still referred to locally as Bourne in the 1930s.

East Grinstead (SSX, England): east green place (*Grenesteda* 1121, *Estgrenested* 1271). The second element, *stede*, is discussed under Ashtead. The compound with *grēne* 'green', occurs in at least six place-names, and as two of these happened to be in the county of Sussex, they were distinguished from the late thirteenth century onwards by the prefixes 'east' and 'west'.

Easthouses (MLO, Scotland): (the) east house (*Esthus* 1241, *Esthouse* 1345, *Eisthousis* 1590–1). From Old English *ēast* and *hūs*. The singular form is not only the earliest but also the dominant one amongst the recorded spellings.

East Kilbride (LAN, Scotland): St Brigid's church (*Kellebride* 1180, *Kelbride* 1230, *Kilbrid* 1359). From Gaelic *Cill Brighde*; for *cill* see Kilmarnock. There were 15 saints called Brigid, the most famous of them being Brigid of Kildare who died in 525. The saint's name goes back to an Early Celtic *Brigantia* 'the high one'. West Kilbride is in Ayrshire.

Eastleigh (HMP, north of Southampton, England): east clearing (*Estleie* 1086, *Estleg* 1242). Since 'east' is already prefixed to *lēah* in this name at the time of the Domesday Survey, it was probably part of the original name. This example is therefore to be distinguished from numerous places originally called *Lege* to which 'east' (or 'west') was prefixed in the thirteenth century. Close aquaintance with the history of the area might make it possible to identify the settlement in relation to which Eastleigh was named, but there is no obvious answer to be deduced from the one-inch map.

Eastwood (NTT, England): east clearing (*Estewic* 1086, *Estweit* 1165, *Est Twait* 1166, *Estthweyt* 1223, *Estwood* 1575, *Eastwait alias Eastwood* 1608). This is a hybrid name, from Old English *ēast* and Old Norse *þveit*. The Old Norse term meant 'forest-clearing' and later 'meadow'. Eastwood is surrounded by English names in *-ley*, and the well-wooded

81

nature of the country probably contributed to the substitution of English *wood* for the original second element. There are several names in this area which show Scandinavian influence, another being Kirkby-in-Ashfield. It is not clear in relation to which place Eastwood was the east clearing; perhaps the reference is to its being east of the River Erewash.

Ebbw Vale (MON, Wales): vale of River Ebwy (*Eboth* 1101–20, *Ebod* 12th cent., *Ebbot c.* 1200, *Ebboth* 1296, *Ebuyth Vaur* 1348, *Ebothvaghan* 1353, *Ebboth* 1409, *Eboth* 1585, *Ebbwy Fychan* 1593, *Eboth* 1653, *Ebw Vawr* 1705). Welsh *Ebwydd* < *eb*- 'horse' + (1) *gwyth* 'anger', or (2) *gŵydd* 'wild', or (3) suffix -*wydd*, *wyth*. The first element *eb*- certainly suggests a connection between the name of the river and horses, and the second element might refer to the rapid course of the stream. 'Ebbw Vale' is a nineteenth-century artificial name for the town which grew around the iron-works which were built on the site of the farm *Pen-y-cae*—'top of the field'—(*Pen-y-cae* 1832, *Penycae* 1849). Welsh *pen* 'end, top' + definite article *y* 'the' + *cae* 'field'. The new settlement was known as Pen-y-cae until it was superseded by Ebbw Vale. The current Welsh form is *Glynebwy* [Welsh *glyn* 'valley' + *Ebw*], a translation of Ebbw Vale. The form developed as *Ebwydd, Ebwyth* > *Ebwy* > *Ebw*.

Eccles (LNC, England): (Romano-British Christian) church (*Eccles c.* 1200). This name is derived from British *eclēsia* 'church', a loan-word from Latin *ecclesia*. It occurs in a number of English place-names, uncompounded as here, or in combination with Old English words such as *healh* (as in Eccleshill STF, Ecclesall YOW), *feld* (as in Ecclesfield YOW), *hyll* (as in Eccleshall LNC, YOW), *tūn* (as in Eccleston LNC, CHE), and *lēah* (as in Exley YOW). The best explanation of its occurrence in place-names is that in each instance it denoted a building recognised by the pagan Anglo-Saxon settlers as a Christian church, a phenomenon for which they would have no English word. Christianity was the official religion of the later Roman Empire, and was well established in Britain before the end of the Roman period.

Edinburgh (MLO, Scotland): the fortress *Eidyn* (*Eidyn, Din Eidyn, Eidyn gaer*, etc. *c.* 600 (*c.* 1250); *Oppidum Eden* 10th cent. (14th cent.), *Dun Edene* 12th cent., *Dun Edenn* 1348; *Edenburge* 1126, *Edeneburg* 1142, *Edinburg c.* 1143; *Eduenesburg* 1120, *E(d)winesburg c.* 1128). The forms quoted are the Welsh (Cumbric), Gaelic, and English forms, the latter two being adaptations of the first. Edinburgh is still *Dùn Eideann* in Gaelic to-day.

It is perhaps necessary to refute again the idea that the name Edinburgh has developed from Old English *Eadwinesburh* 'Edwin's fortress'. There are three main reasons why this theory cannot be correct: (a) Edinburgh was besieged by the Angles in 638 five years after King Edwin of Northumbria (617–33) had died in battle; (b) the name occurs in its Early Welsh form in the *Gododdin* poem around 600, i.e. before Edwin's kingship; (c) spellings like *Edwinesburg* (with a -*w*- and a possessive -*s*-) are confined to the twelfth century and therefore reflect a certain scribal pseudo-learned tradition, no more, for spellings without these two letters abound before, during, and after that period. 'Edwin's fortress' is therefore a scribal etymology of the twelfth century which is impossible to defend but which has lingered on in history books as a convenient explanation, especially in view of the fact that we do not know what Eidyn, the name of the fortification, meant. Perhaps the meaning was not known in the seventh century either, which is why both Gaels and Angles had to be content with a part-translation, rendering *Din* as *Dùn* and *-burgh* respectively, but merely adapting *Eidyn* phonologically.

Egham (SUR, England): Ecga's village (*Egeham* 933, *Eggeham* c. 1060, *Egham* 1201). This is a name of the same type as Amersham.

Elgin (MOR, Scotland): little Ireland (?) (*Elgin* 1136, 1150–53, 1160). Gaelic *Eilginn* is supposed to be a locative case of *Eilgin*, a diminutive of *Elg* or *Ealg*, one of the Gaelic names for Ireland in the Dark Ages. The same term appears in Glenelg, a district-name in western Inverness-shire.

Elland (YOW, England): estate by the river (*Elant* 1086, *Eiland* 1167, *Elande* 1202). The name refers to the position of the place on the south bank of the River Calder. The compound *ēa-land* 'river' or 'water-land' is recorded in Old English as a compound noun meaning 'island', but in this place-name it is perhaps more likely to be an *ad hoc* compound describing the position of this particular estate. Elland is one of a group of names which have *-land* as

their final element, others being Greetland ('gravel-land'), Stainland ('stone-land'), Norland ('north land'), and Barkisland ('land belonging to a man named Bark'). This was probably an area where arable farming was not practised until late in the Anglo-Saxon period, and *land* may mean 'newly-cultivated land'.

Ellesmere Port (CHE, England): this is the town which grew up where the Ellesmere Canal reached the Mersey, see Stourport. The scheme for making the canal was launched at Ellesmere SHR in 1791. The Shropshire name means 'Elli's lake'. The place in Cheshire was called Ellesmere Port as early as 1796, but there was a local preference for the name Whitby Wharf or Whitby Locks, and the railway station was called Whitby Locks when it was opened in 1863. Whitby is a genuine place-name, of Scandinavian origin, meaning 'white village'.

Elstree (HRT, England): Tidwulf's tree (*Tiðulfes treow* a. 1086, *Tidulvestre* 1188, *Idolvestre* 1254, *Idelestre* 1320, *Illestre* 1487, *Elstre* 1598, *Idelstrey alias Elstrey* 1675). The loss of initial *T-* is due to a misunderstanding of the Middle English phrase which meant 'at Elstree', the initial *T-* of the place-name being mistaken for the final *-t* of the preposition *at*. The earliest reference is not to a settlement but to a boundary-mark (possibly an actual tree) on the boundary of an estate at Aldenham. This suggests that while Elstree is formally a name of the same type as Braintree, Coventry, and Oswestry, the meaning in this instance may be 'tree on the boundary of an estate belonging to

Tidwulf'. The settlement at Elstree appears to have grown up at a cross-roads which divides the village into four parts, lying respectively in the parishes of Aldenham, Elstree, Stanmore, and Edgware. The eponymous Tidwulf could have been the owner of one of the four estates which met at this point.

Ely (CAM, England): eel district (*Elge c.* 730 Bede's Ecclesiastical History, *Elige c.* 900 Anglo-Saxon Chronicle, *Eligbyrig* 1036 Anglo-Saxon Chronicle, *Eli c.* 1100 Anglo-Saxon Chronicle). The original second element was *gē* 'district', a word belonging to the earliest period of English place-name formation, which is also the final element of the county-name Surrey ('southern district'). Bede refers to the *regio* called *Elge*, which makes it clear that this was one of the 'regions' or 'provinces' which were the administrative divisions of the Anglo-Saxon kingdoms before they were organised into shires. Because Ely is an island in the Fens, *gē* was confused with *ieg* 'island', and the spellings *Elige*, *Eligbyrig* show this confusion. *Eligbyrig* means 'Ely town', and probably reflects the status of the place as an ecclesiastical centre (see Bury St Edmunds). The economic importance of the eels continued long after the Anglo-Saxon period.

Epping (ESX, England): (?) the people of the look-out place (*Eppinges* 1086, *Upping* 1227). In this name the suffix -*ingas* (which is discussed in the *Introduction*, p. 16) has been added to a topographical term. The numerous -*ingas* names of Essex include several which are of this type, as well as many of the type represented by Barking, in which the first element is a personal name. Nazeing, the adjacent parish to the north-west of Epping, means 'the people of the spur of land'. In Epping, the topographical term is Old English *yppe*, a rare place-name element, which is a derivative of *upp*, and is recorded mainly with reference to buildings, where it can mean a dais at the end of a hall, or an upper chamber. More promising for place-name purposes is the single reference in which Latin *spectacula* is glossed *yppe vel weardsteal*. *spectacula* means here not 'things looked at', but 'place from which things are looked at'. The alternative gloss to *yppe*, *weardsteal*, means 'watch-place', and the equivalent term *weardsetl* occurs in place-names in that sense, sometimes referring to an Iron Age hill-fort. Probably *yppe* means 'look-out place', and in Epping it may refer to the ridge south of the town which is covered by the remains of Epping Forest, and perhaps specifically to the hill-fort called Ambersbury Banks at the north end of this ridge. Uppingham RUT is the village of another group of people called *Yppingas*; in this instance, *yppe* may refer to the ridge west of Uppingham.

Epsom (SUR, England): Ebbi's village (*Ebbesham c.* 973, *Ebsham* 1297, *Epsam* 1404, *Ebisham alias Epsom* 1718). This is a name of the same type as Amersham.

Esher (SUR, England): ash-tree district (*Æscæron* 1005, *Esshere* 1062). The second element is Old English *scearu* 'share', which sometimes means 'boundary' in place-names, but is considered to mean 'district' in this name and in Waldershare, KNT.

Evesham (WOR, England): land in a river-bend belonging to *Ēof* (*Eofeshamme c.* 1020). Old English *hamm* has the same significance as in Buckingham, and the sites of the two towns are very similar. Pensham and Birlingham, to the west of Evesham, are also names in *-hamm* referring to places enclosed by loops of the River Avon.

Evesham had several alternative prefixes in Old English. It is *Ethom* ('at the river bend'), *Cronuchomme* ('river-bend frequented by cranes'), *Ecguines hamme* ('Ecgwine's river-bend', from Bishop Ecgwine who founded the monastery), and in one charter it is referred to simply as *Homme*.

Evington (LEI, England): estate associated with Eafa (*Avintone* 1086, *Evington* 1254). This is a name of the same type as Addington.

Ewell (SUR, England): river-source (*Euuelle* 933). A large stream which is one of the head-waters of the Hogs Mill River rises at Ewell.

Exeter (DEV, England): Roman town on the River Exe (*Exanceaster c.* 900 Anglo-Saxon Chronicle). Exe is a Celtic river-name, which simply means 'water'. In Roman times the town was called *Isca*, the ancient form of the river-name.

Exmouth (DEV, England): (place at) the mouth of the River Exe (*Exanmuða c.* 1025 Anglo-Saxon Chronicle). The early spelling refers to the actual river-mouth (which is mentioned in the Chronicle because a Danish army landed there in 1001), not to the town, which is of comparatively recent origin. The village here (which John Leland in about 1540 called 'a Fisschar Tounlet, a litle withyn the Havyn Mouth') became a seaside resort in the eighteenth century.

F

Failsworth (LNC, England): (?) enclosure with a special type of fence (*Fayleswrthe* 1212). The second element, Old English *worð*, is sometimes compounded with a first element denoting a type of enclosure, as in Haywards Heath and Letchworth. Other instances, not in this volume, are Hurworth DRH (from *hurð* 'hurdle') and Shuttleworth DRB, LNC, YOW (from *scytels*, perhaps meaning 'a bolt'). On the analogy of these names, it has been suggested that the first element of Failsworth is an unrecorded word **fēgels*, derived from *fēgan* 'to join', and denoting a particular type of fence.

Falkirk (STL, Scotland): the speckled church (*Egglesbreth c* 1120 (1165–70); *Eiglesbrec, Egglesbrec* 1166; *Varia Capella* 1166; *la Veire Chapelle* 1301; (la) *Faukirk* 1298, *Fawkirk* 1391; *Fauskyrk* 1564; *Falkirk* 1458). One of the most interesting Scottish place-names especially as it is recorded in various languages of which the above are only significant sample spellings. In short, the story of the name is roughly this: It started out as a Gaelic **Eaglais B(h)rec* before 1080 (with a reasonable possibility of an earlier Cumbric name). By 1166 it had been translated into English although there is initially only indirect evidence for

this in the Latin *Varia Capella* and the Norman French *la Veire Chapelle*. This new English name is *Faw Kirk* containing as its first element Middle English *fawe, faȝe* 'variegated, of various colours'. By false analogy with such Scots words as *ba'* (< *ball*), *fa'* (< *fall*) etc., a new spelling *Falkirk* is produced from the middle of the fifteenth century onwards which in turn has given rise to a new pronunciation, i.e. one pronouncing the -*l*- which is still silent in the pronunciation of the Falkirk people themselves. *Fauskyrk* only occurs on two sixteenth-century maps. The modern Gaelic name is still *An Eaglais Bhreac* 'the speckled church'.

Falmouth (CRN, England): (place at) the mouth of the River Fal (*Falemuth* 1235). The meaning of the river-name (*Fæle* 969) is not known.

Fareham (HMP, England): village among ferns (*Fernham* 1086, *Fereham c.* 1130). A number of other place-names with *fearn* as first element have also lost the -*n*-, instances being Farley STF, Farleigh KNT, SOM, and Farlow SHR.

Farnborough (HMP, England): fern-covered hill (*Ferneberga* 1086). The hill may be the one surrounded by the 250 foot contour which has

Farnborough Park at its southern end. The same name occurs in Berkshire, Kent, and Warwickshire, and, in the modern form Farmborough, in Somerset. Farnham SUR is about six miles south.

Farnham (SUR, England): fern-covered river-meadow (*Fernham c.* 686, *Fearnhamme c.* 900). Farnham is beside the River Wey, and is an excellent example of *hamm* (discussed under Buckingham) in the sense 'river-meadow'.

Farnworth (LNC, south of Bolton, England): enclosure among ferns (*Farnewurd* 1185). Old English *worð* occurs fairly frequently with wild plant-names.

Fauldhouse (WLO, Scotland): house on unploughed land (*Fawlhous* 1523, *Falhous c.* 1540). A compound of Old English *f(e)alh* 'ploughed land', later 'fallow land', and *hūs* 'house'. From the sixteenth century onwards (*Faldhous* 1559–60), the first part of the name was confused with Scots *fauld* 'fold'.

Faversham (KNT, England): (?) village of the smith (*Fefresham* 811, *Fæfresham c.* 935). The first element is generally assumed to be an Old English loan-word from Latin *faber*, but the word is not recorded except in this place-name. The suggested derivation is interesting, as Faversham is adjacent to a small Romano-British settlement (at Syndale House, west of the town), and the grave-goods in Anglo-Saxon burials near Faversham suggest that there was a centre of fine metal-working here during the pagan Anglo-Saxon period. Possibly the metal-working was already established when the

English settlers came, so that they referred to it in naming the place, and the industry then continued after the settlement.

Felixstowe (SFK, England): (?) holy place of St Felix (*Filchestou* 1254, *Filchestowe* 1291, 1375, *Fylthestowe* 1359). Old English *stōw* (discussed under Bristol) frequently means 'religious place' in place-names, and a high proportion of names in -*stow* have a saint's name as first element, and refer to churches dedicated to the saint. St Felix was the first bishop of East Anglia, and the seat of his bishopric was at Dunwich, further up the Suffolk coast. It is generally assumed that Felixstowe was named from him, but the early spellings at present available cannot be said to prove this. In fact they suggest that a different first element has been remodelled by association with Felix, but the material available is not full enough to allow us to come to any definite conclusion in this respect.

Ferryhill (DRH, England): wooded hill (*Feregenne* 10th cent., *Ferie c.* 1125, *Ferye on the Hill* 1316, *Ferye on ye mount* 1646). Ferryhill is at the eastern end of a ridge. Old English *fiergen* 'wooded hill' became *Ferye*, and -*on the Hill* (now shortened to -*hill*) was probably added to prevent confusion with Ferrybridge YOW. This last name (which refers to a ferry across the River Aire) appears as *Ferie*, *Feria*, *Fery*, etc. in most references of the eleventh and twelfth centuries, and it would be necessary to distinguish the two places from each other as both are on the Great North Road.

Filton (GLO, England): hay farm (*Filton, Fylton* 1187, *Fylton of the Hay* 1542). The meaning of the name must have been forgotten long before 1542; and the addition *of the Hay* is interesting evidence for the continuity of agricultural specialisation. The good meadow land at Filton is referred to in the names Broad Mead, to the north, and Southmead, to the south-west.

Fishguard (PEM, Wales): fish yard (*Fissigart* 1200, *Fissegard, id est, Aber gweun* 1210, *Fisgard* 1290, *Fissingard* 13th cent., *Fiscard* 1397, *Fishcard* 1496, *Fisshegarth* 1543). Old Norse *fiskigarðr* 'yard for catching or keeping fish' rather than English *fishgarth* 'enclosure for catching or keeping fish'. Scandinavian influence is fairly strong in Pembrokeshire, but some forms above betray English spellings.

The Welsh name is *Abergwaun* 'mouth of the River Gwaun' (*Fissegard, id est, Aber gweun* 1210, *Aber Gwavn* 15th cent., *Aber gwayn* 1566, *Abergwain* 1586, *Aberguain als. Fiscard* 1698). Welsh *aber* 'estuary' + *Gwaun* (river-name). *Gvoun* 13th cent., *Gweun* 13th cent., *Goweyn* 1483, *Gweyn* 1500.) Welsh *gwaun* 'marsh, moor, wet meadow'.

Fleet (HMP, England): stream (*Le Flete* 1506). Old English *fléot* is more common in coastal names and usually means 'estuary, inlet, creek', but there are some instances in which it clearly refers to a small inland stream. Byfleet SUR, Fletton HNT, and Fleet Marston BUC are other names in which it has this meaning.

Fleetwood (LNC, England): the town was laid out in 1836 by Sir Peter Hesketh Fleetwood, the owner of Rossall Hall (now a public school south-west of the town), and was named after him.

Flint (FLI, Wales): flint, hard rock (*Le Chaylou* 1277, *le Flynt* 1277, *Le Cayllou* 1278, *Flind* 1277, *Flint* 1284, *le Fflynt* 1300, *Flynt* 1368, *y flynt* 14th cent., *Flynt* 1400, *y Fflint* 1450, *y fflint hen* 1468, *y fflynt* 1566). English *flint* 'flint, hard rock', because the castle was built on a rocky ledge in the River Dee. The Old French forms are *caillou* 'flint'. The definite article in the early English forms has disappeared, except in Welsh *Y Fflint*. The Welsh form *Caer Gallestr* (*K. Gallestr* 1604, *Caer Gallestr* 1757) is an antiquarian translation which gained no currency. Welsh *caer* 'fort' + *callestr* 'flint'.

Flixton (LNC, England): Flik's estate (*Flixton* 1177). This name occurs also in Suffolk (two examples) and the East Riding of Yorkshire. The personal name is of Danish origin, as is *Urm* in the nearby Urmston, and these two names indicate a Danish strain in the population of this region south-west of Manchester, Davyhulme, in the same region, contains Old Norse *hulm* 'island, water-meadow'.

Folkestone (KNT, England): (?) Folca's stone (*Folcanstan* c. 697, 824, 830, c. 833, 844, *Folces stane* 946). Folkestone is the meeting place of a 'hundred', and if the first element is a personal name the formation is similar to that of other hundred-names listed under Boston. Alternatively, the first element might be the genitive of an unrecorded weak

89

form (*folce*) of the word *folc* 'people'. The name would then mean 'stone of the people', which might be a way of saying that it was a stone marking a meeting place.

Forfar (ANG, Scotland): unexplained (*Forfar* 1137, *Forfare c.* 1200). All attempts to find a suitable and acceptable etymology have so far been unsuccessful.

Fraserburgh (ABD, Scotland): its earlier name was *Faithlie* which was erected into a free burgh of barony on 2 November 1546. In 1592 it is called *burgum et portum de Fraser*, and in 1601 *Fraserburgh*, after Sir Alexander Fraser of Phillorth. Its nickname in Buchan and the Scottish north-east is *The Broch*.

Frinton-on-Sea (ESX, England): (?) Friða's estate (*Frientuna* 1086, *Frien-ton*' 1158, *Frichintona* 1212). This may be a name of the same type as Addington. Alternatively, the first element could be a word *friðen* meaning 'protected'.

Frome (SOM, England): (place by) the River Frome (*Froom* 705, *Frome* 955). There are five English rivers with this name, the other four being in Dorset, Gloucestershire (two examples), and Herefordshire; and the Welsh form of the name occurs in Ffraw in Anglesey. It is a British name, which means 'fine, fair, brisk'. The River Frome in Somerset and Wiltshire is quite long, and there are a number of settlements on its banks. Perhaps Frome was the earliest of these, since a reference to the river was felt to distinguish it from other places.

G

Gainsborough (LIN, England): Gegn's fortified place (*Gegnesburh, Gægnesburh* 1013 Anglo-Saxon Chronicle, *Gainesburg* 1086). This is a name of the same type as Aylesbury. When Swein Forkbeard, King of Denmark, invaded England in 1013, he sailed down the Trent as far as Gainsborough, where he disembarked and was accepted as king by the leading men of the Danelaw; his choice of this place as a temporary headquarters may indicate that the settlement had some defences.

Galashiels (SLK, Scotland): the *shiels* on Gala (Water) (*Galuschel c.* 1360, *Gallowschel* 1416, *Galoschelis* 1468). Scottish *shiel* 'hut, cottage, temporary shelter' has developed from Middle English *schele* which especially referred to 'a shepherd's hut on the summer pastures'. (The rivername is *Galche, Galue* 1143–4, *Galhe* 1180, etc.) Although Old English *galga* 'gallows' has by some been taken to be the basis of it, there is really no semantic support for this notion. It is much more likely a pre-English river-name whose meaning we do not know.

Garforth (YOW, England): ford by the gore (*Gereford* 1086). The same name occurs in Berkshire with the modern form Garford. The change of Old English *ford* to *forth* is fairly common in north-country place-names; and the early spellings of Garforth (many of which have *Gere-* instead of *Gare-*) have been influenced by the Old Norse word *geiri*, which is cognate with Old English *gāra*. The meaning of *gāra* in place-names has not yet been determined with any precision. It is a derivative of *gār* 'spear', and is considered to mean 'a triangular plot of ground'. This does not, however, seem particularly appropriate in the case of Garforth and Garford, and if the topography of all the place-names containing this word were considered, other possible meanings might emerge. Some sites, especially those of Langar NTT and Plungar LEI (which are quite close to each other) suggest a meaning 'narrow strip of raised ground in a marsh'.

Gateshead (DRH, England): the head of the goat (*Caprae Caput c.* 730 Bede's Ecclesiastical History, *Gatesheued* 1196). There are about 40 English place-names of the same type as Gateshead, consisting of *hēafod*, 'head', and the genitive singular of an animal, bird, or reptile name, other examples being Hartshead LNC, Ravenshead NTT. The suggestion was once made that these names referred to a custom of marking a meeting-place by the erection of a sort of totem pole, bearing either an actual head or a representation of one, but there is little reason to think that meeting-places are commonly referred to and in general the attempts to demonstrate a pagan religious significance for these place-names are far from conclusive. There is room for a systematic investigation of the topography of all place-names containing *hēafod*, irrespective of the type of first element. The word is used in place-names in various transferred senses, such as 'headland, summit, upper end, source of a stream', and the topographic significance may be decisive in most names of the Gateshead type. The first elements might then refer to the frequenting of the topographical feature by a particular bird or beast. On this interpretation, Gateshead would mean 'headland where a goat is frequently seen'. Another possibility is that there was at these places a hill or a rock which bore a rough resemblance to an animal's head.

Gelli Y (BRE, Wales), see *Hay*.

Gillingham (KNT, England): village of the family or followers of Gylla (*Gillingeham, Gyllingeham* 10th cent.). A compound of a folk-name in *-ingas* with Old English *hām* 'village', this type of name is discussed more fully in the *Introduction*, p. 18.

Girvan (AYR, Scotland): unexplained (*Girven* 1275, *Gervan* 1328). The name of the town is surely derived from the river at the mouth of which it lies. However, Gaelic *gearr abhainn* 'short river' is quite unacceptable, and one suspects a river-name of

pre-Gaelic origin. It is not clear whether, when he takes Ptolemy's *Vindogara* to have been near Girvan, Watson (p. 27) considered them to be etymologically connected. For the second element in V. he compares Gaelic *gar, garan* 'thicket', in which case *Vindo-garan* would mean 'white thicket'.

Glasbury (RAD, Wales): 'market town of the monastic community' (*Clastbyrig* 1056, *Glesburia* 1191, *Glasbur* 1291, *Glasebury* 1296, *Glasbury* 1298, *Classebury* 1322, *Glasburgh* 1331, *Glesbiri* 1536–9). Welsh *clas* 'monastic community, sanctuary, cloister', + Old English *burh* 'fortified place, borough, market town'. This is a hybrid Welsh–English name. The Welsh form is *Clas(-ar-Wy)* 'community on the River Wye' (*i'r Clâs c.* 1450, *y klas ar wy* 1566). For *Wye*, see *Rhaeadr*.

Glasgow (LAN, Scotland): green hollow (*Glasgu* 1136, *Glascu* 1165–78, *Glasgo, -gu, -cu, -ku* 14th cent.). Gaelic older *Glaschu*, now usually *Glascho*. Originally a British name for the chief ecclesiastical centre of Strathclyde, composed of the adjective *glas* 'green' and the noun Welsh *cau* 'hollow'. This British form, with mutation of *c* to *g*, has survived in present Anglicised usage. There is, however, also the Gaelic form which properly aspirates *c* to *ch* after the adjective. This may go back to a true Gaelic parallel in British times, a compound of Gaelic *glas* 'green' and Irish *cua* (Old Irish *cue*) 'cup, hollow'.

Glenrothes (FIF, Scotland): as far as can be ascertained, this name of Scotland's second New Town first appeared in print in the *Draft New Town (Glenrothes) Designation Order, 1948*, published as a memorandum by the Secretary of State for Scotland. The first part presumably refers to the valley of the River Leven, and the second element was chosen because the Fife Coal Company had begun the construction of the nearby modern Rothes colliery in 1946. Historical associations of the Earls of Rothes with the 'Glenrothes' area, particularly with Leslie, are of course many centuries old.

Glossop (DRB, England): Glott's valley (*Glosop* 1086, *Glotsop*' 1219). Old English *hop*, used of remote valleys, is common on both sides of the Pennines, in the Welsh Marches, and on the English/Scottish border.

Gloucester (GLO, England): Roman town called Glevum (*coloniae Glev*' 2nd-cent. Latin inscription, *Brittannico sermone Cair Gloiw Saxonice autem Gloecester c.* 800 Nennius's *Historia Brittonum, Gleawan ceaster c.* 900 Anglo-Saxon Chronicle, *Gleweceaster* 984, *Glowecestre, Glouuecestre* 1086, *Glowster* 1618, *Gloster* 1666). This is a name of the same type as Cirencester. The Romano-British name *Glevum* is probably derived from a Celtic stem meaning 'bright'. Popular etymology (which frequently affects the Old English development of Romano-British names) may have caused Old English *glēaw* 'wise, prudent', and later the stem of the verb *glōwan* 'to glow', to be substituted for the original first element.

Glynebwy (MON, Wales), see *Ebbw Vale*.

Godalming (SUR, England): Godhelm's people (*æt Godelmingum c.* 880, *Godelminge* 1086, *Godhelming* 1173, *Godalminges* 1221). This is a name of the same type as Barking (see *Introduction*, p. 18).

Golspie (SUT, Scotland): gold village or Gulli's v. (*Goldespy* 1330), Gaelic *Goillsbidh*. This is a Norse name in *býr* 'homestead, village'. The first element is not very easily etymologised. It may be the word *guld* 'gold', as in the Norwegian *Guldbringen, Guldaakeren, Guldhang*, etc., or it may be a man's name, like *Gulli*. Similar names in Norway show the same ambiguity.

Goole (YOW, England): stream (*gulla in Merskland* 1356, *Gulle in Houk*', *aque Gulle* 1362). The reference of 1362 is to the building of a new bank to prevent flooding of the river called *Gulle*. This stream-name is derived from a Middle English word *goule* or *gole*, which occurs in a few minor place-names, and which survives in dialect in Lancashire, Yorkshire, Somerset, and Devon with various meanings including 'ditch, natural watercourse, deep trench'. The word was influenced by Old French *goule* 'throat', but was probably of independent Germanic origin, and may be derived from an unrecorded Old English term. The canal called Dutch River may be the straightened course of the old stream from which Goole is named. Possibly the use of the name *Gulle* for it in the fourteenth century implies that some work had already been done towards making it a drainage channel, but it is not certain that the word was primarily used for a canalised stream in Middle English.

Gorleston-on-Sea (NFK, England): (?) Gurl's estate (*Gorlestuna* 1086, *Gurlestona* 1130). The query arises from there being no such personal name as *Gurl* on record. The place-name Girlington, which occurs in the West and North Ridings of Yorkshire, appears to contain a personal name *Gyrla*, however, and *Gurl* could be related to this. The word *girl*, which is first recorded in the thirteenth century meaning a young person of either sex, may have been derived from an unrecorded Old English word, and this would provide a stem from which personal names could be formed.

Gosforth (NTB, England): ford of the geese (*Goseford* 1166). The same name occurs at least four times elsewhere; in Cumberland and Northumberland these names show the north-country confusion of -*d* with -*th*, the others have the modern form Gosford. North of Newcastle the A1 crosses two small streams, one south and one north of the modern town of Gosforth. One of these stream-crossings may have been the original 'ford of the geese'.

Gosport (HMP, England): market town where geese were sold (*Goseport* 1250). There are three Old English words, all with the form *port*, which are difficult to distinguish from each other in place-names, and were probably liable to some confusion in the Old English period. These are:

(1) *port* 'a haven, a harbour', a loan-word from Latin *portus*; this is discussed under Portsmouth.

(2) *port* 'a town, a market town, a market', found in various examples of the name Newport. This is of uncertain origin, and may be derived either from Latin *portus* 'harbour', or from the word discussed under (3).

(3) *port* 'a gate, the entrance to a walled town'. This is a loan-word from Latin *porta*, and is rare in place-names.

Portsmouth Harbour was called *Port* from (1), and Portsmouth and other names discussed with it are derived from this. Gosport, in spite of its position on the other side from Portsmouth of the entrance to the Harbour, should be dissociated from these names. Probably it is of much later origin, and contains *port* (2), which is also found in Newport IOW.

Gourock (RNF, Scotland): the rounded hillock (*Over et Nether Gowcokis* 1628, *Ouir et Nether Gowrockis* 1661); from Gaelic *guireag* 'a pimple'.

Grangemouth (STL, Scotland): mouth of the Grange Burn. Founded in 1777 by Sir Lawrence Dundas in connection with the Forth and Clyde Canal, begun in 1768 and opened in 1790, but closed to navigation since 1963. It stands where the small Grange Burn flows into the River Carron, after having passed the site of Abbot Grange from which it takes its name. *Grange* which is from Old French *grange*, means 'granary'.

Grantham (LIN, England): Granta's village (*Grantham, Granham, Grandham* 1086). This is a name of the same type as Amersham.

Gravesend (KNT, England): (place at) the end of the grove (*Gravesham* 1086, *Grauessend* 1157).

94

Grays (ESX, England): this is an example of a post-Conquest owner's name being added to a place-name, and then replacing the place-name in local use. The full name of the place is Grays Thurrock. Thurrock is Old English *þurruc*, only recorded in the sense 'bilge of a ship', but probably meaning 'a place where filthy water collects (as in a ship's bilge)' and here applied to a large stretch of marsh by the Thames, west of Tilbury. The three settlements named from the marsh were felt to need distinguishing prefixes or suffixes in the medieval period. Two of them eventually became known as Little and West Thurrock, while Grays Thurrock (*Turruc* 1086, *Turrokgreys* 1248, *Grayes* 1399, *Grace* 1547, *Grace Thurrock* 1552) was named from Henry *de Grai*, to whom it was granted in 1195, and who derived his surname from Graye in Normandy.

Greenock (RNF, Scotland): sunny knoll (*Grenok c.* 1400, *Greinok* 1635). It is Gaelic *Grianaig*, dative of *grianag* 'a sunny knoll'.

Grimsby (LIN, England): Grīm's village (*Grimesbi* 1086). This is a Danish name of the same type as Corby. Danish names are very common in the area.

Guildford (SUR, England): ford by golden sand (*Gyldeforda c.* 880, *Gildeford* 1086). F. G Mellersh has pointed out that the ford cannot have been on the site of the present bridge, where the current would have been too strong. It was probably at St Catherine's, where the Pilgrim's Way crosses the river, and below St Catherine's is a golden sandy escarpment. The spelling of *c.* 880 shows that the first element is a noun or place-name (not the adjective *gylden*). Perhaps *Gylde* 'golden one' was the name of the escarpment. The ridge now called Hogs Back west of Guildford was earlier called Guildown (*Geldedon* 1195). This may be elliptical for *Gyldeford-dūn* 'Guildford Down'.

Guisborough (YON, England): (?) Gígr's fortified place (*Ghigesburg, Gighesborc* 1086, *Giseburgh c.* 1130). This may be a name of the same type as Aylesbury, with an Old Norse, instead of an Old English, personal name as first element. There is, however, no certain record of the Norse name *Gígr*, which has been suggested.

95

H

Haddington (ELO, Scotland): farm associated with *Hada* (*Hadynton* 1098, *Hadintunschira c.* 1139, *Hadingtoun c.* 1150). Probably identical with Haddington (LIN, England; *Hadinctune* 1086, *Hadingtun* 1212). For the significance of *-ingtūn* names, see *Introduction*, p. 18.

Hale (CHE, England): river-meadow (*Hale* 1086). This name is derived from *halh* in the sense discussed under Bramhall. The River Bollin forms the southern boundary of the parish.

Halesowen (WOR, England): the valleys (*Hala* 1086, *Hales Regis* 12th cent., *Hales Owayne* 1272). This is the plural of *halh*, for which see Arnold, Bramhall, Hale. The precise meaning is not certain in this instance, but the ground here is much broken, and 'valleys' seems a reasonable translation. Owen was a Welsh prince who married a sister of Henry II and became lord of Hales in 1204.

Halifax (YOW, England): (?) area of coarse grass in a nook of land (*Halifax, Halyfax c.* 1095). This is a difficult place-name, which has given rise to much discussion. The most recent, and most authoritative, suggestion is that the final element is an Old English word *gefeaxe* (from *feax* 'hair', used in place-names to describe rough grass, and a collective prefix *ge-*) and the first element either *halh* 'nook of land', or *hall* 'rock'. In the early seventeenth century the name was thought to mean 'holy hair', and this gave rise to strange legends, one about a beheaded maiden, and another involving the head of John the Baptist.

Hamilton (LAN, Scotland): doubtful. Until 1445, the name of the village and barony was Cadzow (*Cadihow* 1150, *Kadihou* 1222, *Cadyow* 1359) of uncertain, but probably Cumbric, derivation. On the erection of the barony of Cadzow into the lordship of Hamilton, the castle, church, and village names were also changed to Hamilton. It is said that the name was brought from England by the Hamilton family; in that case it may well be identical with Hamilton LEI (*Hamelton c.* 1125, *Hameldon* 1220–35) which is either '*Hamela*'s farm' or 'bare hill' (Old English *hamel* 'maimed'). If, on the other hand, it is of local origin, such explanations would make the name too early, and one might consider the suggestion that it is a corruption of *Haugh-mill-town*. This, however, must be viewed with considerable caution, especially in view of the fact that the family name first occurs in

1296 as *Wauter fiz Gilbert de Hameldone*. There was also a *Gilbert de Hameldun*, clericus, in 1292. The personal name seems to favour the derivation from *hamel dūn* 'bare hill', as well as English, particularly Northern English, origin.

Harlech (MER, Wales): fair slab of stone (*Hardelagh*, 1290–2, 1294–5, *Harthelegh* 1316, *Harlech* 14th cent., *Hardlech* 14th cent., *Harddlech* 1450, *Cappel Harddlech* 1590, *Harlech* 1586). Welsh *hardd* 'fair, handsome' + *llech* 'stone, slab'. The name probably refers to the high crag on which the castle stands, and was known before the Norman castle was built. It occurs in the second Branch of the Mabinogi. The English forms *Hardelagh, Harthelegh* are approximations of Welsh *Harddlech*. The *-dd-* was lost early in spoken Welsh.

Harlow (ESX, England): army-mound (*Herlawe* 1045, *Harlawe* 1254). The final element, Old English *hlāw*, very frequently refers to a tumulus, but can be used of a natural hill. The Roman temple near Harlow Railway Station stood on top of a small hill, which was surrounded by a ditch, and one end of which had been artificially scarped. This slightly artificial appearance might have caused the hill to be called a *hlāw* by the Anglo-Saxons. The first element is Old English *here* 'army', which is the word regularly used in the Anglo-Saxon Chronicle for the invading Viking army. There is very little evidence for Danish settlement in Essex, but the county suffered a great deal from Danish raids, and was part of the Danelaw. Harlow may have gained its name from some events during the Viking invasions

of 865–92, or the later ones of 991–1016. There was another instance of the name in Essex, a field at Little Maplestead, which was *Le Herlawe* fourteenth century, *Harlow Hill* 1935; and it is possible, though not certain, that Harlow Hill near the Roman Wall in Northumberland, and Harlow Hill YOW near Harrogate have the same etymology.

Harpenden (HRT, England): harp-valley (*Herpedene c.* 1060, *Harpedene* 1196, *Harpendena* 1285). Harpsden OXF has the same etymology. Both places are on the southern edge of the Chiltern Hills, and in both cases the valley is long, narrow, and shallow. In the case of Harpenden it is probably the valley to the northwest of the town, along which the A6 runs. It is very difficult to say why the word *harp* (Old English *hearpe*) should have been used to describe these valleys.

Harrogate (YOW, England): road to the cairn (*Harwegate* 1332, *Harougat* 1333). This is a Scandinavian name, the final element being Old Norse *gata* 'road, street', which is often found in street-names in areas where there was Norwegian or Danish settlement.

Hartlepool (DRH, England): (?) bay near the stag island (*Herterpol c.* 1180, *Herterpul c.* 1190, *Hertelpol* 1195). The 'pool' is Hartlepool Bay, but the history of the first part of the name is not entirely clear. It is connected with a monastery called *Heruteu* mentioned in Bede's Ecclesiastical History. Bede translates *Heruteu* 'insula cervi' (i.e. 'island of the stag'), and there seems no doubt that this is the correct etymology.

The seventh-century monastery is thought to have been on Hartlepool Peninsula (the 'island' of the place-name), where some building remains and inscribed stones have been found which are almost certainly connected with it. An area inland from Hartlepool was called Hartness (*Heorternesse c.* 1050, *Heorternysse c.* 1130). This name is a compound of *heorot-ēg* 'hart-island', with Old English *hȳrness*, used in place-names of a district under special jurisdiction; it probably refers to the district being in some way dependent on the monastery. It has been suggested that Middle English *Herterpol* (later turned into Hartlepool by the common confusion of -*r*- and -*l*-) arose from the influence of *Herternes*, the Middle English form of the district-name. The relationship of Hart, the name of a village about three miles inland, to Hartlepool poses considerable difficulties, in the absence of a detailed study of the place-names of this area.

Harwich (ESX, England): army-camp (*Herewic* 1248, *Harewyche* 1470). Old English *herewic* is a compound noun recorded in literary sources with this meaning. In the name Harwich it probably refers to a camp of the Danish army during the invasions of 865–92 or those of 991–1016.

Harwood, Great (LNC, England): grey wood (*Majori Harewuda a.* 1123, *Magna Harwod* 1303). There are several other instances of this name in England. 'Great' was prefixed for distinction from Little Harwood, west of Great Harwood and separated from it by Rishton.

Probably both settlements were named from the same extensive wood.

Haslemere (SUR, England): hazel-pool (*Heselmere* 1221, *Haselmere* 1255). The pond has apparently disappeared, but the settlement probably arose here because of the convenient water supply which it afforded.

Haslingden (LNC, England): valley where hazel-trees grow (*Heselingedon* 1242, *Haselendene*, *Heselindene* 1246). The town is situated in a valley surrounded by high moors.

Hastings (SSX, England): Hæsta's people (*Hastinges* 1086). This is a name of the same type as Barking. For both see *Introduction*, p. 18. Such names are very common in south Sussex. The *Hæstingas* are mentioned in historical records in connection with events in 771 and 1011. In 1011 they were still regarded as distinct from the South Saxons, and it seems likely that their territory corresponded to the Rape of Hastings, which is roughly the eastern third of the county of Sussex.

The actual town of Hastings does not appear to have been referred to simply by the tribal name until about the date of the Norman Conquest. In the Burghal Hidage of about 915 and in the Anglo-Saxon Chronicle under the year 1050 it is called *Hæstingaceastre* 'Roman town of the *Hæstingas*', and this name probably arose because of the ruins of the small Romano-British settlement here. *Hæstinga* on pre-Conquest coins is probably an abbreviation for *Hæstingaceastre*. This may have

99

alternated with the name *Hæstinga-port*, 'market town of the *Hæstingas*', which occurs in the Anglo-Saxon Chronicle under the year 1066; it is noteworthy that in the same entry the chronicler also uses *Hæstingan*, which is the dative of the tribal name, probably with reference to the district, not the town. The Bayeux Tapestry has *Hestenga ceastra* once, and *Hestenga, Hestinga* (perhaps the abbreviation used on the coins) in two other inscriptions. The name of the tribe is used for the town in the Domesday Survey, and regularly after 1100. Most reference books cite a form *Hastingas* from a charter of 790, but this charter is a forgery.

Hatfield (HRT, England): heath-covered open land (*Haethfelth c.* 730 Bede's Ecclesiastical History, *Hæþfelda c.* 900 Anglo-Saxon Chronicle). This is a common place-name, sometimes appearing in the modern forms Hadfield or Heathfield. In spite of the rather bleak picture conjured up by the name, Hatfield HRT must have been a settlement able to offer reasonable accommodation by the year 679, when it was the meeting-place of an ecclesiastical council.

Hatfield (YOW, England): heath-covered open land (*Haethfelth c.* 730 Bede's Ecclesiastical History, *Hedfeld* 1086). This is the same name as Hatfield HRT. In this instance it refers to the great tract of marshy moorland east of the town, which was the site of a battle in 632, at which King Edwin of Northumbria was killed. Bede's Ecclesiastical History says this battle was fought 'on the plain which is called Hatfield', so although this is the earliest record of

the name it is not a reference to the settlement. There is another early reference to the district (*hæþ feld lande*) in the Old English document known as the Tribal Hidage, but the first application of the name to the settlement appears to be that in the Domesday Survey.

Havant (HMP, England): Hama's spring (*Hamanfunta* 935, *Havehunte* 1086, *Hafhunte* 1256). The final element is *funta*, discussed under Chalfont. The *-m-* of the personal name Hama was assimilated to the *f-* of *funta*, and later *-funte* was changed to *-hunte*, as in many of the place-names with this final element. A high proportion of the names containing *funta* are in Hampshire.

Haverfordwest (PEM, Wales): west ford used by bucks (*Haverfordia* 1191, *Haverford* 1204, *Averford* 1228, *Hareford* 1283, *Haversford* 1304, *Hereford alias Hareforde* 1385, *Heverford West* 1448, *Herefordwest* 1471, *Herford* 1536–9, *Harffort* 1597). Old English *hæfer* 'he-goat, buck' + *ford*. Locally pronounced *Harford*. *West* was probably added to distinguish it from *Hereford* (Hereford-shire). Welsh forms (*Hwlffordd*, etc.) are approximations of the English ones (*Hawlfford* 14th cent., *Hwlffordd* 15th cent., *Hawrfford* 15th cent., *Hwlfford* 1566, *Hwlfford* 1591, *Hulphord* 1598, *Hwlfordh* 1722). In these forms *-l-* replaces *-r-* and *-dd-* replaces *-d*.

Hawarden (FLI, Wales): high enclosure or farm (*Haordine* 1086, *Hauardina* 1093, *Hawerthin* 1232, *Hawirdyn* 1275, *Haworthyn* 1288, *Hawardin* 1322, *Hawardyne* 1392, *Hawarden* 1439, *Hawerden* 1523,

Harden 1610). Old English *hēah* 'high'+*worðign* 'enclosure'. Hawarden is on rising ground above the River Dee. Locally pronounced *Harden*.

The Welsh form is *Pennarlâg* 'height of Alatog' ([*Koet*] *pennardlaoc* [v.l. *pennarddlac, pennarthlak*] 14th cent., [*Kastell*] *pennardlaoc* 14th cent., *Pener lak* 1560–90, *Pen ar lag* 1566, *Pen yr lak* 1606, *Hawarden* Brit. *Pen ar Lâk c.* 1700, *Pennardhalawg* 1722). Welsh *pennardd* 'height, high ground'+ *?alaog*. *Alaog* could be a personal name from *alafog* [Welsh *alaf* 'cattle'+adjectival ending] or an adjective 'rich in cattle', or from *alaw* 'water lily'. English 'high worthing' is probably a translation of Welsh *pennardd*. The enclosure may have been used to store cattle.

Hawick (ROX, Scotland): village surrounded by a hedge. (*Hawic* 1165–9, *Hawyc* 1264–6, *Havewyk* 1296). A compound of Old English *haga* 'hedge' and *wīc* 'village, etc.' In Scotland, *wīc* usually refers to a dependent farm, like a dairy-farm, for instance.

Hay (BRE, Wales): fence, enclosed forest *Haya* 1144, *Haia* 1166, *La Haye* 1278, *Haya* 1254, *La Haye* 1405, *the Hay* 1536–9). Old English *(ge)hæg* 'fence, enclosed forest'. A fuller form occurs in *Haia taillata* 12th cent., which represents French *la haie taillée* 'cut, hewn hedge or fence'. Another Latin form is found in *Sepes Inscissa* 1181–93. The full Welsh form is *Y Gelli Gandryll* (*Gelli gandrell* 1614), where *candryll* means 'shattered, broken'. The usual Welsh form is *Y Gelli* ([*i'r Gelli c.* 1450, *y Gelli* 1566). As *Celli* means 'grove, copse, woodland', this suggests that *Hay* is used in the later sense of *(ge)hæg* 'a part of a forest fenced off for hunting', and that *sepes* above may be a mistranslation.

Haywards Heath (SSX, England): heathland of the enclosure with a hedge (*Heyworth* 1261, *Haywards Hoth* 1544, *Haywarde, Hewards Hethe* 1603, *Hayworths Hethe* 1607). The name was originally *Heyworth*, and *Hethe* was later added to the genitive of this. See Failsworth.

Heanor (DRB, England): high ridge (*Hainoure* 1086, *Henouere* 1232, *Henore* 1355, *Heighnor* 1516). Heanor is on a hill. Old English *ofer* 'slope, hill, ridge', which is fairly common in Derbyshire names, occurs also in Codnor, two miles north.

Helensburgh (DNB, Scotland): named after Lady Helen, daughter of William, Lord Strathnaver, and wife of Sir James Colquhoun of Luss who first advertised the land of Malig or Milrigs for feuing in January 1776. Initially it was still known as Mulig or the New Town but then renamed.

Hemel Hempstead (HRT, England): homestead in the district called *Hæmele* (*Hamelamestede* 1086, *Hemelhamsteda* 1167, *Hamel Hamsted* 1222, *Hemlamstede* 1339, *Helmpsted* t. Henry 8, *Hemlamsted alias Hempsted* 1541). The district-name *Hæmele* is recorded in a document of about 705. It derives from a word *hamol* 'maimed, mutilated', which occurs in place-names in various topographical senses, usually with *dūn* 'hill', as in the widespread name Hambledon. In the present instance, it refers to the broken nature of the

101

country round Hemel Hempstead, with its steep hills and deep valleys. The two parts of the name were run together to give *Hemlamsted*, which became *Hempsted*, but the original full spelling was restored in modern times.

Hemsworth (YOW, England): Hymel's enclosure (*Hamelesuurde*, *Hilmeuuord* 1086, *Hemelsword c.* 1138, *Hymesworth* 1382, *Hemmesworth* 1431, *Hemsworth* 1556). Old English *worð* is very frequently combined with a personal name, and there are thirty names of this type in the West Riding, including Cudworth, four miles south-west of Hemsworth.

Hendy-gwyn-ar-Daf (CRM, Wales), see *Whitland*.

Henley-on-Thames (OXF, England): high wood (*Henleiam c.* 1140, *Hanlea* 1188). The first element of Henley is Old English *hēah* 'high' (*hēan* in the dative case). The compound with *lēah* 'wood, clearing' has given rise to numerous place-names with the modern forms Healaugh, Healey, Heeley, Handley, Hanley, as well as Henley. In some instances, including this one, the 'high wood' must have overlooked a settlement site on low ground. The frequent occurrence of the name is probably due to the strong visual impact produced by a wood in a dominating situation. Thames is a Celtic river-name meaning 'dark river' or simply 'river'.

Hereford (HRE, England): army ford (*Hereford* 958). An army ford may have been one wide enough for a body of men to cross in broad ranks. In this instance, the reference would be to the Roman road from Leintwardine to Monmouth, which crosses the River Wye at Hereford. Little Hereford near Tenbury, near the boundary between Herefordshire and Shropshire, appears in Domesday Book as *Lutelonhereford*. Probably both places were independently named Hereford, and this was causing confusion in the late Old English period, which led to the prefixing of *lȳtlan* (dative of *lȳtel* 'small') to the less important place.

Herne Bay (KNT, England): corner (*Hyrnan c.* 1100, *Herne* 1269). The early references are to the village of Herne, inland from the coastal resort. Old English *hyrne* is used in various topographical senses in place-names, such as 'a recess in the hills, a curving valley, land in a river-bed'. None of these seems appropriate to Herne KNT, which is on a low, flat-topped ridge. It has been suggested that the district was so called because it was the north-east corner of the mainland of Kent, as opposed to the Isle of Thanet.

Hertford (HRT, England): hart ford (*Herutford c.* 730 Bede's Ecclesiastical History, *Heorotforda c.* 900 Anglo-Saxon Chronicle). The same name occurs in Cheshire, Northumberland, and the North Riding of Yorkshire, with the modern forms Hartford, Hartforth; and Old English *heorot* is a very common first element in place-names.

Heysham (LNC, England): brushwood village (*Hessam* 1086, *Hesham c.* 1190). The first element is the word from which Hayes GTL is derived.

Heywood (LNC, England): high wood (*Hewude, Heghwode* 1246, *Hewod* 1323, *Hayewode* 1324, *Hewode* 1330). The area is not very high, but the wood may have been thought of in relation to Bury, which is lower.

High Wycombe (BUC, England): at the dwellings (*æt Wicumun* c. 970, *Wicumbe* 1086, *Wicumbedena* 1157, *Chepingwycomb* 1478, *Estwicombe* 1509, *Magna Wykeham* 1545). The reference of about 970 is the only pre-Conquest one which is likely to refer to this place. High Wycombe is sometimes identified with *Wichama* in King Alfred's will and *West-wicam* from a will of 944–6, but there is nothing to support the first identification, and the second place is much more likely to be Westwick near St Albans HRT. *Wicumun* probably represents *wicum* (the dative plural of *wic*, discussed under Aldridge) with the addition of another dative plural ending because there were two settlements, High and West Wycombe. West Wycombe is *West Wicumbe* 1195. The name was no doubt considered to end in *cumb* 'valley', and this has influenced its development. High Wycombe was also known as Magna W., East W., and Chipping W., the last prefix meaning 'market'. The river-name Wye is probably a back formation. Elsewhere a derivation 'valley of the R. Wye' is given; this is unlikely, as the valleys here are the sort for which *denu*, rather than *cumb*, is used in place-names.

Hinckley (LEI, England): Hynca's forest-clearing (*Hinchelie* 1086, *Hinkelai* 1176). This is a name of the same type as Barnsley.

Hindley (LNC, England): river-meadow frequented by does (*Hindele* 1212, *Hindeleye* 1259). The same name occurs in Northumberland and (in the modern form Hiendley) in the West Riding of Yorkshire. It is not certain whether *lēah* means 'wood', 'forest-clearing', or 'meadow' in this instance. The association with does seems appropriate to woodland, and Horwich Forest, where deer would be preserved, is a few miles to the north; but the land round Hindley is marshy, and there are a number of names in the vicinity, including Leigh, in which *lēah* seems more likely to have its late sense of 'meadow'.

Hitchen (HRT, England): (place in the territory of the) tribe called *Hicce* (*Hiccam* c. 945, *Hicche* 1062, *Hiz* 1086, *Hichene* 1147, *Hitchin alias Hutchin* 1618). This was originally the name of a group of people who are called *Hicca* in the eighth-century document known as the Tribal Hidage. The dative plural (*Hiccum*) of the tribal name became attached to the place, and the -*n* of the modern form derives from the dative ending -*um*. The river here has been called Hiz in modern times by people familiar with the spelling in Domesday Book. The meaning of *Hicce* is unknown, but Ekwall suggests a river-name related to Welsh *sych* 'dry'.

Hoddesdon (HRT, England): Hodd's hill (*Hodesduna, Hodesdone* 1086, *Hodson* 1649). The modern town is to the east of the hill.

Holmfirth (YOW, England): the wood belonging to Holme (*Holnesfrith*

1274, *Holnefrith c.* 1300, *Holme Frithes* 1302, *Holmesfryth* 1392, *Hulmefirth* 1657). Holme, about 2½ miles south-west, means 'holly-tree', from Old English *holegn*. Firth is Old English *fyrhð*, which sometimes becomes Thrift in modern names.

Holyhead (AGL, Wales): holy headland (*Haliheved* 1315, *Holiheved* 1332, *Le Holehede* 1394, *Holyhede* 1395, *the Holy hedde* 1536–9, *Hollihead* 1596, *Holy Head* 1610). Old English *hālig* 'holy' + *hēafod* 'head-(land)'. The name refers to the striking landmark of Holyhead Mountain. 'Holy' recalls the well-known ecclesiastical settlement of St Cybi. The Welsh name is *Caergybi* (with earlier variants *Castrum Cybi* and *Castle Cybi*)—([o] *gaer gybi sant* 14th cent., *kaer gybi* 14th cent., *Castro Kyby* 1291, *Castrum Cuby* 1283, *Karkeby* 1316, *Castelkyby* 1310, *Chastel Cubii* 1353, *kaer gybi* 1566, *Caercubie alias Holyehead* 1577). Welsh *caer* 'fort' + Welsh personal name *Cybi*.

Holywell (FLI, Wales): holy well (*Helelwele* 1247, *Haliwell* 1254, *Hallewelle* 1285, *Halywall* 1320, *Halwell* 1332, *Holywell* 1465). Old English *hālig* 'holy' + *wielle* 'well'. The reference is to the famous St Winifred's Well which according to the Life of Beuno, bubbled up at the spot where Gwenfrewi's head was rejoined to her body after she had been decapitated. The town is called in Welsh *Treffynnon* 'well town' (*Treffynnon* 1329, [*kastell*] *treffynnon* 14th cent., *trer ffynnon* 1566, *trer ffynnon alias llanwenfrewy* 1590, *Tre Phynon c.* 1700. *Holy Well* (*Wallice Trefynnon alias Gwenfrewi* 1763). Welsh *tref* 'town' + *ffynnon* 'well'. The

church was *Llanwenfrewi* 'church of Gwenfrewi' (see above examples). The well is known in Welsh as *Ffynnon Wenfrewi*. 'Winifred' is an English approximation of *Gwenfrewi*.

Horley (SUR, England): forest-clearing in a horn-shaped area (*Horlee* 1199, *Hornle* 1230). The word *horn* is here used, as it is in Horley OXF, of the land between two streams. There is probably no connection between this name and Horne, about three miles east, where the word appears to refer to a small hill-spur, but an etymology 'woodland belonging to Horne' is a possible alternative.

Horsham (SSX, England): horse village (*Horsham* 947). The same name occurs in Norfolk.

Horwich (LNC, England): grey wych-elms (*Horewych* 1254, *Horwyge* 1539, *Horridge* 1641). This was originally the name of a forest which belonged to the barony of Manchester. It appears to have been given the status of a chase, or private forest, in 1249. The first element is Old English *hār* 'hoar', and the second is *wice* 'wych-elm'.

Hove (SSX, England): (?) hill shaped like a hood (*La Houue* 1288, *Huua* 1291, *Houe* 1332, *Hoove* 1675). This is generally assumed to be Old English *hūfe* 'hood, head-covering', which does not seem to occur in place-names except in this instance. It could be a nickname for a house, but is perhaps more likely to refer to a natural feature. The topography will be obscured in so built-up an area, but a person closely acquainted with the town might nevertheless be able to identify some feature which could have been felt to resemble a hood.

104

Hoylake (CHE, England): sandbank channel (*Hyle Lake* 1687). The settlement is a modern one, originating in an hotel built for sea-bathers in 1792, and expanding greatly in the nineteenth century. Before that the name referred to a deep, narrow channel running between the north-west coast of the Wirral and a great sandbank called East Hoyle Bank. (West Hoyle Bank is a larger sandbank on the other side of Hilbre Island). *Lake* is probably Old English *lacu*, one meaning of which was 'side-channel'. *Hoyle* (the sandbanks' name) is considered to an Old English word *hygel*, 'heap' or 'cluster'. The early topography can be evaluated from the nineteenth-century Ordnance Survey map.

Hucknall (NTT, near Nottingham, England): (?) Hucca's river-meadow (*Hochenale, Hochehale* 1086, *Huccenhal'* 1163, *Hokenhale Torkard* 1287, *Huckney Torquet* 1700). The name appears also in Ault Hucknall DRB, about 11 miles north, and Hucknall under Huthwaite NTT, which is between Hucknall and Ault Hucknall. These can hardly be three independent occurrences of the same compound, and it is generally assumed that Hucknall was the name of a district within which the three settlements were situated. An alternative explanation would be that the two villages at Hucknall under Huthwaite and Ault Hucknall were founded by migrants from Hucknall near Nottingham, and the new settlements took the same name as the parent village. This type of transference of a name from one village to another appears to have taken place in Much and Little Wenlock SHR; but the whole question of the use of one name for several settlements requires study.

If Hucknall was a district name, a precise etymology is hardly possible. If, however, it was first applied to Hucknall near Nottingham, the meaning of *halh* may be 'river-meadow' (see Bramhall), as the place is situated on gently sloping land west of the River Leen. This Hucknall is recorded in Domesday Book, whereas the other settlements do not appear in records until considerably later. The family of Torkard, whose name is used to distinguish this place from the others, owned the manor in 1195.

Huddersfield (YOW, England): Hudræd's open country (*Oderesfelt, Odresfeld* 1086, *Huderesfeld* 1127, *Huddredisfeld* 1241, *Huddresfeld* 1248, *Hodersfeld* 1280) This is a name of the same type as Cuckfield.

Hull (YOE, England): (?) the deep river (*þare ea Hul* 'the river Hull', *c.* 1025, *amnem Hull c.* 1085). There are two suggestions about the origin of the river-name. It could be a Scandinavian name, meaning either 'the deep one' or 'river which flows in a cut channel', or it could be a Celtic name, possibly meaning 'the muddy one'.

The settlement here has been known by several different names, which were apparently in use for overlapping periods of time. It was called *Wyke* from about 1160 to the late thirteenth century, and *Southwyke* in the first half of the fourteenth century. This is either Old English *wīc* (discussed under Aldridge) or Old Norse *vík* 'creek, inlet'. The name Kingston came into use after 1292, when Edward I exchanged lands elsewhere for the port here. This name usually appears with the additions -on Hull, -upon Hull, etc. From the early thirteenth century the town could be referred to simply by the river-name, and it is *portum de Hull, villa de Hull* in a number of thirteenth-century references. This alternation between the full name, Kingston upon Hull, and the shortened form, Hull, persists to the present day.

Huntingdon (HNT, England): huntsman's hill (*Huntandun* 973, *Huntendon* 1212, *Huntindon* 1225, *Huntyngdon* 1286). There is rising ground to the west and to the north of the town, and either could be the *dūn*.

Hutton (ESX, England): settlement on a hill-spur (*Houton* 1200, *Ho – – – now called Hoton* 1347). Hutton Hall is on a promontory, south of the town. In the Domesday Survey the place is called *Atahov* 'at the hill-spur'. This was shortened to *Hoo*, and the short form continued in occasional use after the new formation with -*ton* became current. A document of 1323 calls the place *Hoo*.

Huyton (LNC, England): estate with a landing-place (*Hitune* 1086, *Huton* 1243, *Huyton* 1311). Local knowledge might say whether either the R. Alt or Ditton Brook was suitable for navigation, as the name implies.

Hyde (CHE, England): estate assessed at one hide (*Hyde* 1285). The hide was originally the amount of land which could support one household, so its acreage varied according to the productivity of the soil. It became the formal unit of assessment for taxation. A normal entry in the Domesday Survey gives the number of hides an estate is considered to contain, often stating that the number was greater or less in the time of King Edward, which does not mean that the size of the estate has altered, only that its assessment has been raised or lowered. In place-names, the word is often combined with numerals, as in Fifehead DOR, Fifield GLO, OXF, WLT ('five hides'), Nynehead SOM ('nine hides'), Tinhead WLT ('ten hides'), Toyd WLT ('two hides'), Trenthide DOR ('thirty hides'). When it occurs alone, as in this name and many others, it presumably refers to land with an assessment of a single hide.

Hythe (KNT, England): landing-place (*Hype* 1052 Anglo-Saxon Chronicle). Old English *hȳth* occurs in some thirty ancient settlement-names, including Chelsea and Erith GTL, Huyton LNC. The term is used in place-names of a landing-place on a river, so although Hythe (like Bulverhythe SSX) is by the coast, the landing-place was probably a short distance inland.

Ilkeston (DRB, England): Ēalāc's hill (*Tilchestune* 1086, *Elkesdone* early 11th cent., *Helchesdun c.* 1160, *Ilkestone* 1276). There has been confusion of *dūn* with *tūn*, and the spelling from the Domesday Survey has an initial *T-*, which is really the final *-t* of the preposition *at*. The *dūn* is the ridge between the River Erewash and Nutbrook.

Ilkley (YOW, England): unexplained. (*hillicleg c.* 972, *yllicleage c.* 1030, *Illiclei* 1086, *Ylkeley* 1176, *Ilkley* 1198). For a discussion as to whether Ilkley is Ptolemy's *Olicana* see *Introduction*, p. 22.

Inverness (INV, Scotland): Nessmouth (*Inuernis* 1171–84, *Inuernys* 1189–99). Gaelic *Inbhir Nis*, from *inbhir* 'a confluence'. The river-name which has also given rise to the name of the loch appears in the Anglicised form in the old nominative, whereas *Inbhir Nis*, *Abhainn Nis* 'River Ness', *Loch Nis* 'Loch Ness' show the Gaelic genitive. The name of the river first occurs as *Nesa* in Adamnan's seventh-century life of Columba. This must stand for an earlier **Nesta* which itself is presumably from **Ned-tā* 'the roaring or rushing one', from the Indo-European root **ned-* 'to sound, to roar, to rush'. The second part of Durness

(Durham) is probably the same. Ness is either one of the earliest Celtic river-names in Scotland or even pre-Celtic though Indo-European.

Inverurie (ABD, Scotland): Uriemouth (*Nrurin* 9th cent., *Ennroury* 1172, *Inuerurie*, *Innerurin* 1199). As in Inverness, the first element is Gaelic *inbhir* 'a confluence', referring to the confluence of the Urie with the Don. The river-name (*Vry* 1244, *aqua de Ouri* 1261) has never been convincingly explained; its ending *-ie* is, of course, very common in the Scottish north-east.

Ipswich (SFK, England): Gip's port (*Gipeswic c.* 975 Coin, 993 Anglo-Saxon Chronicle). There are a number of place-names in which 'town' or 'port' is the appropriate translation of *wīc* (see Greenwich, Norwich, Sandwich).

Irvine (AYR, Scotland): from the river of the same name (*Yrewyn* 1258, *Irwyn* 1296). This is of Early Celtic origin and probably identical with the River Irfon in Wales. Similar *n-* formations are quite common amongst this early nomenclature, but the etymology is still obscure.

Iver (BUC, England): brow of a hill (*Evreham* 1086, *Eura* 1175, *Evre* 1220, *Iver* 1382). Old English *yfre* may refer in this instance to the slightly raised position in relation to Colne Brook. The *-am* of the Domesday spelling is a Latin accusative ending.

Jarrow (DRH, England): the fen people (*Gyruum c.* 730 Bede's Ecclesiastical History, *Jarwe* 1228). The name *Gyrwe* occurs in Old English sources as that of a group of people who lived in the fen districts round Peterborough NTP. It is derived from a word meaning 'mud'. The relationship between the Durham place-name and the fenland tribe-name is uncertain, but it is quite likely that the place-name referred originally to a detached portion of the *Gyrwe* who had moved from the Fens to the south bank of the Tyne. Place-names which refer to this sort of migration are discussed under Spalding and Uxbridge.

Jedburgh (ROX, Scotland): enclosed homestead on the River Jed (*Gedwearde c.* 1050 (12th cent.), *Gedwirth* 1177 (16th cent.), *Jedword* 1147–50, etc.). The first element is the so far unexplained river-name Jed; this is compounded with Old English *worð* 'an enclosure', later 'an enclosed homestead'. The earliest spelling indicates a variant *weorð*, with substitution of *ea* for *eo* before *r* plus consonant, as in Northumberland. The element *-worth* was replaced by *-burgh* at an early date because it had become an infrequently used term. It is preserved, however, in the nearby *Bonjedward* (*Bonjedworth* 1321) which has Gaelic *bun* 'foot' as its first element. The incoming Gaels must have taken **Jedward* to be the name of the river.

Johnstone (RNF, Scotland): John's farm (*Jonestone* 1292, *Johnstoun* 1594). The town was founded in 1781 in connection with industrial developments, especially the erection of a large cotton-mill. It is not known who John was.

K

Keighley (YOW, England): Cyhha's forest-clearing (*Chichelai* 1086, *Kyhhelay* 1234, *Kytheleg* 1263, *Kyghley* 1273, *Keghelay* 1365, *Keighley* 1571). This is a name of the same type as Barnsley. The development of Old English -*hh*- (in the personal name *Cyhha*) to -*gh*-, pronounced -*f*-, is regular, and is found also in such words as *laugh* and *tough*. This explains the modern spelling Keighley. In Middle English, however, this -*gh*- represented a sound which was liable to interchange with the sound represented by the spelling -*th*-. The early forms for Keighley show this interchange of -*gh*- and -*th*-, and -*th*- is preserved in the modern pronunciation.

Kelty (FIF, Scotland): hard water (*Quilte* 1250, *Quilt*, *Quhilt* 1329–70), from Gaelic *Cailtidh*, a reduced form of Celtic *Caleto-dubron* 'hard water'. It is not clear, however, which water-course is meant, and the second element may, in fact, have been different.

Kendal (WML, England): valley of the River Kent (*Kendala c.* 1190, *Kentdall* 1591). These spellings refer to the valley. The town of Kendal was called *Cherchebi* in 1086, *Kirkebi*, *Kyrkebi* in the twelfth century. This is a common Scandinavian name, *kirkju-bȳr*, meaning 'village with a church'. The need to distinguish this place from Kirkby Lonsdale and Kirkby Stephen, in the same county, led to the addition of the district name, as in *Kircabikendala c.* 1095, *Kirkby in Kendal* in the thirteenth and fourteenth centuries, *Kirby Kendal* in the fifteenth century. The use of the affix alone as the name of the borough has been noted in 1452 (*burgus de Kendale*), but the full form of the name is found occasionally until the eighteenth century. Kent is a Celtic river-name of uncertain meaning; -*dale* is Old Norse *dalr*.

Kenilworth (WAR, England): Cynehild's enclosure (*Chinewrde* 1086, *Chenildeworda* early 12th cent., *Kiningwurde* 1122, *Kenildewurtha* 1164, *Chenelingwurthe* 1194, *Kelingworth* 1316, *Kenelworth alias Killingworth* 1598). Cynehild is a woman's name. Old English *worð* is very frequently compounded with a personal name, and in these instances it may have much the same significance as *tūn*, and other words for a settlement or an estate. The early spellings for Kenilworth (of which only a small selection is given here) show considerable diversity, and the irregular form *Killingworth* was frequently used in the seventeenth century. This is partly due to the common confusion between *n* and *l*, but there

111

may have been some influence from Killingworth NTB and Kilworth LEI; the last name sometimes appears as *Kilingworth*.

Kennoway (FIF, Scotland): unexplained (*Kennachin* 1183, *Kennachyn, Kennachi* 1250, *Kennoquhy c.* 1510). In the Aberdeen Breviary (*c.* 1510) St Caynicus is given as patron of Kennoway, but there seems to be no confirmation of this statement which is probably based on a mistaken derivation of the name for Cainnech.

Kettering (NTP, England): (?) Cytra's people (*Cytringan* 956, *Keteiringan c.* 963, *Cateringe* 1086, *Ketering c.* 1200, *Keteringes* 1227). This may be a name of the same type as Barking GTL, but there is no personal name on record which would make a satisfactory base. It has been suggested that it might contain a short form of the recorded personal name Cūthfrith. Ketteringham NFK consists of the same folk-name (*Cytringas*) and *hām*.

Keynsham (SOM, England): Cǣgin's land in a river-bed (*Cægineshamme c.* 1000, *Cainesham* 1086). Keynsham is situated at the base of a large loop in the River Avon, and *hamm* is probably used here in the same sense as it is in Buckingham and Evesham.

Kidderminster (WOR, England): Cydela's monastery (*Chideminstre* 1086, *Kedeleministre* 1154, *Kidemenistra* 1168, *Kidelministre* 1212, *Kydermunstre* 1275). There is a charter of A.D. 736 by which King Æthelbald of Mercia gives to an ealdorman named Cyneberht land 'in the province to which was applied by men of old the name

Ismere, by the river called Stour' for the foundation of a monastery. In another charter, dated between 757 and 775, Cyneberht's son, Ceolfrith, gives this land called Stour in the province of Ismere, along with another estate, to the Bishopric of Worcester. In this charter Ceolfrith describes himself as an abbot. It is possible that Stour in Ismere was the old name of Kidderminster, that Cyneberht's monastery was the *mynster* of the place-name, and that his son Ceolfrith was one of its earliest abbots. The province called Ismere is known to have extended at least from Ismere House north-east of Kidderminster to King's Norton near Birmingham. The only difficulty is that the documents make no mention of Cydela, who appears in the place-name as the owner of the monastery; but the fact that his name begins with C- suggests that he belonged to the same family as Cyneberht and Ceolfrith, and he could have been an elder brother of Ceolfrith. The name Stour in Ismere was still used for this estate in a charter of 781, but this could have co-existed with a local name which referred to the monastery.

The change from *Kedeleministre* to *Kydermunstre* is due to the common confusion between *l* and *r*, helped in this instance by the final *-re* of the name.

Kidwelly (CRM, Wales), see *Cedweli*.

Kilbirnie (AYR, Scotland): Brendan's church (*Kilbyrny* 1413, *Killburney* 1584–96). St Brendan's Fair used to be held there on 28 May. The first element is Gaelic *cill* 'church', for which see Kilmarnock.

Kilmarnock (AYR, Scotland): (St) Mo-Ernoc's church (*Kelmernoke* 1299). Gaelic *Cill Mhearnaig*. Gaelic *cill* 'church, churchyard' is a loanword from Latin *cella* which has also given English *cell*. In the archaeological sense it refers to what has been called a 'developed cemetery'. In our name, as in Kilsyth and Kilwinning, the second element commemorates a particular saint. There appear to have been 22 saints called *Mo-Ernóc*. *Mo* 'my' is quite common as a term of endearment in front of saints' names.

Kilsyth (STL, Scotland): (St) Syth's church (*Kelvesyth* 1210, *Kelnasydhe* 1217, *Kilsyth* 1239). The saint in question is not mentioned in any of the Calendars. The *-ve-* and *-na-* (for *-ua-*) in the earliest spellings are reflecting aspirated forms of *mo* 'my' (see *Kilmarnock*).

Kilwinning (AYR, Scotland): (Thy) Finnén's church (*kilwinin* 1202–7, *Kilwynnyn* etc. 1222). The present name and its historical spellings probably represent a Welsh (Cumbric) form *Gwynnion* of the saint's name, but in Arran Gaelic Kilwinning is still known as *Cill Dingeain* (for Cill D'Fhinnéain). Finnén is said to be a diminutive of St Findbar of Moyville who died in 579. For *cill* see *Kilmarnock*.

King's Lynn (NFK, England): pool (*Lena, Lun* 1086, *Lynna* c. 1105). This name is derived from the Celtic word discussed under Lincoln. The administrative district here was called the hundred of *Lynware* in the eleventh century; this means 'Lynn people'. King's Lynn was earlier *Lynn Episcopi* because it belonged to

the Bishop of Norwich; the modern prefix came into use after Henry VIII acquired it from the Bishop by an exchange.

Kinross (KNR, Scotland): head of the promontory (*Kynros* c. 1144, *Chinross* c. 1150, *Kinross* c. 1214), from Gaelic *cinn*, an oblique case of *ceann* 'head, end' and *ros* 'projection, promontory' (see Montrose). The name must derive from the site of the church at the end of a point projecting in to Loch Leven.

Kirkby (LNC, England): church village (*Cherchebi* 1086, *Kyrkeby* 1228). This is a Scandinavian name, common in regions of Danish and Norwegian settlement. This instance, and the one discussed under Kendal, are probably Norwegian.

Kirkby-in-Ashfield (NTT, England): church village (*Chirchebi* 1086, *Kirkeby* 1212, *Kirkeby in Esfeld* 1216). This is a Danish instance of the name discussed under Kirkby LNC. The district-name Ashfield, 'open land with ash-trees', was added for distinction from other Kirkbys; see *Sutton-in-Ashfield*.

Kirkcaldy (FIF, Scotland): fortress of the hard fort (*Kircalethyn, Kircaladin, Kircalathin, Kircaladinit, Kircaldin* all 12th cent.). The first element is not Scots *kirk* but Welsh *caer* 'fortress' for which see *Introduction*, p. 14. This was pleonastically added to an existing compound of Welsh *caled* 'hard' and *din* 'fort, in an earlier form **Caleto-dūnon* hard fort'.

Kirkcudbright (KCB, Scotland): St Cuthbert's church (*Kircuthbright* 1296, *Kirkcudbrich* 1325, *Kirkcudbrith*

113

1495). Names of this type have been termed 'inversion compounds' because they seem to have their elements in the wrong order, with the basic element coming first. This is, however, only true from an English (or Germanic) point of view, whereas the word order would be quite correct in a Gaelic (or Celtic) context. We must therefore see names like Kirkcudbright together with others of the Kilbride, Kilmarnock, Kilbirnie type (which see) and must assume substitution of Norse *kirkja* 'church' for Gaelic *cill*. This was, of course, only possible in a bilingual situation when Norse and Gaelic speakers lived side by side in Galloway. The position is, however, even more complex because in addition to Gaelic word order and a Norse first element, Kirkcudbright contains the name of an Anglian saint as its second part. It is therefore a good focal point for the various linguistic and ecclesiastical influences in our area at the time when the name was coined and first used.

Kirkintilloch (DNB, Scotland): Fort at the head of the eminences (*Caerpentaloch* 10th cent., *Kirkentulach c.* 1200). As the earliest reference shows, the name was originally Welsh but by the tenth century the last element which may have been *bryn* or the like had already been translated into Gaelic. Two hundred years later Welsh *pen* 'head, end' had also become Gaelic *cenn*. Like Kirkcaldy not a *Kirk*-name!

Kirkwall (ORK, Scotland): church bay (*Kirkjuvágr c.* 1225, *Kyrkvaw* 1364), from Old Norse *Kirkju-vágr* 'church bay'. For *vágr* compare Stornoway. The modern spelling first occurs in 1488 and must represent an attempt at re-interpreting the last element on the analysis of Scots *wa'* for wall, *fa'* for fall, *ba'* for ball.

Knighton (RAD, Wales): farm of the young men (*Chenistetone* 1086, *Cnicheton* 1193, *Cnihtiton* 1230, *Knihteton* 1237, *Knighton* 1303, *Knygthton* 1346). Old English *cniht* 'youth, servant, soldier' + *tūn* 'farm'. This is one of the early English names found at or west of Offa's Dyke. The Welsh name is *Trefyclo* for an earlier *Trefyclawdd* 'farm by the dyke' (*p. saint Edwart yn Ref y klawdd* 'Parish of St Edward in Trefyclawdd' 1566, *Knighton in Walche caullid Trebuclo* 1536–9, *Trebuclo pro Treficlaudh* 1586). Welsh *Tref* 'farm' later 'town' + definite article *y* + *clawdd* 'dyke'.

Knottingley (YOW, England): forest-clearing of Cnotta's people (*Notingeleia* 1086, *Knottingley c.* 1120, *Cnottingaleia c.* 1160). This is a name of the same type as Bingley.

Knutsford (CHE, England): Cnūt's ford (*Cunetesford* 1086, *Knottisford* 1282). Cnūt is a Scandinavian personal name. The 'ford' may have been a causeway across the marshy ground south of Tatton Mere, rather than a river-crossing.

114

L

Lacharn (CRM, Wales): origin obscure (*Talacharn* 1191, *Thalkan* 1283, *Tallacharn* 1363, *Talycharn* 14th cent., *Tallagharn* 1403, *Talacharn c.* 1450, *Laugharne als Tallaugharn*, 16th cent., *Talacharne* 1536–9, *Lacharne* 1536–9). Welsh *tâl* 'end'+obscure element *-acharn*. *Talacharn* in the earlier examples was the commote, later lordship, of that name. The earliest name for the site of the castle was *Abercoran* 'mouth of the brook Coran' (*Abercorran* 1191, *Aber Coran*, 14th cent., *Abercorran* 1536–9, *Abercorran c.* 1700). Welsh *cor(r)an* (?) 'little one'. *Lacharn* (*Laugharne*) for the town is an abbreviation of (*Castell*) *Talacharn*. *Laugharne* (pronounced *Larn*) is an English spelling.

Lampeter (CRD, Wales), see *Llanbedr Pont Steffan*.

Lanark (LAN, Scotland): (the) glade (*Lannarc* 1187–9, *Lanarc* 1175–89, *Lanerk* 1275). From Welsh *llannerch* 'a clear space, a glade'. Compare Rhosllannerchrugog DEN.

Lancaster (LNC, England): Roman fort on the River Lune (*Loncastre* 1086, *Lanecastrum* 1094, *Loncastra* 1127). See Chester and Doncaster; Old English *cæster* (the Anglian form of *ceaster*) probably means 'Roman fort' in this instance, as there is not known to have been a civil settlement at Lancaster. Lune is a Celtic river-name, perhaps connected with the Irish word *slán* 'healthy, sound'.

Lancing (SSX, England): Wlanc's people (*Lancinges* 1086, *Launcyng* 1288). This is a name of the same type as Barking GTL and Hastings. In this part of Sussex, between the Rivers Adur and Arun, there is a dense cluster of *-ingas* names, which suggests that the groups of people referred to cannot have been very large.

Largs (AYR, Scotland): slopes (*Larghes c.* 1140, *Largas* 1179). From Gaelic *leorg* 'a slope' to which an English plural *-s* has been added. This may either reflect a Gaelic plural or be the result of two or more places being called *Larg*, like Upper and Lower, Easter and Wester L., etc.

Larkhall (LAN, Scotland): (?) Lark's hall (*Laverockhall* 1620). The juxtaposition of Scots *laverock* and English *lark* looks so conclusive, and yet this name has never been fully explained.

Laugharne (CRM, Wales): see *Lacharn*.

115

Leamington Spa (WAR, England): farm on the River Leam (*Lamintone* 1086, *Lementona* early 12th cent.). Leamington Hastings, further up the Leam, is also named from its position by the river. This type of name is fairly common in this part of the Midlands, other instances being Bishop's and Long Itchington, both named from the River Itchen. Leam (Old English *Leomena*) is a Celtic river-name derived from a word meaning 'elm'. Other examples of this river-name are found in Lymington HMP and in Lympne KNT.

Leatherhead (SUR, England): grey ford (*Leodridan c.* 880, *Ledred* 1155, *Lethered* 1470, *Letherhed* 1504, *Ledred alias Lethered* 1604, *Leatherhead* 1630). This name was solved for the first time in 1980, when R. Coates established that it is Celtic, containing the word which became Welsh *llwyd* 'grey' (found also in Lichfield) and the ancestor of Welsh *rhyd* 'ford'. Leatherhead is thus an important addition to the corpus of names which indicate substantial British survival south-west of London; see Caterham, Croydon, Penge.

Leeds (YOW, England): people living near the river called *Lāt-* (*Loidis c.* 730 Bede's Ecclesiastical History, *Ledes* 1086, *Liedes* 1191, *Leedes c.* 1245, *Leeds* 1518). This is a Celtic name, *Lādenses*, formed from an earlier name of the River Aire. The river-name means 'the violent one'. Bede refers to *Loidis* as a *regio*, which means that it was the name of a recognised administrative unit, and the district appears to have extended at least from the present town to the villages of Ledston and Ledsham,

about 10 miles south-east, since these have the name Leeds as first element. Hastings is another example of the process by which a folk-name became attached to a single settlement.

Leek (STF, England): brook (*Lec* 1086, *Leke* 1247). This is probably ON *lækr* 'brook' applied to a late settlement. Other instances of the name are Leake NTT, YON and Leck in Tunstall LNC. The area is not one where there was dense Scandinavian settlement, but there are places called Hulme to the north-east and north-west, which indicates some Danish speech. Leek probably refers to the small tributary of the River Churnet which flows through the town.

Leicester (LEI, England): (?) Roman town of the people called *Ligore* (*Ligera ceaster* 917 Anglo-Saxon Chronicle, *Ligora ceaster* 942 Anglo-Saxon Chronicle, *Ledecestre* 1086, *Legrecestra* 1130, *Leirchestre* 1205). The final element of this name is *ceaster*, referring to the remains of the large Roman town here. The first element presents considerable difficulty. There is a village called Leire 10 miles south-west of Leicester, which is *Legre* 1086, *Leire* 1227, and seems to be identical with the first element of Leicester. It has been suggested that this was a river-name, identical with Loire in France, and was a name of the small tributary of the River Soar by which Leire stands. Leicester, however, is on the Soar itself, at some distance from this tributary, and as Soar appears to be an ancient Celtic river-name also, Leicester cannot be named from a river called *Legra*. The further suggestion has been made that an Old English folk-name *Ligore* was formed from the river-name, and that Leicester was named from the folk, whose territory could have extended this far. The Bishop of Leicester is referred to in a document of 803 as *Legorensis civitatis episcopus*; this is a Latinisation of the English name *Ligoraceaster*.

The district name *Legor* may have been used by the Welsh in the sixth century as a general name for all the Middle Anglian tribes, and may be the origin of the Welsh *Lloegr*, used by early Welsh poets as a name for England.

Ratae, the name of the Roman town, might have been expected to survive, but has not done so.

Leigh (LNC, England): meadow-land (*Leeche, Legh* 1276). In view of the situation of Leigh at the north-western edge of a large expanse of marshy land, this may be a name of comparatively late origin, which came into use after *lēah* had lost its association with woodland and acquired its modern meaning of 'meadow'. Several names in the parish (Hopecarr, Morleys, Blackmoor) refer to marsh.

Leigh-on-Sea (ESX, England): forest-clearing (*Legha* 1226). This is one of a group of names containing *lēah* in what must have been forested country west of Southend. Rayleigh is in the same group.

Leighton Buzzard (BDF, England): herb-garden (*Lestone* 1086, *Lechtone* 1173, *Leghton* 1247). Old English *lēactūn* means literally 'leek enclosure', but as the word is used to translate Latin *ortus olerum* it

seems fair to translate the place-name 'herb-garden'. In other literary references *lēactūn* seems to mean simply 'garden'. It has given rise to a number of place-names, with a variety of modern forms, such as Lacton, Latton, Laughton, Letton. In this name, as in Appleton 'orchard', *tūn* has its early sense 'enclosure'; this remained in a few compounds long after the word had progressed to its later meanings 'farm' or 'estate'.

Buzzard first appears as an addition to Leighton in 1287. It is a French family-name, derived from the word 'buzzard'.

Lerwick (SHE, Scotland): mud bay (*Lerwick* 1625), from Norse *leir vik*. It does not seem to have been mentioned in the Sagas.

Letchworth (HRT, England): (?) enclosure with a lock (*Leceworde* 1086, *Luchewrth c.* 1190). It has been suggested that the first element of Letchworth is an unrecorded Old English word *lycce* related to *loc* 'lock, bar, bolt'. This would give a compound similar to those discussed under Failsworth. The suffix *-worth* is rather common in village- and town-names in north Hertfordshire and the adjacent part of Bedfordshire.

Leven (FIF, Scotland): elm-water (*Levin c.* 1535). The name of the river at the mouth of which Leven stands must have been in Gaelic *Leamhain*, like the river which flows out of Loch Lomond into the Clyde. The original form was probably **Lemonā*, from Primitive Celtic **lemo-* 'elm'. This name has numerous identical equivalents in England,

117

from Devon to Cumberland. It also occurs in *Lac Leman* in Switzerland.

Opposite Leven, on the west bank of the river, is Innerleven (*Innerlewyn* 1388) 'Leven-mouth', and one feels that Leven, too, started out as a name somewhat like that and was later shortened.

Lewes (SSX, England): the tumuli (*Læwe, Læwes c.* 959, *Lewes* 1086). Old English *hlǣw* in this name has generally been considered to mean 'hill', with reference to the high ground on either side of the town. *hlǣw* and *hlāw* are, however, the regular Old English terms for burial-mounds, and as the hills east and west of Lewes are dotted with tumuli, a reference to these seems to give a more meaningful etymology. There is some interchange between singular and plural in the early spellings, but the plural forms predominate. Lew in Oxfordshire is the same name in the singular, probably also referring to a tumulus.

Leyland (LNC, England): untilled land (*Lailand* 1086, *Leiland* 1212). Leyland occupies low ground by the River Lostock, and the name may refer to the use of much of this for pasture and meadow, rather than arable.

Lichfield (STF, England): open land near *Letocetum* (*Lyccidfelth c.* 730 Bede's Ecclesiastical History). *Letoceto* occurs in the Antonine Itinerary as the name of the Roman town at Wall, on Watling Street, about two miles south of Lichfield. This is a Celtic name, meaning 'grey wood'. Its reappearance (in the Old English form *Licced*) as the first element of Lichfield may be due to the survival of the wood-name, which could have applied to a large area. But in spite of the distance between the two places it may be a reference to the Roman town. The remains at Wall are still impressive, and they may have seemed the most noteworthy feature in a large stretch of country when the English place-name came into use.

Lincoln (LIN, England): Roman *colonia* by the lake (*Lindon c.* 150 Ptolemy, *Lindum colonia* late 7th cent. Ravenna Cosmography, *Lindocolina c.* 730 Bede's Ecclesiastical History, *Lindcylene* 942 Anglo-Saxon Chronicle, *Lincolia* 1086). This is a rare instance of a Romano-British name surviving with very little alteration and without the addition of *ceaster* into Anglo-Saxon times. A *colonia* was a Roman settlement established for the benefit of retired legionary soldiers. The one at Lincoln (which was established about A.D. 90) was named from its proximity to a wide part of the River Witham, referred to as a 'lake' by the British word *lindo-*, which corresponds to modern Welsh *llyn*.

Linlithgow (WLO, Scotland): lake in the damp hollow (*Linlitcu* 1124–47, *Linlidcu* 1138, *Lythcu* 1299, *Lithgw c.* 1200, *Lynlythgw* 1366). These five examples are representative of at least 280 different spellings. They mainly fall into two categories, those with and those without *Lin-*. The assumption must be that *Lithgow* and the like was the name of the place itself, as it is still in local usage to-day, and that Linlithgow is really the name of the lake. The whole name is a compound of Welsh *llyn* 'lake', *llaith* 'damp', and *cau* 'a hollow', as in Glasgow.

Littlehampton (ssx, England): small settlement (*Hantone* 1086, *Hamtone* 1229, *Hampton* 1230, *Lyttelhampton* 1482). It is impossible at present to give a precise translation of Old English *hāmtūn*, which is not on independent record, but occurs in a great many place-names, often by itself and often with a distinguishing first element. A detailed study of all these place-names would certainly shed light on the significance of the compound. Little- is a late addition to the Sussex name, possibly to avert confusion with Southampton.

Littleover (DRB, England): small settlement on the ridge (*Parva Ufre* 1086, *Lytle Oure* 1517). Littleover and Mickleover are situated on the same low ridge. Mickleover was the earlier settlement, originally called *Ufer*, which means 'ridge'. After the establishment of the secondary settlement at Littleover, Mickleover became 'great Over', with the Middle English prefix *Muchele-* which sometimes becomes Much in place-names.

Liverpool (LNC, England): pool with clotted water (*Liuerpul c.* 1190, *Liuerpol* 1211). The place is named from a tidal creek, now filled up, once known as The Pool. The first element is the word *liver*, which appears to be used in the same sense in the names Livermere SFK and Liversedge YOW.

Livingston (WLO, Scotland): Leving's farm (*Uilla Leuing* or *Leuingi* 1124–52, *Leuiggestun* 1153–65, *Levingstun* 1214–16, *Levyngstoun* 1281, *Livingstoun* 1331–53). The man called

Leving who gave his name to the farm is well known from a number of charters of the same period as the first documentation of the place-name. *Leving* derives from Old English *Lēofing* (a derivative of *leof* 'dear') and occurs several times in Domesday Book. Livingston is Scotland's fourth 'new town'.

Llanandras (RAD, Wales), see *Presteigne*.

Llanbedr Pont Steffan (CRD, Wales): church of Peter at the bridge of Stephen (*Lanpeder* 1284, *Lampede* 1291, *Lampader* 1298–1300, *Lampeter Pount Steune* 1301, *Lampeder Talpont* 1303–4, *llanbedyr tal pont ystyuyn* 14th cent., *Lampeder tal pont stevyn* 1407, *ll. bedr bont ystyfyn* 1566, *Llanbeder pont Stephen* 1654). Welsh *llan* 'church' + Pedr (St Peter). The distinguishing element *Tâl Pont Steffan* is Welsh *tâl* 'end' + *pont* 'bridge' + *Steffan* (Stephen). Stephen was probably an early Norman. The element *tâl* was dropped. *Lampeter* is a hybrid and anglicised form. The town is locally called *Llambed*, with the normal development of -*nb*- as -*mb*-.

Llandaf(f) (GLA, Wales), see *Cardiff*.

Llandeilo (CRM, Wales): church of Teilo (*Lanteliau Maur* 1130, *Lanteylavaur* 1281, *Lanteylau* 1289, *Lanteylou Vaur* 1318, *Llandeilaw vawr* 14th cent., *Llandeilo Vaur* 1397, *Llandeylo* 1513, *Llandilo Vawr* 1656). Welsh *llan* 'church' + *Teilo* (saint's name). The distinguishing element *mawr* 'great' marks its importance as an early church of Teilo. The local pronunciation is *Llandilo*.

Llandovery (CRM, Wales), see *Llanymddyfri*.

Llandrindod Wells (RAD, Wales): church of the Trinity (*Llandynddod* 1535, *Llandrindod* 1554–8, *Llandrindod* 1588, *Llandryndott* 1612, *Llanydrindod* 1760). Welsh *llan* 'church' + *trindod* 'trinity'. The church was originally *Llanddwy* 'church of God' (*Lando* 1291). Welsh *llan* 'church' + *Dwy(w)* 'God'. *Wells* is a nineteenth-century addition referring to the chalybeate springs.

Llandudno (CRN, Wales): church of Tudno (*Llandudno* 1291, *Lantudenou* 1376, *Llann Tudno* 1538, *Ll. dudno* 1590, *Llandidno* 1680). Welsh *llan* 'church' + *Tudno* (saint's name).

Llandysul (CRD, Wales): church of Tysul (*Landessel* 1291, *Lantissill* 1299, *Llandussull* 1407, *Llandussyl* 1547, *ll. dyssyl* 1566, *Llandissill* 1674). Welsh *llan* 'church' + *Tysul* (saint's name).

Llanelli (CRM, Wales): church of Elli (*Lann elli* 1160–85, *Lannethey* 1282, *Lanetly* 1291, *Lannethelly* 1311, *Lanelthy* 1360, *Llanelly* 1446, *Llanelli* 1553, *Llanelli* 1606). Welsh *llan* 'church' + *Elli* (saint's name).

Llanelwy (FLI, Wales), see *St Asaph*.

Llanfair Caereinion (MTG, Wales): church of Mary in Caereinion (*Llanveyr* 1254, *Lanveyr* 1291, *ll. fair* 1566, *Llanvair in Krynion* 1579, *Llanvaire in Kerynion* 1596–7, *Llanvair Careinion* 1691). Welsh *llan* 'church' + *Mair* (Mary). The distinguishing element is *Caereinion*, the name of a cantref 'fort of Einion' (*Keriniaun* 1263, *Kerenniaun* 1276, *Kerrenion* 1279, *Kereynon* 1290,

Kereignon 1352, *Kaerinion* 1420). Welsh *caer* 'fort' + *Einion* (personal name).

Llanfairfechan (CRN, Wales): little church of Mary (*Annueyr* 1254, *Lanueyr* 1284, *Llanvayr* 1291, *Llanvair Vechan* 1475, *Ll. fair fechan* 1566, *Llanvair Vechan* 1698). Welsh *llan* 'church' + *Mair* (Mary) + *bechan* 'little'. So called because there was a large Marychurch at Conway.

Llanfair-ym-muallt (BRE, Wales), see *Builth Wells*.

Llanfyllin (MTG, Wales): church of Myllin (*Llanvelig* 1254, *Lanvyllyn* 1291, *Lanvethlyng* 1309, *Llanvilling* 1543, *Ll. fyllinn* 1566, *Llanvylling* 1691). Welsh *llan* 'church' + *Myllin(g)* (saint's name).

Llangadog (CRM, Wales): church of Cadog (*Lancadauc* 1281, *Lankadoc* 1284, *Llangadok* 1289, *Langadok* 1326, *Llanngadawc* 14th cent., *Ll. Cadog Fawr* 1590, *Llangadock Vawr* 1606). Welsh *llan* 'church' + *Cadog* (saint's name). The epithet *mawr* 'great' is sometimes added to mark its importance among the churches of Cadog.

Llangefni (AGL, Wales): church near River Cefni (*Llangevni* 1254, *Llangevni* 1398, *Llangefne* 1481, *Llangefny* 1505, *Ll. gefni* 1566, *Llangefny* 1651). Welsh *llan* 'church' + *Cefni* (river-name) (*Avon Kefni* 1536–9, *Keuenye* 1610). *Cefni* could be either from *cafn* 'dip, hollow', or more probably from *cefn* 'ridge', referring to a river having its source on a ridge.

The church is dedicated to St Cyngar (*sancti Kyngar* 1481, *Llangyngar* 1509).

Llangollen (DEN, Wales): church of Collen (*Lancollien* 1234, *Llancallen* 1254, *Thlangothlan* 1284, *Langollen* 1291, *Llangollen* 1391, *Ll. gollen* 1566). Welsh *llan* 'church' + *Collen* (saint's name).

Llanidloes (MTG, Wales): church of Idloes (*Lanidloes* 1254, *Thanidloys* 1280, *Thlanidleys* 1286, *Llanydelas* 1375, *Ll. Idlos* 1566, *Llanidloes* 1603). Welsh *llan* 'church' + *Idloes* (saint's name).

Llanrwst (DEN, Wales): church of Gwrwst (*lhannruste* 1254, *Lannwrvst* 1291, *Lan Ourost* 1334, *Llanwrwst* 1398, *Llanrowest* 1433, *Llanrwst* c. 1560). Welsh *llan* 'church' + *Gwrwst*, *Grwst* (saint's name). The stress is on the second syllable.

Llantrisant (GLA, Wales): church of the three saints (*Landtrissen* 1246, *Thlanatrissent* 1297, *Llanytrisein* 1321, *Lantrissen* 1424, *Ll. y Trissaint* 1566, *Lantressan* 1292, *Lantrissan* 1381, *Llantrissan* 1530, *Llantrissant* 1668). Welsh *llan* 'church' + def. art. *y* + *sant* (singular) 'saint' or *saint* (pl.) 'saints'. There are two sets of forms, one with the singular *sant*, the other with the plural *saint*. The name of the town finally settled down as *Llantrisant*. The three saints are Illtud, Gwynno, and Dyfodwg.

Llanwrtud (BRE, Wales): church of Gwrtud (*Llanwrtid* 1553, *Ll. Wrtyd* 1566, *Llanwrtid* 1596, *Llanurtyd* 1605, *Llanwrtyd* 1695). Welsh *llan* 'church' + personal name *Gwrtud*. The church, however, is now dedicated to St David. *Wells* was added to the name in the nineteenth century with reference to the healing springs.

Llanymddyfri (CRM, Wales): church near the waters (*Llanamdewri* 12th cent., *Lanamdeveri* 1194, *Lanemdevry* 1250, *Landevery* 1280, *Lanymdevery* 1383, *Llanymthevery* 1485, *Llanymddyvri* 1450–85, *Llanymthevery* 1587, *Llanymddyfri* 1612). Welsh *llan* 'church' + *am* 'near' [cf. *Amlwch*] + *dyfri* (a derivative of *dwfr* 'water'). The name *Dyfri* appears in late examples for a brook in and near Llanymddyfri (*Devery* 1485, [*D*]*eueri* 1536–9), and may be an alias for the modern *Bawddwr* (Welsh *baw* 'dirt' + *dŵr* 'water, stream'). It is not at all certain, however, that *Dyfri* is a genuine brook name. If it is, *Llanymddyfri* would mean 'church near the brook Dyfri'. The name is locally pronounced *Llanddyfri* (with loss of *ym*). The form *Llandovery* is a stereotyped English spelling which has nothing to commend it, cf. *Aberdovey* for *Aberdyfi*.

Loanhead (MLO, Scotland): top of the lane (*Loneheid* 1618). A compound of Old English *lane* and *hēafod* 'head'.

Lochgelly (FIF, Scotland): (?) white loch (*Lochgellie* 1606) from the loch of the same name. This surely contains a Gaelic name *Geallaidh* 'the shining one' which also occurs several times as a stream-name. It is formally identical with Old Irish *gelde* 'shining', on the basis *gel* 'white', Modern Gaelic *geal*.

Lochgilphead (ARG, Scotland): the head of Lochgilp (*Lochgilpshead* 1650), Gaelic *Ceann Loch Gilb*. The loch-name is said to derive from the Gaelic word *gilb* 'chisel', because of its shape.

London (GTL, England): unexplained (*Londinium* c. 115 Tacitus, 4th cent. Antonine Itinerary, *Lundinium* late 4th cent. Ammianus Marcellinus, *Lundonia* c. 730 Bede, *Lundene, Lundeneceaster* c. 890 Old English Bede, *Lundenburg* c. 900 Anglo-Saxon Chronicle).

Like most of the place-names recorded from Roman Britain, London is a Celtic toponym adopted by the Roman administrators. An attempt to rename the town *Augusta* in the 4th cent. was not successful. London is one of a small class of Romano-British names (including Dover and York) which survived without the permanent addition of an Old English word.

The meaning of *Londinium* has unfortunately resisted the efforts of Celtic philologists. For a long time it was explained as 'town of Londinos', from a hypothetical personal name considered to be based on a word *londo-* 'bold'. This has to be abandoned because the -*u*- of the Old English spellings shows that the Celtic name had ō, and the vowel in *londo-* is short. *Lund-* is the regular spelling in Old and early-Middle English documents. The later spelling with *o* (which does not represent the pronunciation) is a convention to avoid confusion of *u* and *n* in writing. This substitution of *o* for *u* before and after nasal consonants and the letters *v* and *w* had become very common by 1300.

For references to towns and boroughs now in the Greater London area, see Greater London Names (p. 193).

Long Eaton (DRB, England): long farm on an island (*Aitune* 1086,

Eitun 1176, *Long Eyton* 1288, *Longeaton* 1577). The site was probably felt to be an island because it was enclosed on three sides by the Rivers Trent and Erewash. *Long* was prefixed to distinguish this place from Little Eaton north of Derby, which has the same· etymology. It is impossible to say why some settlements are called 'long' and others 'short' in place-names.

Eaton, Eton, and Eyton sometimes derive from Old English *ēa-tūn* 'farm on a river', and sometimes (as in this instance) from *ēg-tūn* 'farm on an island'.

Lossiemouth (MOR, Scotland): at the mouth of the River Lossie. Laid out by the town of Elgin in 1698 when the construction of a harbour also began. The *port of Lossy* is mentioned in 1383 but was probably further up the river.

The river-name is probably identical with Ptolemy's *Loxa* in location and derivation although the modern name shows an additional suffix *-odiā*. Some prefer an interpretation as Gaelic *Uisge* (or *Abhainn*) *Lossa* 'river of herbs' and take *Loxa* to be the old name of the River Findhorn. If, as is more than likely, the second element of that name is not only pre-Gaelic but pre-Celtic, then this chronological sequence is, of course, not possible.

Loughborough (LEI, England): Luhhede's fortified place (*Lucteburne* 1086, *Luchteburc* 1186). This is a name of the same type as Aylesbury and Bromborough. No historical associations suggest the existence of a fort at Loughborough, so the *burh* may in this instance have been a fortified manor-house. For the development of Old English *-hh-* to *-gh-*, pronounced *-f-*, see Keighley.

Loughton (ESX, England): Luca's estate (*Lukintone* 1062, *Lochetuna*, *Lochintunam* 1086, *Lucheton*' 1200, *Lucton c.* 1315, *Lughton* 1331, *Lufton* 1512, *Lowton* 1525, *Laughton* 1586). The Old English form was either *Lucantūn* or *Lucingtūn*. When the name had contracted to *Lucton* it contained the combination *-ct-*, which often produced a modern spelling *-ght-* (see Leighton Buzzard). The modern pronunciation of Loughton (Lowton) treats *-gh-* somewhat as it is treated in the word *plough*.

Louth (LIN, England): the loud one (*Lude, Ludes* 1086, *Luda* 1093). The name was originally that of the River Lud, on which Louth is situated. The substitution of *-th* for *-d* is an occasional characteristic of place-names in the north and east of England. See *Introduction*, p. 25.

Lowestoft (SFK, England): Hloðvér's homestead (*Lothu Wistoft* 1086, *Lothewistoft* 1212, *Lowistoft* 1219). This is a Danish place-name, see Corby. Old Danish *toft* seems to have meant 'the plot of ground in which a dwelling stood'. It is fairly common in the Danelaw, but occurs mostly in the names of small settlements; it is particularly common by itself in the name Toft.

Luton (BDF, England): farm on the River Lea (*Lygtun c.* 925 Anglo-Saxon Chronicle, *Loitone* 1086, *Luitun* 1156, *Luton* 1195). Lea is a Celtic name, possibly meaning 'light river'. Luton and Limbury are near the source of the Lea, and are both named from the river. The earliest spelling of Luton is from a forged charter, but the place-name may have been copied from a genuine early document.

Lymington (HMP, England): farm on the River Lymen (*Lentune* 1086, *Limington* 1186, *Liminton* 1196). Lymington has the same etymology as Leamington WAR. After Lymington had been named from the river, the river-name was forgotten, and in modern times it has been re-named Lymington River from the settlement.

Lytham St Annes (LNC, England): (place) at the slopes (*Lidun* 1086, *Lythum c.* 1190). This is the dative plural of Old English *hlið* 'slope', referring in this instance to the sand-dunes along the coast. These would be very noticeable before the area was built-up, and would stand in marked contrast to the flat ground inland. St Annes is a modern town named from a church built in 1872–3.

M

Macclesfield (CHE, England): Maccel's open land (*Maclesfeld* 1086). The personal name Maccel is not on record, but a name Macca occurs in a number of place-names, and Maccel would be a regular formation from the same stem. The element *feld* is fairly frequently compounded with a personal name (see Cuckfield). Although there was a royal forest here after the Norman Conquest, the place-names in the immediate vicinity of Macclesfield do not suggest that the district was heavily wooded in pre-Conquest times.

Machynlleth (MTG, Wales): field or plain of Cynllaith (*Machenleyd* 1254, *Maghkanthleyt* 1295, *Maghhenelet in Keveylok* 1310, *Machynllaith* 1385, *Maghinlleygh* 1386, *Maghynllaith* 1504, *Machynllaith* 15th cent., *Machynlleth* 1676). Welsh *ma*- 'plain, low-lying ground' + pers. name *Cynllaith*. The element *ma*- (Brit. **magos*) is followed by spirant mutation of *t* and *c* in a compound name, cf. *Machen, Mechain, Mathafarn*. *Cynllaith* is probably, though not necessarily, a personal name in place-names, cf. the river and commote of *Cynllaith* in Denbighshire. *Cynllaith* as an adjective means 'kind, gentle', as a noun (also *cunllaith*) it means 'slaughter, destruction'. *-eth* is a dialectal development from *-aith*.

There is no basis whatsoever for the common belief (following Camden) that *Machynlleth* represents the Roman station *Maglona* (more correctly *Maglova*).

The commote in which it stood was *Cyfeiliog* 'territory of Cyfail or Cyfael' from Welsh personal name *Cyfail* (*Cyfael*) + territorial suffix *-iog*.

Maes-teg (GLA, Wales): fair, handsome field (*Maes tege issa* 1543, *maesteg issa, maesteg kenol, maesteg ycha* 1630, *Maestêg issa ur Tir Amable ferch Ievan Dee* 1693, *Maestêg* 1706). Welsh *maes* 'field' + *teg* 'fair'. Formerly a farm divided into three (*isaf* 'lower', *canol* 'middle', *uchaf* 'higher'), in the parish of Llangynwyd, it is now an urban district comprising the former townships of Cwm-du and Llangynwyd Uchaf. The 1693 alias is 'land of Mable (Mabli) daughter of Ieuan Ddu'. The industrial developments of the nineteenth century (iron furnaces) caused a rapid growth in this area, and the earlier name *Y Llwyni* (*y llwyney* 1631) [Welsh *llwyni* plural of *llwyn* 'bush, copse'] was superseded by *Maes-teg*.

Maesyfed (RAD, Wales), see *New Radnor*.

Maghull (LNC, England): mayweed meadow (*Magele* 1086, *Mahale c.*

1200, *Mahhale* 1255, *Maghal* 1219, *Maele* 1323, *Male* 1514). The second element is *halh*, which (as explained under Bramhall) often means 'river meadow' in Cheshire and Lancashire. Old English *mægðe* 'mayweed', occurs also in Mayfield ssx and Maytham KNT. The hard *-g-* of Maghull is not a normal development from *mægðe*, but it may have been cultivated in the modern pronunciation because it seemed appropriate to the spelling. There are sixteenth-century spellings which suggest that the name had become a monosyllable with the medial consonants completely dropped. Presumably, however, these co-existed with other spellings in which the *-gh-* was preserved, and the latter were felt to be more correct, and so caused an adjustment in the pronunciation.

Maidenhead (BRK, England): landing-place of the maidens (*Maideheg'*, *Maidehee* 1202, *Maydenhithe* 1262, *Maidenhead* 1600). The precise meaning of *maiden* in place-names is always difficult to determine. Sometimes it probably refers to ownership (as in Medbury BDF, Maidencourt BRK), but this does not seem appropriate in Maidenhead. The reference could be to the convenient nature of the landing-place, or (more probably) to its being a place where girls were in the habit of assembling. The figurative uses of the adjective *maiden*, such as 'made or used for the first time', cannot be considered, as there is no evidence that they were current before the sixteenth century. The modern form is due to association with the word *maidenhead*.

126

Maidstone (KNT, England): stone of the maidens (*Medestan, Meddestane* 1086, *Maidestan* 1160, *Maydenestan'* 1205). In this name *maiden* probably refers to a place where girls were in the habit of assembling. Other meanings have been suggested for Maidstone, mainly on the basis of a spelling *mægþan stane* from a list of estates liable for work on Rochester bridge. This list is of uncertain date, however, and the spelling it gives for Maidstone does not outweigh the other evidence, all of which suggests that the name has the same first element as Maidenhead.

Maldon (ESX, England): hill marked by a cross (*Mældune* 913 Anglo-Saxon Chronicle). Other instances of the same name are Maulden BDF, Malden SUR, and Meldon NTB. Old English *mæl* has a variety of meanings, but it is well evidenced in the sense 'Christian cross', and this seems the most likely in place-names. Old English *cristelmæl*, which certainly means 'crucifix', also occurs in place-names, instances being Christian Malford WLT, Christelton CHE, Christmas Hill WAR, and Kismeldon DEV, which last name is a parallel to Maldon. That the Anglo-Saxons sometimes erected a cross on a prominent hill is established by some boundaries, dating from A.D. 966, relating to an estate at Newnham Murren OXF; these run *up on wearddune þær þæt cristel mæl stod*, 'up on the watch-hill, where the crucifix stood'. The cross at Maldon may have been erected as a focus for religious services, and it is tempting to suggest that it was the forerunner of the church.

Maltby (YOW, England): Malti's village (*Maltebi, Malteby* 1086). This is a name of the same type as Corby. Maltby LIN and YON are identical.

Malvern (WOR, England): bare hill (*Mælfern c.* 1030, *Malferna* 1086, *Maluernia* 1130). This is a typical example of a Celtic place-name, which must have been in use during the Roman period and was passed on to the Anglo-Saxons. It is the older type of Celtic compound, in which the adjective (a word corresponding to modern Welsh *moel* 'bare') precedes the noun (a word corresponding to Welsh *bryn* 'hill'). During the sixth century A.D. the new type of Celtic place-name came into being, in which the defining element follows the noun; a name of this later type in Worcestershire is Pensax 'hill of the Saxons'. The Malvern hills are a notable landmark from all directions, so this is an instance of the type of natural feature which is most likely to keep its pre-English name because it is known to so many people. From being used in compounds of this type, *moel* was felt to mean 'bare hill', and some Welsh hills are simply called y Foel. The English adjective *calu*, of identical meaning, also came to be used as a substantive in the hill-name The Callow, which occurs in Shropshire.

Manchester (LNC, England): Roman town called *Mamucium* (*Mamucio* 4th cent. Antonine Itinerary, *Mameceaster* 923 Anglo-Saxon Chronicle, *Mamecestre* 1086, *Manchestre* 1330). This is a name of the same type as Cirencester. Romano-British *Mamucium* is of uncertain etymology. The change from *Mam-* to *Man-* appears to have taken place in the fourteenth century. The adjective Mancunian is presumably based on a form *Mancunio*, which occurs in one manuscript of the Antonine Itinerary, but is considered to be a corruption of *Mamucio*.

Mansfield (NTT, England): open land by the River Maun (*Mamesfelde* 1086, *Manesfeld* 1202, *Maumefeld* 1244, *Maunsfeld c.* 1250, *Mauncefeld* 1515, *Mancefeld* 1520). There are some bounds of part of Sherwood Forest, dating from 1232, which mention a place called *Mammesheued* about four miles south-west of Mansfield. This could mean either 'top of the hill called *Mam*' or 'source of the river called *Mam*', since *hēafod* (see Gateshead) is used in both these transferred senses. The River Maun does, in fact, rise near this spot, but as there is no known river-name of this kind, and as there is good evidence for a hill-name Mam, it seems preferable to regard *Mammesheued* as the hill which rises to 570 ft. north of Kirkby-in-Ashfield. The river-name would then be a back-formation (see Bishop's Stortford) from the hill. This process of back-formation must be assumed to have taken place early, as there seems little doubt that Mansfield was named from the river some time before the Norman Conquest. If *Mam* is in fact the name of a hill, it is related to Mamhead DEV and Mam Tor DRB, and may be from a Celtic root meaning 'breast'. The River Maun is *Mome* thirteenth century, *Mone* 1335; this was probably influenced by the development of the settlement-name to *Manesfeld, Maunsfeld* etc., and so became Maun.

March (CAM, England): (place) at the boundary (*Merche, Mercha* 1086, *Marche* 1286). Old English *mearc* 'boundary', usually becomes Mark in place-names, but the development to March in this instance has been explained as due to an old locative ending *-i*. If this is so, the name must date from the earliest stage of the Anglo-Saxon settlement. The nature of the boundary is uncertain; it might be the northern edge of the region called Ely.

Margate (KNT, England): (?) gap in the cliffs by a rock called The Mare (*Meregate* 1254, *Mergate* 1258, *Margate* 1293). Margate is generally interpreted as 'gate leading to the sea'. This is linguistically possible, as *mere* meant 'sea' as well as 'lake' in the Old English and Middle English periods, but the compound would not be very meaningful. Old English *geat* in Margate and in Ramsgate appears to refer to a break in the cliffs, and there is nowhere such a gate could lead except to the sea. Possibly one of the rock formations here was known as 'The Mare'; see Cowes for a similar use of animal names.

Market Harborough (LEI, England): (?) hill where oats are grown (*Hauerberga* 1177, *Mercat Heburgh* 1312). Haverhill SFK is a similar compound. The first element of both is probably Old Norse *hafri* 'oats', in which case the names are hybrids, with a Norse first and an English second element. The existence of a similar word (*hæfer* in Old English and *hafr* in Old Norse) which means 'a he-goat' makes it impossible to give a definite etymology, however. A payment by the township of Harborough of three marks for the privilege of having a market is recorded on the Pipe Roll for the year 1203.

Maryport (CUM, England): named after Mary Senhouse, whose husband made a harbour here between 1750 and 1760. The settlement was earlier called *Elnefoot*, from its position at the mouth of the River Ellen.

Matlock (DRB, England): oak tree where councils are held (*Meslach* 1086, *Matlac* 1196, *Matloc* 1204, *Mathlac* 1233). The first element is Old English *mæðel* 'speech, assembly, council', probably referring to a meeting-place. Matlock is not known to have been a hundred meeting-place, so the nature of the assembly is uncertain. Matlask NFK means 'council ash'.

Melton Mowbray (LEI, England): middle farm (*Medeltone* 1086, *Melton* 1200, *Melton Moubray* 1284). Old English *middel* was influenced by Old Norse *meðal*, and this caused the name to become Melton instead of Middleton or Milton. Mowbray is from Roger de Moubray, who owned the place about 1125.

Old English *middel-tūn* has given rise to a great many place-names. There are at least 6 Meltons, 33 Middletons, and 27 Miltons, all from this source. They are presumably each named from their situation in relation to two other places with more distinctive place-names. In the case of Melton Mowbray, however, it would be very difficult to identify the other two settlements.

Menai Bridge (AGL, Wales): bridge over the River Menai (*Porthatheu* 1291, *Portaythowe* 1294, *Porthaethwy* 1316, *Porthaythoy* 1413, *Porthaithwye* 1589, *passago de Porthaythwye* 1651, *Porthaethwy Ferry* 1795). Welsh *porth* 'ferry' + tribal name *Daethwy; Porth Ddaethwy > Porthaethwy*. The commote in which it stood was *Dindaethwy* (Welsh *din* 'fort' + *Daethwy*), (*Dyndaythou* 1291, *Dyndaetho* 1304). Porthaethwy was one of the recognised crossing-places between Anglesey and the mainland. It is normally called *Y Borth* in Welsh. The English form *Menai Bridge* followed the completion of the bridge by Telford in 1826. The River *Menai* is *Mene* 11th cent., *Menei* 13th cent., *Meney* 1379, *Menai* 1455. Welsh *mon* (cf. *myn* in *myned* 'go'?) + suffix -*ai*, with the meaning of 'flow, stream'?

Merthyr Tudful (GLA, Wales): grave of Tudful (*Merthir* 1254, *Merthyr* 1281, *Merthur* 1296, *Merthyr Tutuil* 13th cent., *Merthyr Tydfyl* 1566, *Merther-Tidvill* 1680, *Merthyr Tydvil* 1760, *Merthyr Tydfil* 1833). Welsh *merthyr* 'grave of a saint, or churchyard consecrated with his bones' [Lat. *martyrium*] + *Tudful* (saint's name).

Mexborough (YOW, England): Mēoc's fortified place (*Mechesburg* 1086, *Mekesburgh* 1234, *Mexburgh* 1529). This is one of a group of names discussed under Conisbrough.

Middlesbrough (YON, England): middlemost fort (*Midelesburc c.* 1165). Old English *middel* (discussed under Melton Mowbray) occasionally appears in place-names in the superlative, *midlest*. Possibly this is a relatively late name, and *burh* means 'town' rather than 'fort'. It would be interesting to identify the two places in relation to which this is the middlemost.

Middleton (LNC, England): middle farm (*Middelton* 1194). Names with this meaning are discussed under Melton Mowbray. In this instance, 'middle' may refer to the position in relation to Manchester and Rochdale.

Midsomer Norton (SOM, England): north settlement where there is a midsummer festival (*Midsomeres Norton* 1248, *Midsummernorton* 1269). Norton is a very common name which raises problems similar to those discussed under Melton. Norton, however, can be explained by reference to one earlier settlement with a more distinctive name, whereas two are needed to explain Melton, Middleton, etc. Midsomer is considered to refer to the festival held on the day of St John.

Milford Haven (PEM, Wales): sandy estuary (*de Milverdico portu* 1191, *Mellferth* 1207, *Milford* 1219, *Muleford* 1293, *Milford Haven* 1394, *Milford Havyn* 1453, *Milforde Havon* 1595). Old Norse *melr* 'sand-bank, sand-hill' + *fjǫrþr* 'fiord'. The early references are to the haven itself, since the town is modern. The form *Milford* is probably due to English influence, and *haven* was added later when the original meaning was lost.

The Welsh form is *Aberdaugleddyf* 'mouth of the rivers Cleddyf' (*Aber Dav Gleddef* 15th cent., *Aber . . . Dau Gleddau* 15th cent., *Aberdugledheu*

129

1586). Welsh *aber* 'mouth'+*dau* 'two'+*Cleddau*, *Cleddyf* (river-name). The two rivers are the Eastern Cleddau (Cleddau Ddu) and Western Cleddau (Cleddau Wen)—(*Cledeu* 1191, *ad fluvium qui dicitur Gladius* 13th cent., *Cledyf* 14th cent., *aque de Clethi* 1326, *Gledy* 1394, [*hyd*] *Gleddav* 15th cent., *Klethey* 1603, *Clethe Wen* 1603, *Clethy ffv.* 1698). Welsh *cleddau, cleddyf* 'sword' +*du* 'black' or *gwen* 'white'. The name of the river belongs to that class of river-names which are taken from tools or arms, either because they cut or slice through the land, or whose waters shine, cf. *Gele* in *Abergele*, *Cyllell* 'knife', *Nodwydd* 'needle', etc.

Milngavie (DNB, Scotland): has been variously explained as Gaelic *muileann-gaoithe* 'wind mill' or *meall na gaoithe* 'hill of the wind', but its early spellings (*Mylngavie* 1669, *Milngavie* 1685) are not really conclusive. Pronounced *Mill-guy*, with the accent on the second syllable.

Mirfield (YOW, England): (?) open land where festivities are held (*Mirefeld* 1086, *Mirifeld* 1246, *Merefelde* 1293, *Murfeld* 1531). This etymology assumes that the first element is Old English *myrgen* 'joy, pleasure', and that the -*n*- has been lost, as it often is in this position. If this is correct, Mirfield is of similar meaning to Wakefield, and there is another parallel in Berkshire, Gainfield Farm in Buckland, which means 'open land of the games'. Alternatively, the first element of Mirfield could be the adjective *myrig* 'pleasant' (which is fairly common in place-names), and the reference would then be to the

natural characteristics of the place, not to human activities.

Mold (FLI, Wales): high hill (*Mohald* 1254, *Montem Altum* 1278, *Moald* 1284, *Mold* 1297, *Mohaut* 1297, *Monhalt* 1358, *Mohault* 1428, *Mohawt* 1439, *Mould* 1581). Norman French *Mont-hault* 'high mount'. These forms developed as *Montalt* > *Moltalt* > *Mohaut* > *Mohault* > *Mold*. The name describes the site of Mold. The Welsh form is *Yr Wyddgrug* 'the tomb-mound' (*Gythe Gruc* 1280–1, *kastell yr wydgruc* 14th cent., *y wytgruc* 15th cent., *Yr Wyddgrug* 16th cent., *yr wydd gryc* 1566, *y Wydhgryg vulgo y Wyrgryg*, *c.* 1700). Welsh *y(r)* definite article+ *gwydd* 'sepulchre, tomb, memorial' +*crug* 'mound'. In Welsh the combination -*ddgr*- sometimes becomes -*rgr*-. The element *gwydd* also appears in *Y(r) Wyddfa* 'Snowdon', where *gwydd* refers to a stone cairn on the summit. Norman French *Mold* and Welsh *Y(r) Wyddgrug* refer to the Bailey Hill.

The commote and lordship of which Mold was the centre were called respectively *Ystrad Alun* 'vale of the River Alun' (*Stratalwen* 1291, *Estradelon* 1323, *Stradalun* 1327–8, *Ystrad Alun* 1450, *Estradelun* 1536–9, *Ystrad Alyn c.* 1700). Welsh *ystrad* 'strath, vale'+river-name *Alun*. For *Alun* cf. *Alun* 1337, *Alyn* 1383–4, *Alun* 1457, *Alun* 1550, *Alyn* 1612. Welsh *alun* < *al-* 'wander, meander' +suffix -*un*, cf. Celtic *Alaunos*, *Alauna*.

The English name for the lordship was *Moldsdale* 'vale of Mold' (*Mouhautisdale* 1275, *Moldesdale* 1437, *Mohuntsdall* 1493, *Vallis Mot'alti* 1508, *Mohauntsdale* 1561,

130

Molesdale yn Walsch caullid Stredalen 1536–9). *Mold* + Old English *dæl* 'dale'.

Monmouth (MON, Wales): mouth of the River Mynwy (*Munwi Muþa* 11th cent., *Monemude* 1086, *Munemuda* 1190, *Monmouth* 1267, *Monemuta* 14th cent., *Munmouth* 1441, *Monnemouthe* 1553). Welsh *Mynwy* + Old English *muþa* 'mouth'. The name of the river is *Mingui* (*Myngui, Mynugui, Mynui, Minugui c*. 1150, *Mona* 1250, *Monue* 1410, *Munwey cambrice Mone* 1536–9, *Monowe* 1567, *Munno, Munow* 1577, *Monowe* 1578, *Monnowe* 1637). Welsh *Mynwy* may be connected with the Celtic tribe *Menapii*, or the root *myn-, men-* 'go', cf. *Menai*.

The early Welsh name for the town is Abermynwy 'mouth of the River Mynwy' (*Aper Mynuy, Aper Myngui c.* 1150, *Aber Mynwy* 14th cent.). Welsh *aber* 'mouth' + *Mynwy*. The later form is *Trefynwy* 'town of Mynwy' (*Tre Fynwe* 1606).

In English the form *Mynwy* developed as *Monnow*. In the name of the town *Monnowmouth* became *Monmouth*.

Montgomery (MTG, Wales): (*Montgomeri* 1086, *Muntgumeri* 1086, *Monte Gumeri* 1166, *Mongomery* 1211, *Mungumberi* 1227, *Moungomery* 1292, *Mount Gomery* 1313). The first castle of Montgomery was built by Roger de Montgomery before 1086 at Hen Domen, and was named after his castle of Montgommery in the department of Calvados, Normandy. The second castle of Montgomery was commenced on the present site in 1223–4. This was known first in Welsh as *Castell Baldwin* 'the castle of Baldwin' (*kastell baldwin* 14th cent., *castell baldwin* 14th cent.) Welsh *castell* 'Castle' + *Baldwin*. Montgomery was granted to Baldwin de Bollers in 1102, and probably the castle took its name from him. The later Welsh name is *Trefaldwyn* 'town of Baldwin' (*Trefaldwyn* 1440, *Montgomerike in Walche Treualuine* 1536–9, *Trefaldwin* 1566, *Trefaldwin* 1586, *Tre'Valdwin* 1722, *Tre Faldwyn* 1810).

The county takes its name from the town, i.e. *Sir Drefaldwyn*. As *tref* is feminine it mutates the following consonant, and since mutated *-f-* can be from *-b-* or *-m-*, *Trefaldwyn* was incorrectly thought to be for *Tre* + *Maldwyn* and *Maldwyn* is sometimes used in Welsh for the county.

Montrose (ANG, Scotland): moor of the promontory (*Munros c.* 1178, *Vetus Monros a.* 1200). Gaelic *Mon-rois*. In this compound, *mon* is a short form of *monadh* 'moor' and *ros* means 'a promontory or wood'.

Morecambe (LNC, England): this is a modern name, due to the identification by Lancashire historians of the bay here with a place in Ptolemy's Geography called *Morikámbē*. This identification was first made by Whitaker, who published a *History of Manchester* in 1771, and it led to the name Morecambe Bay being generally adopted and used for the town, which grew up as a result of the expansion of the holiday industry in the nineteenth century. It seems reasonably certain that the estuary called *Morikámbē* by Ptolemy was the estuary at Lancaster, but the modern name Morecambe is an antiquarian revival, not a genuine survival from Romano-British times.

131

Morpeth (NTB, England): murder path (*Morthpath c.* 1200, *Morpeth* 1200). Old English *morð* 'murder', has been noted in two other place-names, Mortgrove HRT ('murder grove') and a lost *morþhlau* in Kineton WAR ('murder tumulus'). Probably the road which crossed the River Wansbeck at Morpeth had an evil reputation. Dupath CNW means 'thief path', and may indicate a similar state of affairs.

Motherwell (LAN, Scotland): Our Lady's Well (*Modyrwaile* 1363, *Modervale* 1373, *Moderwell* 1626). For the time being, we have accepted the literal meaning of the name as the correct one, although the earliest spellings are a little difficult to explain in this context. As a burgh, Motherwell has since 1920 been combined with Wishaw. This is likely to be identical with the Warwickshire Wishaw (*Witscaga* 1086, *Wiðshada* 1166) in which the second element is Old English *scaga* 'wood' whereas the first part may be either Old English *wiðig* 'willow' or *wiht* 'bend'. Wishaw LAN is on record in 1696 in its modern form.

Mountain Ash (GLA, Wales): mountain ash (*Aber Pennarthe* 1570, *Tir Aber-Penarth* 1666, *Tyr Aberpennar* 1771–81). Welsh *aber* 'mouth' + brook name *Pennar*. The brook is *Penar* 1536–9, *Pennar Brook* 1792. *Pennar* is probably for *Pennardd* (cf. the forms *Pennarth*), the name of the mountain where the brook rises, i.e. Welsh *pennardd* 'height'. This is more probable than the other possibilities, i.e. *pen* 'head, top' + *garth* 'ridge', or *pen* 'head' + *arth* 'bear'. The town grew rapidly during the industrial expansion of the nineteenth century, and local tradition has it that the landowner, John Bruce Pryce, arbitrarily bestowed the name 'Mountain Ash'. The Welsh name remains as *Aberpennar*.

Musselburgh (MLO, Scotland): mussel borough (*Muselburge* 1070–930, *Muchselburg* 1201), from Old English *muscle* 'mussel' and *burh* 'borough, town'. A famous mussel-bed lies just off-shore.

Nairn (NAI, Scotland): (the submerging) river (*Inuernaren* 1189–99, *Invernaryn* 1204, *Inuernarren* 1208–15, *Narne* 1382), Gaelic *Inbhir Narunn*. As the early forms show, Nairn was quite clearly originally Invernairn 'Nairn mouth' (compare Inverness). The town-name was later shortened so that now it looks identical with the river-name, Gaelic *Abhainn Narunn*. The name of the water-course is one of the oldest in Britain; as an *n*- stem **Narō(n)* it is the same as the Illyrian river-name *Narōn* (now Narenta) and has relatives in various parts of Central Europe. The Indo-European root on which all these names are based is **ner-* 'to penetrate, to submerge'.

Nantwich (CHE, England): famous salt-works (*Wich* 1086, *Nametwihc* 1194, *Nantwich* 1281). Nantwich is one of several inland salt-working places which could be referred to at least up to the time of the Domesday Survey simply as *Wich*. The others are Droitwich WOR and Northwich and Middlewich CHE. Droitwich and Nantwich eventually acquired prefixes of similar meaning, Droitwich being the 'princely' Wich, and Nantwich the 'named' Wich.

There has been much discussion of the precise meaning of *wic* in these names. The most recent opinion is that one of the meanings developed by the word was 'salt-works'. Other meanings are discussed under Aldridge, Greenwich, and West Wickham.

Nant-y-glo (MON, Wales): coal brook (*Nantygloe* 1752, *Nant-y-glo* 1832). Welsh *nant* 'brook' + definite article *y* 'the' + *glo* 'coal'. This is another of the industrial towns which developed in the early nineteenth century. The iron furnaces date from about 1809. A church was established in 1844 under the parish church of Aberystrwyth (see Blaenau). *Coalbrookdale* occurs a little lower down the valley of the Ebwy Fach as a translation of *Nant-y-glo*.

Narberth (PEM, Wales): near the hedge (*Nethebert* 1220, *Nerberth* 1291, *Arberth* 1300–25, *Nerberd* 1327, *la Nerbert* 1331, *Nerberth* 1382, *Nerberch* 1535, *Ar berth* 1566, *Narberth* 1612, *Narbarth* 1698). Welsh preposition *ar* 'near, opposite' (cf. *Arfon* under *Caernarfon*) + *perth* 'bush, hedge'. The original form is seen in *Arberth* (1300–25), and this is still used locally. *Narberth* probably stands for *yn Arberth* 'in Arberth'. Traditionally the site of one of the royal courts of Dyfed, the place became the centre of the Norman lordship of Narberth.

Neath (GLA, Wales): (?) shining river (*Nidum* Roman period, *Neth* 1191, *Neth* 1254, *Neth* 1272, *Neeth* 1314). The town takes its name from the river (*Ned c.* 1150, *flumen Ned* 12th cent., *Neth fluvium* 1191, *Neeth* 1306). The Welsh name is *Castellnedd* 'castle of Nedd' (*a chastell nedd c.* 1500, *Kastell Nedd* 1566, *Castell Neth c.* 1700). Welsh *castell* 'castle' + *Nedd*. The Roman fort took its name from the river, and British **nid-* and Welsh *nedd* are possibly to be equated with Latin *nideo* 'shine'. Anglo-Norman forms like *Neth*> *Neath* are an approximation of Welsh *Nedd*.

Nelson (LNC, England): this is a modern name, derived from the Lord Nelson Inn. The inn is marked on a map of 1818, and it gave a name to the new town which grew up here owing to the rapid development of the textile trade. A local board was formed in 1864 for 'the district of Nelson'.

Newark-on-Trent (NTT, England): new work (*Niweweorce c.* 1080). It is impossible to say whether Old English *weorc* means 'fortification' or simply 'building' in this name. There are some place-names in which it appears to refer to an old fortification, such as an Iron Age hill-fort (Workway in Alton Priors WLT) or a town wall (Butterwork in Lincoln), but there are others in which it refers to a new building. The clearest example in this latter category is Newark SUR, which refers to a new priory. Newark SUR is a Middle English name, however, and it may be that in the Old English period, when the Nottinghamshire name probably arose, the meaning 'fortification' is more likely. It has been suggested that Newark NTT was named in distinction to *Old-work*, the name current from about 1230 to 1722 for the Roman ruins at *Margidunum*; but as *Margidunum* is 11 miles away from Newark it is not likely that there is any connection between the names.

Newbury (BRK, England): new market town (*Neuberie c.* 1080). Other examples of this name are Newborough STF, Newbrough NTB, Newburgh LNC, YON. Newport has the same significance. The probable history of Newbury BRK is that Ernulf de Hesdin, who obtained the manor after the Norman Conquest, founded a trading centre which was successful because it was at the point where the road from Oxford to Winchester crossed the River Kennet. *Burh* is here used in the late Old English sense 'town' as in Bury St Edmunds and Peterborough.

Although the name *Neuberie* is used in a charter of about 1080, it had not at that date completely ousted the earlier name of the settlement; Ernulf de Hesdin's estate here is described in the Domesday Survey under the name *Ulvritone*.

Newcastle Emlyn (CRM, Wales): *Novum Castrum de Emlyn c.* 1240 new castle in Emlyn (*Emlyn with New Castle* 1257, *Newcastle Emlyn* 1295, *castle of Emelyn* 1328). The Welsh form is *Castellnewydd Emlyn* 'new castle of Emlyn' (*Castell neuweydd in Emlyn* 1541, *Kastell newydd yn E.* 1566). Welsh *castell* 'castle' + *newydd* 'new' + *Emlyn* (cantref name). The 'new' castle was so called to distinguish it from the 'old' castle at Cilgerran. It is locally called *Castellnewy*, with the characteristic dialectal loss of final *-dd*. The cantref of *Emlyn* (later Norman lordship) was divided into the commotes of *Is Cuch* (administrative centre at Cilgerran) and *Uwch Cuch* (administrative centre at Newcastle) 'land around the glen' (*Emblin, Emelinn* 1130, *Emlin c.* 1150, *Emlyn* 1257, *Emelyn* 1288, 1311, *Emlyn Vchcuch* temp. Hy V, *Emlyn Hysse Keych* 1524, *Emlyn Is Kych* 1593). Welsh *emlyn < am* 'about, around'+*glyn* 'glen'. The Act of Union of 1536 assigned Emlyn Uwch Cuch to Carmarthenshire and Emlyn Is Cuch to Pembrokeshire, with the river *Cuch* as boundary.

Newcastle-under-Lyme (STF, England): new castle (*Nouum Oppidum sub Lima* 1168, *Novum castellum subtus Lymam* 1173). The date of the construction of the castle is not known, but the earliest reference to it is in a charter of 1149, by which King Stephen granted it to the Earl of Chester. In this charter the castle is referred to as the *novum castellum de Staffordshira*. Lyme is a Celtic forest-name, discussed under Ashton-under-Lyne.

Newcastle-upon-Tyne (NTB, England): new castle (*Novem Castellum* 1130, *Nouum Castellum super Tinam* 1168). A castle was built here in 1089 by a Norman named Robert Curthose. Tyne is believed to be a Celtic river-name, from a root meaning 'to dissolve, flow'.

Newmarket (SFK, England): new market (*Novum Forum* 1200, *Novum Mercatum* 1219, *la Newmarket* 1418). This name has the same significance as Newbury and Newport.

Newport (IOW, England): new market town (*Neweport* 1202). The word 'port' is discussed under Gosport. There are at least six examples of the name Newport.

Newport (MON, Wales): new port (*Novus Burgus* 1138, *Novoburgo* 1191, *Nova Villa* 1290, *Neuborh* 1291, *Neuporte* 1322, *Newport upon Husk* 1439). Old English *niwe* 'new'+*port* 'port' and *burh* 'town'. The Welsh name was *Castellnewydd ar Wysg* 'new castle on Usk' (*Castell Newyd ar Wysc* 14th cent., *y Castell Newydd* 15th cent., *y Kastell Newydd ar Wysc* 1566). Welsh *castell* 'castle'+*newydd* 'new'+*ar* 'on'+*Wysg* 'Usk'. In modern Welsh *Castelnewydd(ar-Wysg)*. For *Wysg*, Usk see Usk.

Newport (PEM, Wales): new port (*Nuport* 1282, *Ecclesia de Novo Burgo* 1291, *Newburgh* 1296, *Novus Burgus* 1316, *Newporte* 1325, *Nieuport* 1377, *Nyport* 1492). Old English *niwe* 'new'+*port* 'port' or *burh* 'town'. The Welsh name is *Trefdraeth* 'town near the shore' (*Kastell Trefdraeth* 14th cent., *Tredraith* 1536–9, *Tref Draeth* 1566, *Trevdraeth* 1722, *Newport alias Trefdraeth* 1763, *Newport or Trefdraeth* 1801). Welsh *tref* 'town'+*traeth* 'strand, shore'. The local pronunciation is *Tredraeth*. The name of the strand was *Traeth Edrywy*, but there was another *Edrywy* in Cardiganshire, and it is impossible to say which of the early forms refer to the *traeth* in Trefdraeth.

Newquay (CNW, England): Professor Charles Thomas has supplied the following information: The quay goes back to the medieval period. It was in need of repair in 1439, when an indulgence was granted to contributors to the work. In this indulgence it is spoken of as the *Kaye* at *Tewen Blustry*. Possibly it was deemed 'new' after these repairs, as the earliest occurrence of the English name noted dates from about 1480. The place is called *Newe Kaye* in 1603 in Carew's *Survey of Cornwall*, but Carew complains that in his day the quay which gave rise to the name is unserviceable. The Cornish name for the town is Towan Blistra, from *towan* 'sand-dune', and an uncertain defining element.

Newton Abbot (DEV, England): new farm (*Nova Villa* late 12th cent., *Nyweton Abbatis* 1270). Abbot was added because the place was given to Torre Abbey in 1196.

Newton has been said to be 'probably the most common English place-name'. Newnton, Newington, and Naunton have the same meaning as Newton. Many Newtons have distinguishing prefixes or additions; among the latter may be instanced Newton Aycliffe DRH (Aycliffe is a neighbouring place, probably 'oakwood') and Newton-le-Willows LNC (see *Chester-le-Street* for this type of addition).

New Radnor (RAD, Wales): at the red bank (*Raddrenoue* 1086, *Radenoura* 1191, *Radnore* 1201, *Old Radenouere* 1252, *Rademore Nova* 1277, *New Radenore* 1298, *New Radnore* 1408, *Raddenore* 1459, *Radnor Nova* 1535). Old English *rēad* 'red'+*ofer* 'bank' or *ōra* 'bank'. Old Radnor and New Radnor are about two miles apart. *Old Radnor* is *Pencraig* in Welsh. 'Chief rock' (*Pen Craig* 15th cent.,

Penkraic c. 1562, *pen kraic* 1566). Welsh *pen* 'top, chief'+*craig* 'rock'. *New Radnor* is *Maesyfed* in Welsh 'field or plain of Hyfaidd' (*Maeshyueid* 14th cent., *maessyueid* 15th cent., *Maisseueth* 1586, *o. fysyfed* 1566). Welsh *maes* 'field'+pers. name *Hyfaidd*. When Radnorshire was created by the Acts of Union of 1536 and 1542 the new shire took its name from (New) Radnor, as did the Welsh form *Sir Faesyfed*.

Newton Mearns (RNF, Scotland): new town in the parish of Mearns; (the latter is *Mernes* 1177, *Meornes* 1179) and is identical with the alternative name for Kincardineshire: The Mearns. Both derive from Gaelic *An Mhaoirne* 'the Stewartry', an area administered by a steward or official with delegated authority. 'The Stewartry' is also the other name for Kirkcudbrightshire. *Maoirne* is probably a borrowing from Welsh *maeroni*, from *maer* 'a steward, an officer', a loan-word from Latin (*maior*). *Newtoun de Mernis* is mentioned in 1609.

Newton St Boswells (ROX, Scotland): the new town of the parish of St Boswells. The parish name is *Sanct Boswellis c.* 1120 and *St Boswalls* in 1682. It commemorates *Boisil*, a seventh-century prior of Old Melrose. The older name of the parish, recorded from the twelfth to the seventeenth century, was Lessudden (*Lessedewyn, Lassidewyn, Lessedwin* 1153–1230), with a church dedicated to St Mary. The later parish church was built in 1652 or earlier from the ruins of an older church or chapel dedicated to St Boswell.

Newtown (MTG, Wales): new town (*Newentone c.* 1250, *Nova Villa* 1295, the *Newtown* 1360, *Neueton* 1365, *Newton* 1458, *the newe towne of Kyddweyn c.* 1540). Old English *nīwe* 'new' + *tun* 'town'. The Welsh name is *Trenewydd, Drenewydd* 'new town' (*Drenewyth in Kedewen* 1394, *Drenewyth alias Llanvayr in Kedewen* 1395, *i'r Drev Newydd* 15th cent., *Tref newydd* 16th cent., *y dre newydd* 1566, *Trenewith* 1586, *Tre newydd yng-Hedewen* 1612, *Newtown or Trene-vith* 1680). Welsh *tref* 'town' + *newydd* 'new'. The town was in the commote of *Cedewain* '(?) territory of Cadaw'. Welsh pers. name (?) *Cadaw* + territorial suffix *-ein* (*ing*). The church was *Llanfair-yng-Nghede-wain* 'Church of Mary in Cedewain' (*Llanweyr* 1254, *Thlanveir in Kedewey* 1279, *Lanwoyr* 1291, *Llannvair in Kedeweyn* 1386, *Llanvere in Kedewen* 1395, *new town of Kedewyng alias Llanvair in Kedewyng* 1406). Welsh *llan* 'church' + *Mair* 'Mary' + *yn* 'in' + *Cedewain*.

Northampton (NTP, England): north settlement (*Hamtun* 917 Anglo-Saxon Chronicle, *Norðhamtun* 12th cent. Anglo-Saxon Chronicle). This name consisted originally of the term *hāmtūn*, which is discussed under Littlehampton. North was prefixed for distinction from Southampton, though that name is actually of different origin. The need to distinguish the two arose after the formation of the Midland shires in the tenth century. As there were two shire towns which were by then both called *Hamtun*, there were for a time two administrative units both called *Hamtunscir*, and this led to the prefixing of North- and South-.

Northwich (CHE, England): north salt-works (*Wich, Norwich* 1086, *Northwich c.* 1150). This is one of a group of names which are discussed under Nantwich. It is north of Nantwich and Middlewich.

Norwich (NFK, England): north port (*Norðwic c.* 930 Coin, 1004 Anglo-Saxon Chronicle). The Anglo-Saxon Chronicle records that in 1004 'Sweyn came with his fleet to Norwich'. The best translation of *wīc* in this instance seems to be 'port', and Norwich can be classed with Ipswich as regards the second element. North- probably refers to its position north of Ipswich and Dunwich (which was also a port in medieval times).

Nottingham (NTT, England): village of the family or followers of Snot (*Snotengaham c.* 900 Anglo-Saxon Chronicle, *Snotingaham c.* 925 Anglo-Saxon Chronicle, *Notinge-ham* 1130). This is a name of the same type as Gillingham. The loss of *S-* in the early twelfth century was due to the Norman French tendency to simplify groups of consonants.

Nuneaton (WAR, England): farm by a stream (*Etone* 1086, *Eatona c.* 1155, *Eyton* 1237, *Nonne Eton* 1247). This is a common place-name, usually surviving in the spelling Eaton, but occasionally as Eton or Yeaton. It is derived from the compound *ēa-tūn* 'river-farm', and names from this source are sometimes difficult to distinguish from those derived from *ēg-tūn* 'island-farm'. In the Warwickshire name, *ēa* refers to the River Anker. *Nun-* was prefixed after a Benedictine nunnery was founded here in the twelfth century.

O

Oban (ARG, Scotland): small bay (*Oban* 1643), in Gaelic *un t-Òban Latharnach* 'the little bay of Lorne'. Gaelic *òb* is a loanword from Norse *hóp* 'land-locked bay', and Òban its masculine diminutive.

Oldbury (WOR, England): (?) old hill-fort (*Aldeberia* 1174, *Oldebure* 1270). The second element is *burh*, discussed under Aylesbury. As there are a number of instances of the name Oldbury which certainly refer to Iron Age hill-forts, and as these forts are common in the West Midlands, it is most likely that the translation given here is valid, although the ravaged nature of the landscape precludes the identification of archaeological remains; cf. Wednesbury.

Oldham (LNC, England): old promontory (*Aldholm c.* 1227, *Aldhulm* 1227, *Oldum* 1327, *Owdam* 1546). The second element (discussed under Durham) is Old Norse *holmr*, Danish *hulm*, which meant 'island', later 'river-meadow'. Oldham is situated on a spur of moorland, which juts out into lower ground to the south and west of the town, and in this instance *holmr* may be used (as Old English *hamm* sometimes is) to denote an inland promontory. The first element is probably Old English *ald* 'old', though the significance of the compound is not absolutely clear. There are other names in which *ald* is compounded with a topographical term, e.g. Aldfield YOW, Aldford CHE. In Oldham the meaning might be 'promontory which is the site of an ancient settlement'. As in Durham, there has been confusion of *holmr* with Old English *hām*.

Ormskirk (LNC, England): Orm's church (*Ormeschirche c.* 1190, *Ormeskierk* 1203, *Ormeschurch* 1317). This is a Scandinavian place-name, but there is alternation of Old English *cirice* with Old Norse *kirkja* in the early spellings.

Orm was probably the name of the founder of the church. It was a fairly common personal name in areas of Scandinavian settlement, and it is probably only a coincidence that *Orm de Ormeskierk* appears in the reference of 1203. Old Norse *kirkja* is very common in place-names, but is rare with a personal name, Algarkirk LIN being another of the few examples. Old English names in which *cirice* is compounded with a man's or woman's name are commoner, and include Alvechurch WOR, Baschurch SHR, Lillechurch KNT, Offchurch WAR. In all these instances, the settlement was presumably flourishing before the church

139

was built, and known by some earlier name which the 'church' name displaced.

Ossett (YOW, England): fold frequented by thrushes (*Osleset* 1086, *Oselesete* 1226, *Osset* 1284). The second element is (*ge*)*set* 'dwelling, camp, place for animals, stable, fold'. This is not a common place-name element, but occurs in several Yorkshire names besides Ossett, including Woodsetts YOW and Lissett and Winsetts YOE.

Oswaldtwistle (LNC, England): Oswald's land in a river-fork (*Oswaldestwisel* 1246). Two streams join in the town, and this was presumably considered the distinguishing feature of the land owned here by a man called Oswald.

Stream-junctions are frequently mentioned in place-names, even when the streams are very small. Old English *twisla* is found chiefly in north country names, and there are several examples in Lancashire besides Oswaldtwistle. Another word for a stream-junction is *gemӯðe*, common in the West Midlands in such names as Mitton, Myton.

Oswestry (SHR, England): Oswald's tree (*Osewaldestre c.* 1180, *Croesoswald* 1254). The manor was earlier known as *Meresberie* (1086), *Blancmonasterium* (1160), *Album Monasterium* (1215). Oswestry is a name of the same type as Braintree, Elstree, and Coventry. Interpretation is particularly difficult in this instance because of the ancient local tradition that Oswestry means 'St Oswald's cross' and alludes to the killing of the Christian King Oswald of Northum-

bria by the pagan King Penda of Mercia in A.D. 641.

The application of the name Oswestry to the settlement here cannot be traced back before the mid-thirteenth century. In the Domesday Survey, the manor is described under the name *Meresberie*. This survives as modern Maesbury, a hamlet 2½ miles south of Oswestry, the name of which means 'fortified place of the boundary', with reference to the proximity of Offa's Dyke. There is no possibility of equating *Meresberie* with *Maserfelth*, the name given by Bede as that of the site of the battle of 641, though the two were probably associated in local tradition. A church at *Meresberie* is mentioned in the Domesday account, but nothing is said about the dedication. It is only from a later source, the Cartulary of Shrewsbury Abbey, that we learn that it was dedicated to St Oswald. The monks of Shrewsbury clearly believed, however, that the dedication went back to early Norman times; there is no reason to doubt this, and it is the best evidence for the antiquity of the traditional association with St Oswald. The church is called *ecclesia Sancti Oswaldi* in 1121. The Welsh form *Croesoswald* proves that the name was interpreted as 'cross of St Oswald' from at least the mid-thirteenth century. The English name (*Oswaldestre*), the French name (*Blancmuster*) and the Latin name (*Album monasterium*) all appear frequently in records till 1300, after which *Oswaldestre* becomes the commonest one. The French and Latin names mean 'white collegiate church'.

The English name Oswestry and

140

the traditional association of the site with the death of St Oswald probably date from before the Norman Conquest, and the tradition is probably responsible for the dedication of the church. The Welsh form *Croesoswald* proves that the tradition was accepted by Welsh speaking people in the area. There is nothing in this evidence, however, which proves that St Oswald really was killed here, and it is as likely as not that the whole tradition arises from an Old English place-name of a fairly common type (discussed under Braintree) which meant 'Oswald's tree'. Other names of this type occur in Shropshire (Brimstree, Wittery) and Herefordshire (Aymestry, Cholstrey). There was a similar tradition in Gloucestershire, which associated the site of St Oswald's death with a place called Oswald's Tump in Marshfield. The Gloucestershire place was referred to as *Oswaldescroyz* in 1306, and it may be that Marshfield (*Meresfeld* 1086) was associated with Bede's *Maserfelth*, as Maesbury near Oswestry was.

Otley (YOW, England): Otta's forest-clearing (*Ottan lege c.* 972, *Othelai*, *Otelai* 1086, *Otley* 1434). This is a name of the same type as Barnsley and Keighley. Old English *lēah* is one of the commonest place-name elements in the West Riding.

Oxford (OXF, England): ford used by oxen (*Oxnaforda c.* 925 Anglo-Saxon Chronicle, *Oxenaforda* 1059, *Oxeneford* 1086). The ford has recently been located near Folly Bridge. Other place-names which refer to a ford associated with cattle are Rutherford DEV, Stafford SSX, Sturford WLT. The Latinisation *Oxonia* is frequently used in the twelfth and thirteenth centuries.

P

Paignton (DEV, England): estate associated with Pǣga (*Peintone* 1086, *Peynctone* 1259, *Peingtone* 1267, *Pyngton* 1438, *Paington* 1837). This is a name of the same type as Addington GTL. Old English *Pǣgingtūn* developed to *Paington*, which was the normal spelling in the eighteenth and early nineteenth centuries. The present spelling was substituted by the Railway Company after 1850.

Paisley (RNF, Scotland): church (*Passeleth* 1157, *Paisleth* 1158), Gaelic *Paislig*. From Latin *basilica* 'church' which in Middle Irish had become *baslec*, dative *baslic* 'church, churchyard, cemetery'. The early spellings in -*th* and the medieval Latinised form *Pasletum* are probably due to a misreading of *c* and *t*.

Peebles (PEB, Scotland): shiels (*Pobles* c. 1124, *Pebles* c. 1126). The basis of this name is Welsh *pebyll* 'tent, pavilion' to which an English plural -*s* has been added, presumably because the Welsh original was plural. The form *Pobles* shows Gaelic influence (compare Gaelic *pobull*).

Peel (IOM): the castle (*Pelam* 1399 Charter of Henry IV to the Earl of Northumberland). This is an English name, probably dating from the second half of the fourteenth cen-

tury, when the English government was concerned with the fortifications on St Patrick's Isle. The main castle on the Isle of Man was Castle Rushen at Castletown, and this is called *castrum* in the charter of 1399. The name Peel was not at first extended from the castle to the town, the latter being still called *Holmetown* in the sixteenth century. *Holme* 'island' was the Old Norse name for St Patrick's Isle.

Pembroke (PEM, Wales): end land (*Pennbro* c. 1150, *Pembroch* 1191, *Penbrocia* 1231, *Penbrok* 1245, *Penuro* 14th cent., *Penfro* 15th cent. The county is *Penbrocsira* 1219, *Penbrosyr* 1220, *Pembrok* 1283). Welsh Penfro = *pen* 'end' + *bro* 'land' (British **brog-*, cf. Gaulish *Allobroges*). English forms like *Penbroc* point to an early acquaintance with the name, i.e. the middle stage between British **Pennobrogā* and Welsh *Penfro*, before the -*b*- had become -*f*- (-*v*-) and the -*g*- had disappeared in Welsh. The name originally referred to the cantref which juts out into the sea, and it would have been the 'end land' from the point of view of the rest of the area. For -*nb*->-*mb*- cf. *Lampeter*, *Llambed*.

Penarth (GLA, Wales): end of the hill, ridge (*Ecclesia de Penarth* 1254,

Penharth 1266, *Pennarth* 13th cent., *Penarthe* 1535, *Penarth* 1536–9, *Penarth* 1566). Welsh *pen* 'end, top, head'+*garth* 'promontory, highland'. The name refers to the headland known as Penarth Head. The stress accent is on the second syllable.

Penicuik (MLO, Scotland): hill of the cuckoo (*Penikok* 1250, *Pennycuke* 1306–1424). Identical with an earlier form of Welsh *pen y gog*, apart from the absence of mutation from *c* to *g* in *gog*. However, this is not always shown in Anglicised spellings.

Pennarlag (FLI, Wales), see *Hawarden*.

Penrhyndeudraeth (MER, Wales), see *Portmadoc*.

Penrith (CMB, England): hill ford (*Penrith c.* 1100, *Penred* 1167, *Penreth* 1197). There was also a form of the name in which the *-n-* was dropped, represented by such spellings as *Pureth, Peareth, Perith* from 1271 to 1717, and still surviving in local pronunciation.
Penrith is a Celtic place-name. It is usually stated to refer to the crossing of the River Eamont at Eamont Bridge, about a mile south of the town on the A6, but as the name almost certainly goes back to Roman times it is perhaps more likely to refer to the crossing of the river by the Roman road from Brougham to Carlisle, about a mile south-east of the town. If so, British *pen* 'head, top', may have the meaning 'hill', as the high ground east of Penrith would be felt to overlook this ford.

Pen-y-bont ar Ogwr (GLA, Wales), see *Bridgend*.

Pen-y-cae (MON, Wales), see *Ebbw Vale*.

Penzance (CNW, England): holy promontory (*Pensans* 1332, *Pensant* 1367, *Pensaunce* 1552). This is a Cornish name, identical in meaning with Holyhead. Professor Charles Thomas says that the name was given because of the old chapel of St Mary (now St Mary's parish church), which stood on the central point of the town's coastline.

Perth (PER, Scotland): copse (*Pert c.* 1128, *Perth a.* 1150). Compare Welsh *perth* 'bush, brake, copse'. In Gaelic it is *Peart*, genitive *Peairt*. Since the thirteenth century it has also been known as St Johnstoun, after its church dedication to St John the Baptist. To-day this name survives as the name of a football club. See *Narberth* PEM.

Peterborough (NTP, England): St Peter's town (*Burgus sancti Petri* 1225, *Petreburgh* 1333, *Peterborough alias Borough Saynt Peter* 1588). The Anglo-Saxon settlement here, which was the site of an important monastery founded in the second half of the seventh century, was called *Medeshamstede*, 'Mēde's homestead'. This monastery was destroyed in the Danish wars of the late ninth century. It was restored in the Benedictine revival of the mid-tenth century, and at some time after that the place became known as *Burh* 'the town' (*Burg* 1086, *Medeshamstede qui modo Burg dicitur* 12th cent.). Probably, as suggested in the case of Bury St Edmunds, this new name arose after the place had become an important ecclesiastical centre. The Abbey was dedicated to St Peter.

Peterhead (ABD, Scotland): St Peter's headland (*Petyrheid* 1544). The remains of the old church of St Peter can still be seen at the Kirkton of Peterhead. St Peter is the patron saint of the parish which was originally known as Inverugie (*Inverugy Petri* 1274, *Pettirugy* 1495, *Petterugie alias Peterhead* 1744). In the now extinct Gaelic dialect of Braemar, Peterhead was *Inbhir-uigi*, whereas Gaelic-speaking fishermen from elsewhere call it *Ceann-phadruig*.

Plymouth (DEV, England): mouth of the River Plym (*Plymmue* 1230, *Plimmuth* 1234, *Plummuth* 1281, *Pleymuth* 1292, *Plympmouthe* 1353, *Sutton Prior vulgariter Plynmouth nuncupatur c.* 1450). The earlier spellings refer to the estuary; the parish was originally called *Sutton* ('south farm'). The river-name Plym is generally explained as a back-formation from the name Plympton. The town of Plympton is not actually on the river, but Plympton and Plymstock are two adjoining parishes east of Plymouth whose west boundary is formed by the Plym, and there is no doubt that their names must be connected with the name of the river.

Plympton (DEV, England): farm of the plum-tree (*Plymentun c.* 905, *Plintona* 1086, *Plimtun* 1131, *Plumton* 1167, *Plimpton* 1225, *Plumpton* 1238). The River Plym was probably named from this estate by the process known as back-formation, which is described under Bishop's Stortford.

Plymstock (DEV, England): (?) outlying hamlet connected with Plympton (*Plemestocha* 1086, *Plumstok* 1228, *Plimstok* 1244). Plymstock is the parish south of Plympton. If the original name were Old English *Plymentūnstoc*, this would very probably have been shortened to *Plemestocha* by 1086. Alternatively, Plymstock could be a compound of *stoc* (discussed under Basingstoke) and *plȳme* 'plum-tree'.

Pontefract (YOW, England): broken bridge (*Pontefracto* 1090, *Pumfrate c.* 1190, *Puntfreit* 1226, *Pomfracch* 1443). The site of the bridge has been identified as that of the present Bubwith Bridge, which carries the road from Pontefract to Ferrybridge across a small stream called Wash Dike, and provides an important communication with the Great North Road. The name is recorded in Latin and French, and the modern spelling derives from the Latin form, while the local pronunciation (Pomfret) is derived from the French form. The local form would doubtless be French from the beginning, but the Latin was considered more dignified for documentary use. This French name arose after the foundation of a Priory of Cluniac monks and the establishment of the castle of Ilbert de Lacy. It ousted the English name of the settlement, which was *Taddenescylf* 'Tædden's shelf of land', surviving as Tanshelf, west of Pontefract. The settlement also had a Norse name, *Kyrkebi*, recorded from about 1090 to 1440.

Pontardawe (GLA, Wales): bridge over River Tawe ([br.] *Ar Dawy* 1578, *Ty pen y bont ar tawey* 1706, *Pontardowey* 1707, *Pont ar Dawye* 1760, *Pont ar dawe* 1830). Welsh *tŷ* 'house' + *pen* 'end' + *y* 'the' + *pont* 'bridge' + *ar* 'over' + *Tawe* (river-name). The settlement probably took its name

145

from the house at the end of the bridge. For *Tawe* see *Swansea*.

Pontarddulais (GLA, Wales): bridge over River Dulais (*Ponte ar theleys* 1557, *Dulais bridge* 1578, *Penybont ar ddylays c.* 1700, *Pontarddylais* 1765). Welsh *pont* 'bridge' + *ar* 'over' + *Dulais* (river-name). The settlement grew at the end of the bridge over the River Dulais. *Dulais* is Welsh *du* 'black' + *glais* 'stream'.

Pontllan-fraith (MON, Wales): bridge of the vari-coloured lake (*tre penybont llynvraith* 1492, *tre penbont* 1502, *Pontllynfraith* 1713, *Pontlanfraith* 1782). Welsh *tre* 'farm' + *pen* 'end' + *y* 'the' + *pont* 'bridge' + *llyn* 'lake, pool' + *braith* 'variegated, speckled'. *Llyn* in this name has been superseded by *llan* 'church' by popular etymology.

Pontypool (MON, Wales): bridge of the pool (*Pont y poole* 1614, *Pont-y-Pool* 1680, *Pont-y-poole* 1694, *Pont-y-pool* 1707). Welsh *pont* 'bridge' + *y* 'the' + English *pool*. The town is on the Afon Lwyd, and 'pool' may refer to the river. As with so many other towns in Glamorgan and Monmouthshire industry meant rapid growth of population, and Pontypool grew from a small settlement near the parish church of Trefddyn (Trevethin) 'homestead' (*Throvethin* 1254, *Trefddyn* 1535, *Tref ddyn Kattwc* 1566, *Trevethyn* 1594, *Trevethin* 1612). Welsh *trefddyn* 'fortified farm' < *tref* 'farm' + *dynn* 'fence, height'. The stereotyped spelling *Trevethin* represents Welsh *trefddyn*. Elsewhere *trefddyn* has become *Treuddyn* (as in Flintshire).

Pont-y-pridd (GLA, Wales): bridge of the earthen house (*Pont y Tŷ Pridd,*

Pont y Pridd c. 1700, *Pont y Ty Pridd* 1764, *Pont y Ty Pridd* 1769, *Pont y Pridd or the new bridge* 1781, *New Bridge or Pont yprydd* ˑ1813, *Pontytypridd* 1848). Welsh *pont* 'bridge' + *y* 'the' + *tŷ* 'house' + *pridd* 'earth'. The 'new' bridge was built in 1755, and for some time there were two names. Newbridge was eventually abandoned because of another well-known Newbridge in Monmouthshire.

Poole (DOR, England): the pool (*Pole* 1194). The word refers, as it does in Hartlepool, to an enclosed harbour.

Portchester (HMP, England): Roman fort at the harbour (*Porceastra* 904, *Porteceaster c.* 972). The first element is the Old English name of Portsmouth Harbour, which is discussed under Portsmouth. The second is the word *ceaster*, discussed under Chester. The Roman site here is a particularly impressive fort of the type built in the late third century to protect the south-east against Saxon pirates. In a charter of about A.D. 972 the place is referred to as *illud oppidum*, and this may indicate that the Anglo-Saxons classed it with the walled towns of Roman Britain, rather than thinking of it as a fort.

Portland (DOR, England): estate by the harbour (*Porland* 1086). The place is referred to simply as *Port* in the Anglo-Saxon Chronicle, in a description of a battle against Danish invaders in A.D. 840. The precise meaning of *land* is always difficult to determine in place-names, but as it seems in this instance to be a late Old English addition to an earlier name, 'estate' is a reasonable translation, cf. Elland.

Port Glasgow (RNF, Scotland): founded in 1668 and laid out on the lands of Newark. First known as Newport Glasgow, it was intended to serve as the main anchorage and harbour for Glasgow but the deepening of the Clyde prevented it from developing in this way.

Porthaethwy (AGL, Wales), see *Menai Bridge*.

Porth-cawl (GLA, Wales): sea-kale harbour (*Portcall* 1632, *Pwll Cawl o. Porth Cawl* 1825, *Porth Cawl* 1833, *Port Cawl* 1840). Welsh *porth* 'harbour' + *cawl* 'cabbage, sea-kale'. So called possibly because sea-kale grew in abundance there. *Pwll* is Welsh *pwll* 'pool'.

Portmadoc (CRN, Wales): port of Madocks (*Portmadoc* 1838). William Alexander Madocks enclosed a large area of Traeth Mawr 'the great strand' and built Tremadoc *c.* 1800 'town of Maddoks' (*Tre-madoc* 1810, *Tremadoc* 1838, *Tremadoc* 1851). After building an embankment across the Traeth he obtained an Act of Parliament to construct a port, in 1821. The two names, *Tremadoc* and *Portmadoc* are deliberate creations. If they had been normal Welsh names they would have been *Trefadog* and *Porthfadog*. Portmadoc is known locally as *Port*, and the forms *Porthmadog* and *Tremadog* are used in current Welsh.

The Traeth Mawr which is referred to above is *Trait maur* 1194, *y Traeth Mawr* thirteenth century, *Traithmaure* 1536–9, *Traith Maur* 1586, *Traeth Mawr* 1681–2, *Traeth Mawr* 1795. Near this is *Traeth Bychan* (*Bach*) 'little strand' (*Traith*

Vehan 1536–9, *Traeth Bychan* 1695, *Traeth Bychan c.* 1700, *Traeth Bach* 1795). Welsh *traeth* 'beach, strand' + *mawr* 'great', *bychan*, *bach* 'little'. The two strands are separated by *Penrhyndeudraeth* 'headland of the two strands' (*Penrryn Devdraeth* 1457, *Penryn Duetith* 1536–9, *Penrhyndeudraeth* 1699, *Penrhyn Deudraeth* 1796, *Penrhyn Deudraeth* 1838). Welsh *penrhyn* 'promontory, headland' + *dau* 'two' + *traeth* 'strand'.

Portree (INV, Scotland): harbour near the slope (*Portri* 1549). The popular explanation is that this name dates from a short visit paid to Skye by the Scottish King James V and that it is therefore Gaelic *Port-righ* 'King's harbour'. The local pronunciation, however, proves it to be *Port-righeadh* 'harbour of (the) slope'.

Portslade-by-Sea (SSX, England): (?) crossing-place of the harbour (*Porteslage* 1086, *Portes Ladda c.* 1095, *Porteslade c.* 1182). The stretch of coast is so built up that the topography is obscured, and this makes it difficult to explain the place-name. This is an area in which *port* often means 'harbour', and it is possible that here, as in Portsmouth, *port* is used as a first element in the genitive case. There may have been a harbour before the coast-line was made up. The second element, *gelād*, can mean 'water-course' or 'crossing-place over a river'. If the harbour was long and narrow, as looks possible from the map, there might have been a causeway over it connecting the mainland with the long arm of land which ran parallel to the coast on the seaward side.

147

Portsmouth (HMP, England): the mouth of the harbour called Port (*Portesmuþa c.* 900 Anglo-Saxon Chronicle). The ridge north of Portsmouth Harbour is called Portsdown, and the island which bounds the harbour on the east (on which the town of Portsmouth lies) is called Portsea; these names probably mean 'hill' and 'island of Port harbour'. Old English *port* is a loan-word from Latin *portus*, and the harbour here may have been referred to in Roman times as *Portus*; it was certainly important then, as the presence of the great Roman fort at Portchester indicates. Whether or not there is any continuity from Roman to Anglo-Saxon times, it seems most satisfactory to interpret *Port* as the Anglo-Saxon name for the harbour. An alternative explanation would be to consider *Port* as a man's name, and this interpretation was current in Anglo-Saxon times. The Anglo-Saxon Chronicle ascribes an early English landing here to a chieftain called *Port*, who is said in the annal for 501 to have landed at *Portesmuþa*. There is other evidence of confusion between place- and personal names in the early annals of the Chronicle, however, and this may only indicate that there was from the earliest times a tendency for upper-class commentators to explain place-names in this way.

Port Talbot (GLA, Wales): see *Aberavon*.

Potters Bar (HRT, England): forestgate associated with a family named Potter (*Potterys Barre* 1509, *Potters Barre* 1548). Geoffrey *le Pottere* is mentioned in connection with land in this area in 1294. There are a number of place-names ending in Bar in this part of Herts, and they are thought to refer to gates controlling the entrances to Enfield Chase. Bell Bar is a settlement 2½ miles north of Potters Bar.

Prestatyn (FLI, Wales): priests' farm (*Prestetone* 1086, *Prestattune* 1257, *Pr'statun od le Deke* 1278, *Prestanton* 1279, *Prestaton* 1305, *Prystatun* 1325, *Prestatun c.* 1400, *Prystaton* 1420, *Prestatvn* 1543, *Prestatyn* 1536). Old English *prēosta* 'priests' + *tūn* 'farm'. This is one of the early English place-names in Flintshire the form of which has been changed owing to later resettlement by Welshmen. The accent is on the penultimate syllable in Welsh, and this has preserved the genitive plural ending of *prēosta*. Le *Deke* in 1278 refers to the northern end of Offa's Dyke which ran near Prestatyn. If the name of the place had developed in English it would probably have become *Preston*. It should be noted too that Old English *tūn* became *-tyn* in Welsh. Cf. *Moston* > *Mostyn*.

Presteigne (RAD, Wales): household of priests (*Presteheinede c.* 1250, *Presthemede* 1278, *Prestemede* 1316, *Presthende* 1447, *Presteyne* 1549, *Prestmede alias Prestende* 1552, *Presteine in Walche caullyd Llanandre*, *Prestein in Walsche is caullid Llanandrew* 1536–9). Old English *prēost* 'priest' + *hǣmed* 'society, household'. The forms in *-n-*, if they are not misreadings of *m*, are obscure. The name of the church is in Welsh *Llanandras* 'church of Andreas' (*Ll. andras* 1566, *Lhan Andre* 1586, 1698). Welsh *llan* 'church' + *Andreas*, Andrew (saint's name).

Preston (LNC, England): estate of the priests (*Prestune* 1086, *Prestone* 1166, *Presteton* 1180). This is a common place-name. The first element is in the genitive plural, but it is not necessary to assume that several priests lived at a place so named; the estate could have been an endowment given to maintain a household of priests serving a church situated elsewhere.

Prestwich (LNC, England): priest's dwelling (*Prestwich* 1194, *Prestewyk* 1277, *Prestwidge* 1598). Old English *wīc* (discussed under Aldridge) can refer to a single dwelling, and *prēostwīc* may have been a compound meaning a priest's house. The same name in the modern form Prestwick occurs in Northumberland and Ayrshire.

Prestwick (AYR, Scotland): priest's (or priests') dwelling (*Prestwīc* 1165–73, *Prestwik* 1330). Old English *prēost wīc* 'priest's dwelling' or *prēosta wīc* 'priests' dwelling'. Identical with such names as Prestwick NTB and BUC and Prestwich LNC. This is a surprisingly early example of an English place-name on the Firth of Clyde.

Pudsey (YOW, England): (?) enclosure by the hill called The Wart (*Podechesai* 1086, *Pudekesseya* 12th cent., *Pudekeshay* 1219, *Pudesay* 1294, *Pudeshay* 1309). The final element may be Old English *gehæg*, discussed under Bushey. There is an Old English word *puduc* 'wart', which might have been the name of the steep hill on which the town stands.

Pwllheli (CRN, Wales): salt pool (*Pwllhely* 1292–3, *Porthelli*, *Porthelly* 1350–1, *Purthely* 1355, *Pwllheli* 1510, *Pullely* 1524, *Pwllhelic* 1560–90, *Pwllhelie* 1652–3, *Pwllheli* 1657). Welsh *pwll* 'pool' + *heli* 'brine, salt water'. The second element is more probably the common noun *heli* 'brine' than the personal name *Helig*, despite the form *Pwllhelig*, which savours of antiquarian supposition. Helig ap Glannog is traditionally connected with an inundation of the sea. Forms like *Portheli* may reflect a desire to substitute *porth* 'harbour' for *pwll* 'pool', but may also be due partly to English pronunciation of Welsh *-ll-*.

R

Radcliffe (LNC, England): red cliff (*Radeclive* 1086). The place is believed to take its name from a cliff of red sandstone on the bank of the River Irwell.

Radur (GLA, Wales): oratory (*Radur* 1254, *Rador* 1291, *villam Aradur* 13th cent., *Radur* 1315, *Radur* 1349, *Radur* 1400, *Aradur* 1506, *Rader* 1536–9, *Yr Adur Vawr* 1569, *The Rader* 1610, *The Radder* 1625). Lat. *oratorium*. This interpretation is slightly preferable to suggesting an unattested personal name **Aradur*, although *Radur* does occur. The examples show that the original *Aradur* was misinterpreted as *Y Radur* (with the Welsh definite article *y*), and this was then translated as English *The Radur*.

Raglan (MON, Wales), see *Rhaglan*.

Ramsbottom (LNC, England): valley of the ram (*Romesbothum* 1324, *Ramysbothom* 1540). In this name, as in others with an animal name in the genitive as first element, it is possible that the animal name is used as a personal name, or as a nickname for some feature of the landscape. Ramsbottom lies in the valley of the Irwell, with fairly dramatic hills on either side.

Ramsey (IOM): wild-garlic river (*Ramsa* 1257 Manx Chronicle). This is an Old Norse name, the second element being *á* 'river', which occurs also in Laxey IOM ('salmon river'). Two rivers, those from Sulby Glen and Glen Alden, unite to flow into the sea at Ramsey, but it has been suggested that the 'wild-garlic river' of the place-name was a tiny stream south of these which was called *Strooan ny craue* in the nineteenth century. This Gaelic name means 'the stream of the wild garlic'.

Ramsgate (KNT, England): (?) gap in the cliffs by a rock called The Raven (*Remmesgate* 1275, *Rammesgate* 1298). Margate and Ramsgate are both situated at gaps in the rocks which fringe the coast of Thanet. The first element of Ramsgate is the genitive of *hræfn* 'raven'. It is impossible to say precisely what this means; it could be used as a personal name, could refer to the prevalence of the bird here, or could be a nickname for some natural feature.

Rawtenstall (LNC, England): rough cow-pasture (*Routonstall* 1324). This is one of a group of names the other members of which are in the adjacent part of the West Riding. The others are Cruttonstall, Heptonstall, Rawtonstall (identical with the Lancashire name), Saltonstall, Shackleton, and Wittonstall. Rawtenstall LNC is specifically described as a *vaccary* in

1324, and Saltonstall YOW is called a *vaccaria* in 1315. All the places are on the edge of high moorland, and it seems likely that in this area Old English *tūnstall*, which is one of many terms for a farmstead, had developed a specialised meaning and was used of buildings occupied when cattle were being pastured on high ground.

Rayader (RAD, Wales), see *Rhaeadr*.

Rayleigh (ESX, England): forest-clearing frequented by female roe-deer or by she-goats (*Ragheleiam* 1086, *Raelega* 1173). Old English *rǣge* is used of both animals, so it is impossible to say which is meant, but the name may refer to a clearing in which one or other was frequently seen with its young. There are a number of names which indicate the presence of woodland in this area west and north-west of Southend.

Reading (BRK, England): Rēad's people (*Readingum c.* 925 Anglo-Saxon Chronicle). This is a name of the same type as Barking GTL. Saxon burials of fifth-century date are recorded from Reading, and this is one of the few instances in which such a burial site coincides with a place-name in *-ingas*.

Redcar (YON, England): red marshy land (*Redker c.* 1170, *Readcar* 1653). The land is low-lying, and the rocks are a reddish colour. The name is a hybrid, from Old English *rēad* and Old Norse *kjarr*.

Redditch (WOR, England): red ditch (*La Rededich* 1247, 1300, *The Redde Dych* 1536). The use of the definite article in this name suggests that it arose as a name for an actual ditch,

and is not elliptical for 'place at the red ditch'. There does, however, seem to have been a settlement in the fourteenth century, as the Patent Roll for 1348 records an incident in which a monk of Bordesley Abbey broke into the house of a woman living here.

Redhill (SUR, England): red slope (*Redehelde* 1301, *Redd Hyll* 1588). The name refers to the red sandstone here, also mentioned in the name of Redstone Hill, at the foot of which the town lies. The earliest spelling suggests that the original second element was Old English *hielde* 'slope'. There are a number of names in which this was altered to *-hill* by popular etymology.

Redruth (CNW, England): (?) red ford (*Ridruthe* 1259, *Rudruth* 1283). This is a Cornish name, with first element *rid* 'ford'. The ford was presumably over the small stream west of the town which flows into the sea at Portreath. The course of the A30 through Cornwall is shown on the Ordnance Survey Map of Roman Britain as a Roman road. The name Redruth is not likely to go back to the Roman period, as it is the later type of Celtic compound in which the adjective follows the noun; but the ford was doubtless an important one because it was on this ancient road. Professor Charles Thomas queries the usual etymology 'red ford' on the grounds that the adjective should have become *-reeth* not *-ruth*. He considers that some spellings such as *Ruthdruth* (1317), *Rysdruth* (1431) suggest a second element meaning 'druid', or a personal name such as *Druut*.

Reigate (SUR, England): roe-deer gate (*Reigata c.* 1170). This is a Middle English name, from *reye* (earlier Old English *rǣge*, discussed under Rayleigh) and *gate*. Names of similar meaning are Rogate ssx and Dargetts KNT. The reference is probably to the entrance to a medieval deer-park.

Renfrew (RNF, Scotland): point of current (*Reinfry c.* 1128, *Renfriu* 1147–52, *Reinfrew* 1158), from Welsh *rhyn-frwd*.

Retford (NTT, England): red ford (*Redford* 1086, *Radeford c.* 1155, *Rethford* 1219, *Retford* 1219). This is a fairly common name, usually surviving in the modern form Radford. The reference is to the colour of the soil, which was perhaps exposed by the heavy wear and tear on the tracks leading to the ford. The Nottinghamshire place was sometimes called *Retford in the Clay*, The Clay being a district-name for this part of the county. The Great North Road crosses the River Idle at Retford.

Rhaeadr (RAD, Wales): waterfall (*Raidergoe* 1191, *Raedr'* 1291, *Rayder* 1316, *Rayadyr Gwy* 14th cent., *Raeadr* 15th cent., *Raydre* 1436, *Raiadergwy* 1543, *Rayader Gwy* 1655, *Rhayader* 1744). Welsh *rhaeadr* 'waterfall' + river-name *Gwy*. There was a considerable waterfall here until the building of a bridge in 1780. *Gwy* = River *Wye* 'winding' (*Guoy c.* 800, *Gui, Guy, Guai c.* 1150, *Guy* 1184, *Waye* 1278–9, *aqua Wayam* 1279–80). Welsh *gwy*, cf. Welsh *gwyr-o* 'wind, bend', referring to the winding course of the river.

Rhaglan (MON, Wales): (?) rampart (*Raghelan* 1254, *Ragelan* 1291, *Raclan* 1346, *Ragelan* 1399, *Rhaglan* 15th cent., *Raglan* 1550). Welsh *rhag* 'fore, counter' + *glan* 'bank'. In form the second element could be *llan* 'church', but this would be more difficult to explain in conjunction with *rhag*.

Rhiwabon (DEN, Wales): hill of Mabon (*Rywnabon* (l. *Rywuabon*) 1291, *Riwuabon* 1362, *Riwvabon* 1394, *Riwabon* 1397, *Ruabon* 1461, *Rhiw vabon* 1566, *Ruabon* 1676, *Rhiwabon* 1810). Welsh *rhiw* 'hill' + pers. name *Mabon*. The -*f*- was lost as early as the fifteenth century. *Ruabon* represents a poor English spelling.

Rhondda (GLA, Wales): noisy (river) (*Rotheni* 12th cent., *Rotheni* 1250, *Rodney* 1600, *Rhonddi* 1700). For the two rivers *Rhondda Fawr* and *Rhondda Fach* (or *Fechan*) cf. *Rotheni maur* 1203, *Rodeney vaur* 1536–9, *greate Rodney* 1596–1600, *Rhondda fawr* 1833, *Rotheney vehan* 1536–9, *little Rodney* 1596–1600, *Ronthey the lesser* 1614, *Ronthey vechan* 1666, *Rhonddafechun* 1799, *Rhondda fychan* 1833). The valley was *Glyn Rhoddni* which also became the name of a commote 'glen of the River Rhondda' (*Glenrotheny* 1268, *Glinredney* 1296, *Glynrotheny* 1314, *Glyn Rothne* 1424, *Glin Rotheney* 1526–9, *Glynrotheny* 1614). Welsh *glyn* 'glen, valley'. Welsh *rhoddni, rhoddne* < *rhawdd-*, British *rād-*, cf. Welsh *ad-rawdd* 'tell, relate', Old Irish *rád-* 'speak'. The name of this river is akin to others which are descriptive of noise, tumult, etc., cf. *Llafar, Clywedog, Trystion*, etc. The two forms *Rhoddni* and *Rhoddne* became *Rhonddi* and *Rhondde* by metathesis,

153

but *Rhonddi* disappeared in favour of *Rhondde* which became *Rhondda* dialectally. Rhondda is now a municipal borough.

Rhosllannerchrugog (DEN, Wales): moor, heath of the heather glade (*Rose lane aghregog* 1544–5, *Rhos llannerch Rirgog* 1546, *Rowse* 1698). Welsh *rhos* 'moor, heath' + *llannerch* 'glade, clearing' + *grugog*, adjective from *grug* 'heather'.

Rhuddlan (FLI, Wales): red bank (*Roelend* 1086, *Ruthelan* 1191, *Rothelan* 1241, *Rundlan* 1254, *Ruthlan* 1437, *Rudlan* 14th cent., *Rutlan* 15th cent., *Ryddlan* 1566, *Rhuddlan* 1577–8, *Ruthland* 1582). Welsh *rhudd* 'red' + *glan* 'bank', referring to the River Clwyd. For Clwyd, see *Rhuthun*. Forms in *-land* show English influence.

Rhuthun (DEN, Wales): red fort (*Ruthun* 1253, *Ruthin* 1283, *Ruffin* 1308, *Ruthyn* 1478, *Rhuthun* 15th cent., *Ruthyn* 1535, *Tre Rythyn* 1566, *Ruthyn* 1698). Welsh *rhudd* 'red' + (?) *din* 'fort' or (?) *hin* 'bank, edge'. *Rhuthin* became *Rhuthun* because of the influence of the first vowel *-u-* on the vowel of the second syllable. *Ruthin* is a stereotyped English spelling. *Rhudd* 'red' is descriptive of the colour of the rock. The castle was once known as Y Castell Coch yng gwernfor (*kastell rrvthvn* = *kastell gwernvor* 1545–53). Welsh *castell* 'castle' + *coch* 'red' + *yn* 'in' + *Gwernfor* (i.e. *gwern* 'marsh' + *mawr* 'great'). For *Gwernfor* cf. *Gwernvor* 1579, *Gwern-fore c.* 1700.

Rhuthun was the administrative centre of the cantref of Dyffryn Clwyd 'vale of Clwyd' (*Defrenclut* 1247, *Diffrencloyt* 1277, *Dyffrynclwyt*

1284, *Dyffryn Cloyt* 1291, *Deffrencloyt* 1352, *Deffren cloyd* 1498, *Dyffryn Klwyt* 14th cent., *Diffrin Cluid* 1586). Welsh *Dyffryn* 'broad valley' + *Clwyd*. For Clwyd cf. *Cloid fluvium* 1191, *Cloyt* 1284, *Cloyd*' 1334, *Kloid* 1534, *Clwyd* 1605. Welsh *clwyd* 'hurdle, wattle, lattice', possibly referring to a ford or weir at some point on the river. There is one example of *cluit* (= clwydd) rhyming with *ebruit* (= ebrwydd), but this may not be completely dependable.

Rhydaman (CRM, Wales), see *Ammanford*.

Rhyl (FLI, Wales): the hill (*Ryhull* 1301, *del Hull* 1302, *Hillous*, *Hullhouse* 1351, *Hull* 1351, *Hulle* 1454, *Hull* 1541, *Yrhill* 1578, *Hill* 1600, *Rhyll* 1660, *Rhil* 1706). Old English *hyll* 'hill'. The simple forms *Hull* above seem to be the West Midlands *hull*. The form *Rhyl* is a hybrid of the Welsh definite article *yr* + *hull*. Rhyl was formerly a township in the parish of Rhuddlan, and is called in Welsh *Tre'r-hyl*, from the chief house of 'The Hill' (*Tre'rhul c.* 1700, *Tre-r-hyll* 1612). Welsh *tre* 'township' + definite article *yr* + *hill*. The derivation from English *hill* has always caused some criticism because of the very low-lying site of the township, but *hill* is also used in English place-names for a slight elevation.

Rhymni (MON, Wales): River Auger (*Remni* 1101–20, *Remny* 12th cent., *Rempny* 1296, *Rempney* 1314, *Rempny* 1447, *Rymney* 1541, *Rumpny* 1681, *Rumney* 1760). Welsh *rhwmp* 'borer, auger' + suffix *-ni*. The name is descriptive of a river which bores its way through the land, cf. the river-name *Taradr* with the same meaning. The river gave its name to a church (formerly in Monmouthshire, now in Cardiff) (*Ecclesia de Rempney* 1291, *Ecclesia de Rempny c.* 1348, *Rumney* 1536–9). The Welsh name for this place was *Tredelerch* 'farm of Telerch' (*Tredelerch* 1536–9, *Tref Delerch* 1606, *Tredelogh* 1698, *Tredeler* 1857). Welsh *tref* 'farm' + pers. name *Telerch* [< *Ty* + *Elerch*].

The river-name was also taken for the new industrial town which grew around the iron-works. Rhymni was established as an ecclesiastical parish in 1843 as part of Bedwellty.

Rhymney and *Rumney* are stereo-typed anglicised spellings of *Rhymni*.

Rickmansworth (HRT, England): Ricmǣr's enclosure (*Prichemareworde* 1086, *Richemaresworthe c.* 1180). This is a name of the same type as Isleworth GTL.

Ripley (DRB, England): strip of woodland or strip-shaped clearing (*Ripelei* 1086, *Rippelega* 1176). The same place-name occurs in Hampshire and Surrey. It is a compound of *lēah* 'wood, clearing', with Old English *ripel*. This last word, which means 'strip', is frequently associated with woodland and occurs in modern dialect in the sense 'coppice'. It is impossible to make a final choice between the two etymologies suggested, but the first is perhaps the more likely.

Ripon (YOW, England): (place in the territory of) the tribe called *Hrype* (*Hrypis, Hripis c.* 715 Eddi's Life of St Wilfred, *Inhrypum c.* 730, Bede's Ecclesiastical History *Rypum c.*

1030, *Ripum, Ripun* 1086). The place-name is probably derived from the dative plural of a tribe-name, and is a similar formation to Hitchen. There is no recorded mention of the tribe (as opposed to the place), however, and the meaning of *Hrype* is not known. Repton DRB is generally derived from Old English *Hrypadūn* 'hill of the tribe called Hrype', and probably refers to a settlement made by people from the area of Ripon.

Rochdale (LNC, England): valley of the River Roch (*Rachedale c.* 1195, *Rochedale* 1246, *Rechedale* 1276). The settlement here was earlier called *Recedham* (1086), *Rechedham* (*c.* 1200), *Rachedam* (1296), and the river was *Rached* thirteenth century, *Rachet* 1292. The relationship between river-name and settlement-name poses questions similar to those discussed under Mansfield. It is possible that *Recedham* is the earliest of the names, and that the river was named from the village. Ekwall suggested that *Recedham* contained Old English *reced, ræced* 'hall, house', and *hām* 'village', and that the river-name was a back-formation from this. The only objection to this is that *reced* has not been noted in any other place-name. If the river-name is the original one, it is probably Celtic, but no parallel can be found for it. Whatever the relationship between *Recedham* and the river-name *Raced*, it seems clear that in the twelfth century the river-valley became known as *Rached-dale*, and that this was shortened to *Rachedale*, which supplanted *Rachedham* as the name of the settlement, and led to the formation of a new river-name *Rache*.

Rochester (KNT, England): Roman town called *Hrofi* (*Hrofæscæster, civitas Hrofi c.* 730 Bede's Ecclesiastical History, *Hrofesceaster c.* 900 Anglo-Saxon Chronicle, *Rovecestre* 1086). *Hrofi* is an Old English form derived from the name of the Roman town here, which is recorded as *Durobrivis* in the fourth-century Antonine Itinerary. The Romano-British name means 'the bridges of the stronghold'. The stages by which *Durobrivis* developed into Old English *Hrofi* are complicated, but can be convincingly explained.

The Old English name *Hrofi* probably became current in local use while the full Romano-British name was remembered in learned circles. The Venerable Bede uses *Dorubrevi* as well as the English name, and *Dorobrevi, id est, civitas Hrofi* occurs in a Canterbury document of 844. Bede was not aware that *Hrofi* was a derivative of *Dorubrivis*, and he says that *Hrofæscæster* was named 'after a former chief of it, who was named Hrof'. It has been noted under Portsmouth that there may have been a bias towards this type of etymology among upper-class commentators in the Anglo-Saxon period.

Romiley (CHE, England): spacious clearing (*Rumelie* 1086, *Romilee* 1285). The first element of this name is probably the adjective *rūm* 'spacious'; but it could be a derivative *rūmig*, with the same meaning.

Rotherham (YOW, England): village on the River Rother (*Rodreham* 1086, *Roderham* 1200, *Rotherham* 1461).

The river-name is Celtic, and may mean 'chief river'. In this part of the country, Old English *d* becomes *th* in the neighbourhood of *r*.

Rothesay (BTE, Scotland): (?) Roderick's island (*Rothersay* 1321, *Rosay c.* 1400, *Rothesay* 1401). The second element is clearly Norse *ey* 'island', whereas the first part is probably a personal name. The earliest spelling indicates that this may have been Roderick (or Rudri or Ruari), the son of Reginald, to whom it was granted in 1210. Some say that it was at one time the name of the whole island, whereas others hold that it only applied to the castle surrounded by a moat. The Gaelic name of Rothesay is *Baile Bhóid* 'town of Bute'.

Royton (LNC, England): rye farm (*Ritton* 1226, *Ryton* 1260, *Ruyton* 1327, *Royton* 1577). This is a fairly common place-name, occurring usually in the modern spelling Ryton. It may indicate some sort of agricultural specialisation at the places concerned.

Ruabon (DEN, Wales): see *Rhiwabon*.

Rugby (WAR, England): Hrōca's fortified place (*Rocheberie* 1086, *Rokebi* 1200, *Rukby* 1484, *Rugby* 1525). The spelling in Domesday Book is considered to indicate that this was originally an English place-name of the same type as Aylesbury. Danish influence has caused *-by* to be substituted for *-byrig*. Rugby is three miles west of Watling Street, which was the western boundary of the Danelaw, and there are several Danish place-names in a strip of territory along the English side of this boundary. Badby NTP, also in this strip, is another name in which Danish *-by* was substituted for English *-byrig*.

Rugeley (STF, England): clearing near a ridge (*Rugelie* 1086, *Ruggelega* 1156). The higher ground to the south and west of the town is much broken, and the ridge may have been one of the spurs jutting out from the edge of it.

Rumney (GLA, Wales), see *Rhymni*.

Runcorn (CHE, England): wide bay (*Rumcofa* 915 Anglo-Saxon Chronicle, *Runcoua c.* 1157, *Runcore* 1259). The first element is *rūm*, discussed under Romford. The second is *cofa*, which in literary sources has the meanings 'cave, den, inner chamber'. It seems that in place-names *cofa* could sometimes mean 'recess on a coast', as in the modern derivative *cove*, and that in this instance it refers to the bay formed by the broadening of the Mersey just below Runcorn.

Rushden (NTP, England): valley where rushes grow (*Risdene, Risedene* 1086, *Ressenden* 1200, *Russenden* 1205, *Russheden* 1428). The town lies in the valley of a small tributary of the River Nene. There is another Rushden, of identical origin, in Hertfordshire.

Rutherglen (LAN, Scotland): (?) valley (*Ruthirglen* 1153–65, *Ruglyn* 1300, *Rothirglene* 1315–21, *Ruchirglen* 1368–9, *Ruglen* 1385–9). Whereas the second element is either Welsh *glyn* or Gaelic *gleann* 'valley' (or perhaps a succession of both), the first part is a little troublesome. One would like to see some derivative of British *roudo-s* 'red' in it but this leaves the *-ir-* forms unexplained. Old English *hrȳther* 'cattle' has been suggested with vigour for both Rutherglen and Rutherford ROX but certainly in the case of our name this would be an unlikely combination.

Ruthin (DEN, Wales), see *Rhuthun*.

Ryde (IOW, England): (place at) the stream (*la Ride* 1257). In the dialect of Hampshire and the IOW Old English *ri* 'small stream', became *ride*. The stream which runs into the sea at Ryde is not named on the one-inch map.

S

St Albans (HRT, England): the town grew up round the Abbey which was founded on the traditional site of the martyrdom of St Alban.

The date of St Alban's death may have been A.D. 209. The earliest recorded mention of him is in connection with a visit to his tomb made by St Germanus in A.D. 429. The story of the martyrdom is told in some detail by Bede who was using earlier written sources. Bede says that 'Saint Alban suffered on the twenty-second day of June near the city of Verolamium, which the English now call Verlamacæstir or Uæclingacæstir'. The account he gives points clearly to the site of the saint's execution being that of the later church, on Holywell Hill, across the River Ver from the Roman town. While it is difficult to separate fact from legend, the cult of St Alban has been accepted by historians as a survival from Roman Britain into Anglo-Saxon England, and it has recently been claimed that the monastic church over the saint's shrine was probably founded in A.D. 396–8, which would make this the oldest surviving monastic church in Latin Europe. The settlement which grew up round the church was sometimes called *Sancte Albanes stow* 'holy place of St Alban'. In the Domesday Survey and in many medieval documents it is called *villa Sancti Albani*.

The Roman town was called *Verulamio* by Tacitus (A.D. 50), and variants of this spelling occur in other classical sources. This may be a name of the same type as London, formed by the addition of a suffix *-ion* to a man's name. Bede says that in his day the English called the site of the Roman town *Verlamacæstir* or *Uæclingacæstir*; and *Wæclingaceaster* (later *Wætlingaceaster*) is well recorded in other old English texts. It was still in use at the end of the tenth century. It means 'Roman town of the people of Wæcel', and the first element was transferred from this name to Watling Street. It was probably in the early eleventh century that the name *Sancte Albanes stow* ousted *Wætlingaceaster*.

In the Roman town itself there is another tantalising suggestion of continuity from Roman to Anglo-Saxon times in the siting of the church of St Michael, which is on top of the basilica of Verulamium.

St Andrews (FIF, Scotland): the town where the church and shrine of Saint Andrew are (*Cind righ monaigh* sub anno 747 Tigernach's Annals, *Chilrimunt c.* 1139, *Chilrimund, Kilremund* 1144, *Kilrimont c.* 1150, *Kilrimund* 1153–9, 1160–1, 1163–4;

burgensibus episcopi Sancti Andree 1153–62). In a sense *Kilrimont* is the earlier name of St Andrews but the two names seem to have overlapped for a while; in fact *Kilrimont* continued to be used till the end of the thirteenth century when the town and burgh of St Andrew were already well established. *-rimont* is an Anglicised form of Early Gaelic *Rigmonad* 'royal hill' which itself may be an adaptation of an earlier British or Pictish name. It is preceded by Gaelic *cill* 'church, churchyard', with a side-form *Kin-* (as in the earliest record form) which may be purely a phonological phenomenon or may indicate that a name beginning with Gaelic *cinn*, an oblique form of *ceann* 'head, end' also existed. We may have had a doublet 'church of the royal hill' and 'end of the royal hill'.

This is not the place to discuss the background to the connection between St Andrew, brother of Peter, either with St Andrews or with Scotland. It is sufficient to say that the 'legend of St Andrew' produced the Priory of St Andrew and this in its turn the burgh of St Andrew. The modern form St Andrews is probably a modernised English form of the Scots vernacular *Sanct Androis* or *Androiss*; that the name of the saint was quite often used for the place is shown by such Latin forms as *apud Sanctum Andream*. St Andrews was for long one of the principal pilgrim shrines of Britain.

St Asaph (FLI, Wales): church of Asaff (*Ecc'e de Sco. Assaph* 1254, *Ecclesia Cathedralis de Sancto Asaph'* 1291). Latin *sanctus*, English *saint* + personal name *Asaff*. The Welsh name of the city is *Llanelwy* 'church on the River Elwy' (*Lanhelewey* 1345, *Lanelwy* 1365, *Llannelwy* 1456, *Llan Elwy alias S. Asaphe* 1536–9, *Llanelwy alias St Asaph* 1763). Welsh *llan* 'church' + *Elwy* (river-name) (*Elgu* 12th cent., *Elwy* c. 1300, *Elewe* 1334, *Elwy* 1499, *Elwy* 1549). Welsh *elwy* = verbal element *el-* 'go, drive' + suffix *-wy*.

St Austell (CNW, England): (church of) St Austol (*ecclesia de Austol* c. 1145, *St Austol* 1251). St Austol was a companion of the better-known St Mewan, whose name occurs in Mevagissey.

St Clears (CRM, Wales): church of St Clêr (*ecclesia de Sancto Claro* 1291, *Seint Cler* 1331, *Seyn clier* 1353, *Seynclere* 1413, *Seynt Cler* 1535, *Sain Kler* 1566, *Sainct Cleares* 1659). Latin *Sanctus* 'saint' + (?) *Clarus* (personal name). Nothing is definitely known of this saint. The current Welsh standard form is *Sanclêr*.

St Davids (PEM, Wales): church of David (Dewi) (*yn hy Ddewi* 15th cent., *Dewi o Fyniw* 1566, *Tŷ Deui* 1586, *Ty Dewi* 1722). Welsh *tŷ* 'house' (church) + pers. name *Dewi* (for **Dewydd* < Latin *Dauidus*). *David* (Welsh *Dafydd*) are later learned borrowings from *Dauidus*. The Welsh form *Tyddewi* shows an unusual lenition of *Dewi* after the masculine noun *tŷ*. But there are several examples of this in place-names after such masculine elements as *cae, tyddyn*, etc. especially when the second element is a personal name.

The other Welsh form is *Mynyw* (latinised as *Menevia*) which came to be used for the diocese—(*Miniu* 12th cent., [*y*] *vyniw* 15th cent., *Mynyw*

15th cent.). Welsh *mynyw* 'grove, bush', cf. Old Irish *Cell Muini*. According to the Life of St David he was educated at *Henfynyw* (*Hendmen, Hevene* 1291, *Henvenen* 1284, *Henvynyw* 1513, *Hen Fyniw* 1566). Welsh *hen* 'old' + *mynyw*. In the Welsh Life a Latin form is given *vetus rubus* with a Welsh translation *yr henllwynn* (1346). This is Welsh *hen* 'old' + *llwyn* 'bush, grove'. Henfynyw is an old parish church near Aberaeron in Cardiganshire, and the epithet *hen* probably serves to distinguish it from the better known *Mynyw* to which St David moved.

St Helens (LNC, England): named from the chapel of St Helen. This is first mentioned in 1552, but there was probably a medieval chapel at the road-junction here, and a cluster of houses round it. The town owed its growth to the development of coal-mining, helped by the formation of the Sankey Canal in 1755. It had become a small town by 1800, and was made a borough in 1869.

St Neots (HNT, England): (*S'Neod* 1132, *villa S. Neoti* 1203, *Saint Nede* 1310, *Mon. S. Neoti vulgo nuncupatur Sainte Need* 1542, *St Edes* 1558, *St Neots vulgo St Nedes c.* 1750). The town grew up round a monastery, which was probably founded between 972 and 975. St Neot was a Cornish saint, and an early chronicler describing the foundation says that the founders obtained his relics from Cornwall.

Sale (CHF, England): (place) at the willow-tree (*Sale* 1260, *la Sale* 1285). The name is derived from Old English *sale*, which is the dative of *salh* 'willow' (modern *sallow*).

Salford (LNC, England): willow ford (*Salford* 1086, *Selford* 1253). Old Salford village was on the Irwell, and the name probably refers to a crossing-place on that river. Sale, a few miles south, means 'at the willow-tree'. There is another Salford of identical origin in Beds, but Salford in Oxfordshire and Warwickshire are derived from an earlier *salt-ford*.

Salisbury (WLT, England): (*Searobyrg c.* 900 Anglo-Saxon Chronicle, *Sarisberie* 1086, *Salesburia* 1096, *Searesbyrig* 1123 Anglo-Saxon Chronicle, *Salesbury* 1227, *Saresbury* 1294, *Salsbery* 1575). It is impossible to give a meaningful translation of this name. It arises from a memory of a Romano-British name combined with an English second element *byrig* 'fort' (which was not usually applied to Roman sites). The Romano-British settlement called *Sorviodunum* (4th cent. Antonine Itinerary) lay inside the prehistoric hill-fort at Old Sarum, and *byrig* refers to the massive ramparts. *Sorvio-* (of unsolved meaning) may have been the pre-Roman name of the hill-fort. *-dunum* is a Celtic word borrowed by Latin speakers and used in naming heavily defended sites. *Sorvio-* became *Searo-* in Old English. There is no grammatical reason why *-s-* should have developed in Old English *Searobyrig*, but the name was perhaps associated with names like Amesbury, and a genitival inflection was felt appropriate to the first element, resulting in the form *Searesbyrig*. Norman French difficulty in distinguishing *-r-* and *-l-* produced *Salesburia*, from which the modern form is derived. The alternative form *Suresbury* was often abbreviated to *Sar'* in medieval documents, and this

161

was Latinised to *Sarum* in the fourteenth century. A Norman castle was built inside the hill-fort, and this is called *Vetus Saresbir'* 1187, *Old Saresbury* 1429, *the Olde Castell of Sarum* 1540.

Saltburn-by-the-Sea (YON, England): salt stream (*Salteburna c.* 1185). It has been suggested that the name refers to the alum which is found in this district.

Saltcoats (AYR, Scotland): salt-(workers') houses (*Saltcottis* 1528–9, *Saltcotes* 1548, *Saltcoittis* 1576). Manufacture of salt from salt-pans is recorded at various periods.

Sandbach (CHE, England): sand stream (*Sanbec* 1086, *Sondbache* 1260). The place is by a small tributary of the River Wheelock. The final element is Old English *bece*, *bæce*, which can mean 'valley' as well as 'stream'. Betchton, 2½ miles south-east, which lies on another small tributary of the Wheelock, means 'stream farm'.

Sandown (IOW, England): sandy river-meadow (*Sande* 1086, *Sandham* 1271, *Sandone c.* 1300, *Sandam* 1432, *Sandam or Sandown Fort* 1775). From the situation of the place, in the flat ground between the River Yar and the sea, it seems likely that the final element is *hamm*, discussed under Buckingham. This ending was reduced to an indeterminate vowel + *m*, the *-d* of *Sand-* was then felt to belong to it, and this resulted in the substitution of *-down* for *-ham*.

Scarborough (YON, England): (?) Skarthi's fort (*Escardeburg c.* 1160, *Scartheburg* 1208). There is an Old Norse saga which states that Scar-

borough was built by a Viking called *Þorgils Skarði*, who was in England in A.D. 966–7. *Skarði* was a nickname meaning 'hare-lipped'. It is possible, however, that the place-name was originally a compound of Old Norse *skarð* 'gap', and *berg* 'hill', and that this name was later associated with Þorgils Skarði, and the popular etymology caused the substitution of *borg* 'fort', for *berg*. If the name was originally descriptive of the place, the *skarð* might have been the narrow valley along which the A64 approaches Scarborough from the south.

Scunthorpe (LIN, England): Skúma's hamlet (*Escumetorp* 1086, *Scunptorp* 1245). This is a Danish name, similar to the type discussed under Corby. The element *þorp* is one of the more common habitative words in Danelaw place-names, and it appears to be used in such meanings as 'secondary settlement, outlying farm or small hamlet dependent on a larger place'. Hamlets with names in *-þorp* have not often developed into towns. Names ending in *-thorp* or *-throp* and simplex names such as Thorpe, Thrup, occur outside the Danelaw, but these contain the cognate Old English word *þrop*.

Seaford (SSX, England): ford near the sea (*Saforde* late 11th cent., *Seford* 1180, *Seafourd* 1601). There is no river at Seaford now, but the mouth of the Ouse, now at Newhaven, was in this region until the course of the river was altered by great storms in the sixteenth century. Seaford was still known as the 'old' haven in 1834. The ford was presumably where the road along the coast crossed the old course of the Ouse.

Seaham (DRH, England): village by the sea (*Sæham c.* 1050). As Old English *hām* had a more limited life than Old English *tūn* as a place-name element, it is probable that this name arose at an early stage of the Anglian settlement in Northumbria and is earlier than the relatively common name Seaton.

Selby (YOW, England): village among willow-trees (*Seleby c.* 1030, *Saleby c.* 1070, *Selby* 1221). It is possible that this place was identical with *Sele tune*, mentioned in the Anglo-Saxon Chronicle under the year 779, with replacement of Old English *tūn* by Old Norse *bȳ*. The Old Norse word *selja* 'willow', may have interchanged with Old English *salh* 'willow', and *sele* 'willow copse'. The compound would be identical in meaning with the common name Willoughby.

Selkirk (SLK, Scotland): (?) Hall church (*Selechirche c.* 1120, *Seleschirche c.* 1136, *Selekirke* 1165–1214). The first element is probably Old English *sele* 'hall, dwelling', although a personal name is also possible. However, it is not 'Shielkirk' or 'church of the Selgovae'.

Sevenoaks (KNT, England): seven oaks (*Seouenaca c.* 1100). Attention has been drawn to the curious fact that the corresponding name Siebeneich occurs at least six times in Germany. Old English *seofon* occurs fairly frequently in place-names in combination with tree-names, with words for stones or mounds, or with *welle* 'spring', and there may be a reference to folk-lore in names of this type.

Shanklin (IOW, England): (?) bank by a feature called The Cup (*Sencliz* 1086, *Sentlinge* 1225, *Shenclyng* 1305). The second element may be Old English *hlinc* 'ridge, bank', and the first *scenc* 'cup', perhaps with reference to the waterfall at Shanklin Chine. Knowledge of the topography would be necessary before saying whether the site of the settlement is aptly described by this compound.

Sheerness (KNT, England): (?) promontory shaped like a plough-share (*Scerhnesse* 1203, *Shernesse* 1221, *Sherenass* 1446, *Shirenasse* 1462, *Shiernas* 1579, *Sheerness* 1690). This name has generally been explained as 'bright headland', with first element Old English *scir*; but names containing *scir* usually have earlier and more frequent spellings with *Shire-* than are found for Sheerness. Old English *scear* 'plough-share', seems worth considering, in view of the shape of the promontory. The final element, *næss* (related to *nasu* 'nose'), is fairly common both in coastal and in inland names.

Sheffield (YOW, England): open land by the River Sheaf (*Scafeld* 1086, *Scefeld c.* 1176, *Seffeld* 1193, *Sheyfeld* 1533, *Sheffild* 1543). Sheaf is derived from Old English *scēað* 'boundary', in allusion to the river having once been on the boundary between the kingdoms of Mercia and Northumbria. An alternative form *Sheath* was still in use in 1637, but in most of the early spellings (such as *Scheve* 1183) there has been the common change of -*th*- to -*v*-. In the town-name the change from *Scēað-feld* to such forms as *Seffeld* would be helped by the -*f*- of *feld*, and the

163

town-name probably influenced the river-name.

Shields, North and South (NTB and DRH): temporary huts (South Shields is *Scheles* 1235, North Shields is *Chelis* 1268, *Nortscheles* 1275). The Middle English word *schele* only occurs as a place-name element in the north country and in Scotland, and it is most common in Northumberland. It was used of a shepherd's hut on summer pasture, and it is natural that places with names containing such a word did not as a rule develop into towns. In North and South Shields the word referred to fishermen's, rather than to shepherds', huts. The growth of the fishermen's settlement into a town is documented by a complaint made by the burgesses of Newcastle in 1279. This states that the Prior of Tynemouth has erected a town on one side of the Tyne at *Sheles*, and the Prior of Durham has built another town on the opposite side, and that the fishermen who had their huts there before this development are now selling to the new inhabitants fish which should be conveyed to Newcastle.

Shipley (YOW, England): sheep pasture (*Scipelei* 1086, *Shepele* 1225, *Shiplay* 1468). The final element is *lēah*, which is discussed under Barnsley and Leigh. It is possible that names in which this element is combined with a word for a farm animal arose comparatively late, when *lēah* was losing its original association with woodland. Other names in this category are Booley SHR (first element 'bull'), Bulkeley CHE ('bullock'), Calveley CHE, Cowley GLO, Gateley NFK ('goat'), Horse-

ley DRB etc., Lambley NTT, Oxley STF.

Shirley (WAR, England): bright clearing (*Syrley* c. 1240, *Sherle* 1306, *Shirley* 1403). This name occurs also in three other counties. Some prefer the etymology 'shire clearing', which might refer to position on a county boundary, or to the use of the clearing for meetings such as the shire-moot.

Shoeburyness (ESX, England): Shoebury may mean 'fort by a feature called The Shoe' (*Sceobyrig* c. 900 Anglo-Saxon Chronicle). The Ordnance Survey map shows a patch of rocks in the Maplin Sands off Shoebury Ness which is shaped like a human foot, and a feature here is marked *The Shoo* on a map dating from the first half of the sixteenth century. An alternative derivation is from *scēo* 'shelter', discussed under Richmond. Nothing appears to be known of any fortification here.

Shoreham-by-Sea (SSX, England): village by the steep bank (*Sorham* 1073, *Shorham* 1167). The first element is rather rare, referring in this instance to the fairly steep slope of the downs east of the River Adur. The above spellings actually refer to Old Shoreham, which was inland from the modern town. Shoreham-by-Sea is *Noua Sorham* 1235, *Nywe Shorham* 1288. It is called *Portu* in 1151, when the church of St Mary de Portu was given to Sele Priory. This is probably a Latinisation of the English name *Port* 'harbour', found in Portslade and Portsmouth. It is also called *Hulkesmouth* (1329), *port of Hulkesmouth alias Shorham*

(1457), possibly from a wreck which lay here.

Shotts (LAN, Scotland): steep slope(s) (*Bertrum Schottis* 1552, *Bartrum Schottis* 1616). Old English *sceot 'a steep slope'. The first part of the sixteenth- and seventeenth-century form appears to be a personal name. The present name is possibly a shortened form of Kirk o' Shotts.

Shrewsbury (SHR, England): (?) fortified place of the district called The Scrub (*Scropesbyrig* 1006 Anglo-Saxon Chronicle, *Scrobbesbyrig* 1016 Anglo-Saxon Chronicle, *Sciropesberie* 1086 Domesday Book, *Salopesberia* 1156 Pipe Roll, *Shrobesbury* 1327 Patent Roll, *Shrofbury* 1339 Patent Roll, *Shrousbury* 1339 Close Roll, *Shrovesbury* 1346 Patent Roll, *Shrosbury* 1364 Close Roll). The first mention of Shrewsbury is in a charter of 901, which is said to have been drawn up *in ciuitate scrobbensis*. This is a Latinisation, like those discussed under Leicester and Worcester. The vernacular form of 901 cannot be inferred from it, but the use of *civitas* (unusual for a place which was not the seat of a bishopric) may indicate that *byrig* here refers to a defended settlement of some size, and that this eminently defensible site was a regional centre from the beginning of its history. The first element is likely to be the genitive of a district-name, derived from a word related to Old English *scrybb* 'shrub'. There are several place-names which suggest the existence of a form *scrubb*, and there may have been a third form *scrobb*, found in Shrewsbury and in Shrob Lodge in Passenham NTP. Some confirmation for this suggestion that the first element of Shrewsbury is a district-name is found in the Anglo-Saxon Chronicle under the year 1016. One text (C) has *Scrobsæton* where the other texts have *Scrobbesbyrigscir* for the name of the county. If there were really a group of people called the *Scrobsǣte*, their name would be formed in the same way as *Wreocensǣte* ('dwellers near the Wrekin') and *Magonsǣte* ('dwellers near Maund'), and would consist of a name for a large feature of the landscape and the suffix -*sǣte*. The suggestion that Shrewsbury contains a personal name is not convincing as the evidence given for an Old English personal name *Scrobb* is not satisfactory.

The development of *Scrobesbyrig* to Shrewsbury, with the side-form Salop used for the county, may be tentatively explained as follows: Norman French difficulty in pronouncing consonant groups and in distinguishing -*r*- and -*l*- led to the form *Salopesberia*, in which -*a*- has been inserted into the simplified consonant group (giving *Sarob*-) and -*l*- has then been substituted for -*r*-. *Salopesberia*, with various spellings of the second element, is overwhelmingly predominant in government records of the twelfth and thirteenth centuries. A local form closer to the Old English one must have remained in use, however, and appears in the surname of Geoffrey de *Shrobesbury*, mentioned in 1327. The change of -*b*- to -*v*-, shown in such spellings as *Shrofbury*, *Shrovesbury*, is unusual, and may be due to Welsh influence. The spelling *Shrousbury*, with -*u*- representing -*v*-, may have given rise to a form *Shrowsbury*,

165

owing to the -*u*- being mistaken for a vowel. The spelling *Shrewsbury* arose by analogy with words like *show* and *shrew*, which had for a time two forms, different in spelling and pronunciation. The modern upper-class pronunciation of Shrewsbury preserves the correct vowel in spite of the altered spelling.

Sidmouth (DEV, England): mouth of the River Sid (*Sidemuða c.* 1085). Also on the river are Sidbury and Sidford. The river-name is generally explained as a derivative of Old English *sid* 'large, spacious, extensive, long'. This offers difficulties, as most of the other rivers in the area, such as the Teign, Otter, and Axe, are very much bigger than the Sid. If the names are really to be derived from *sid*, it seems more likely that the river-name is an early back-formation from one of the settlement names, possibly from Sidford. Although Sidford is first recorded in 1283, it may be a much older name, meaning 'spacious ford', and the river-name could have been a back-formation from this before the Norman Conquest. For other early back-formations see Mansfield and Plympton. Derivation from *sid* is not certain, however. The early spellings for Sidbury and Sidmouth include some in which the first element is spelt *Sude-* and *Sede-*. A range of Middle English spellings with -*i*-, -*e*-, and -*u*- generally indicates derivation from Old English -*y*-. There is an Old English word *gesyd* 'miry place', which has never been postulated as a place-name element, but which seems a possible base for a river-name, and would explain the spellings of Sidbury and Sidmouth.

Sittingbourne (KNT, England): stream of Sidu's people (*Sidingeburn* 1200, *Sidingburn* 1232, *Sithingeburn* 1258). This is one of a small class of names in which *burna* has been added to the genitive of a group-name in -*ingas* of the type discussed under Gillingham. Others are Bathingbourne IOW, Collingbourne WLT, Hollingbourne KNT, and Pangbourne BRK. The stream at Sittingbourne rises near the church and flows into Milton Creek.

Skegness (LIN, England): Skeggi's promontory (*Shegenesse* 1166, *Skegenes* 1256). This is a Scandinavian name, probably containing the personal name *Skeggi* found in Skegby NTT. Skegness is not on a promontory, but the coastline may have altered. Alternatively, if the coastline has not altered, the reference may be to the hook-shaped projection south of the town, and the name may mean 'promontory shaped like a beard'. Old Norse *skegg* 'beard', is the source of the personal name *Skeggi*.

Skipton (YOW, England): sheep farm (*Scipton* 1086). Initial Sk- is due to Old Norse influence. The name is fairly common elsewhere in the form Shipton.

Slough (BUC, England): muddy place (*Slo* 1195, *le Slough* 1443). The land by the Thames is very flat here. Bray, on the Berkshire side of the river, is probably derived from a French word meaning 'marsh', and Dorney, between Slough and Bray, has *ēg* 'island', as second element. There are other places called Slough in Bedfordshire and Sussex.

Smethwick (STF, England): smiths' dwelling (*Smedeuuich* 1086, *Smethewic* 1221). The final element is the word *wīc*, discussed under Aldridge. The same name occurs in Cheshire, and *smiða* 'of the smiths', is compounded with other words for a settlement in a number of names, including Smethcott (two in SHR), Smeaton (YOW and two in YON), Smeeton LEI, and Smeetham, earlier *Smetheton*, ESX. Presumably all these place-names indicate some degree of industrial specialisation.

Solihull (WAR, England): (?) muddy hill (*Solihull* 12th cent., *Sulihull* 1242, *Sylhyl* 1340, *Solihull alias Sulhill alias Sillill* 1633). If the first element is an adjective *sylig* (not on record, but a regular formation from *sylu* 'miry place') the reference is probably to the hill south of the church, where the road runs through stiff red clay. An alternative derivation is from an unrecorded Old English word *sulig* 'pig-stye'.

Southampton (HMP, England): estate on a promontory (*Hamtun* c. 900 Anglo-Saxon Chronicle, *Suðhamtun* 962). There is a spelling *Homtun*, which is from a forged charter, but which nevertheless constitutes evidence that the first element is the word *hamm*, which is discussed under Buckingham. In some coastal names this word appears to have had the sense 'promontory'; examples include Topsham DEV, Hamworthy DOR, Bosham and Iham SSX, as well as the present name. The suburb of Northam ('north promontory') occupies a small projection jutting out into the estuary of the Itchen, north of the large promontory occupied by Southampton. The probable reason for the prefixing of *sūð* to *hammtūn* is discussed under Northampton.

Southend-on-Sea (ESX, England): south end (of Prittlewell parish) (*Sowthende* 1481). The place was earlier called *Stratende* (1309) 'end of the Roman road'. This may indicate that there was a Roman road linking the Romano-British settlements at Billericay, Wickford, and Prittlewell, which reached the sea here.

Southport (LNC, England): this is a modern, artificial name. The town grew up round a hotel built at the end of the eighteenth century to cater for the visitors who were frequenting the North Meols district for bathing in the summer. At a house-warming for the hotel a guest christened the place Southport. He may have been thinking of it as south of the resorts of Blackpool and Lytham. The site of the hotel is marked by a lamp with a bronze relief, near the crossing of Lord Street and Duke Street.

Spalding (LIN, England): people of the district called *Spald* (*Spallinge* 1086, *Spaldingis* c. 1115, *Spaldinges* 1199). As mentioned under Epping, the suffix -*ingas* was sometimes added to a place-name. A district-name *Spald* may be inferred from the eighth-century list of tribal divisions known as the Tribal Hidage. This includes a district called *Spalda* (*land*), which appears from its position in the list to be the area round Spalding. *Spalde*, which would be the name of the tribe, is a parallel formation to *Gifle* (from the River Ivel), and *Hicce* (discussed under Hitchin), which also appear in the

Tribal Hidage. The tribe *Spalde* may have been named from a district called *Spald*, and this may derive from an Old English word related to modern German *spalten* 'to cleave', meaning 'ditch, trench'. It could have been a name given to the whole fenland between the Car Dyke and The Wash, and might refer to the Car Dyke (which is a Roman canal), or to the presence of drainage channels throughout the area.

The district called Spaldingmoor and the village of Spaldington in the East Riding of Yorkshire have the genitive of *Spaldingas* as first element. It is unlikely that the territory of the people of Spalding stretched as far north as this and included land on the other side of the Humber. The East Riding names probably refer to a group of people from the Spalding area who had moved to another region.

Stafford (STF, England): ford by a landing-place (*Stæfford* 913 Anglo-Saxon Chronicle, *Statford* 1130). The name is abbreviated to *Stæþ* on tenth-century coins. The etymology given here has been questioned on the grounds that the meaning 'landing-place' is not recorded for Old English *stæð*, which appears in the senses 'bank of a river, shore'; but the cognate Old Norse *stǫð* meant 'landing-place', and it seems necessary to assume this for the Old English word in order to make sense of Stafford. If the etymology is correct, it suggests that there was traffic on the River Sow as well as on the roads which converge on the crossing-place.

Staines (MDX, England): (place at) the stone (*Stane c.* 1050 Anglo-Saxon Chronicle, *Stanes* 1086, *Staines* 1578). The reference is generally held to be to a Roman milestone on the road from London to Silchester, which crossed the Thames at Staines. There is no record of such a milestone, however, and the stone could equally well be a glacial boulder. The name should have become Stone (as it has elsewhere). The change from singular to plural is also irregular, though it can be paralleled in other place-names.

Stamford (LIN, England): stony ford (*Steanford* 918 Anglo-Saxon Chronicle, *Stanford* 1086). Other instances of the name with the modern form Stamford occur in Northumberland and the East Riding of Yorkshire. It is fairly common with the modern form Stanford. Roads from all directions converge on the crossing of the River Welland at Stamford.

Stapleford (NTT, England): ford marked by a post (*Stapleford* 1086). This is a fairly common name; the first element is the word *stapol*, which is discussed under Barnstaple. Perhaps it was necessary to mark this ford over the Erewash because it was not on a major travel-route, and not so well-used that the precise crossing-place was obvious.

Stenhousemuir (STL, Scotland): moor of the stone-house (*de Stan house c.* 1200, *Stanus* 1264, *Stenhous* 1601). Even in the seventeenth century the last element does not yet seem to have been added. The first part means clearly 'stone house'; compare Stonehouse LAN in connection with which another *Muir de Stone-*

hows is mentioned in 1694. *Muir* is the Scottish spelling of *moor*.

Stevenage (HRT, England): (place at) the strong oak-tree (*Stithenæce c.* 1060, *Stigenace* 1086, *Stithehache* 1200, *Stivenach* 1201, *Stithcneche* 1230, *Stiveneche* 1255, *Stethenhach* 1293, *Stephenhache* 1368, *Stevenage* 1511, *Stephyn Hache* 1527, *Stephnage* 1617). Some prefer an etymology 'stiff gate' or 'Stiða's gate', with second element *hæcc*. The spellings with -*hache* could be considered to support this, but other names with *āc* (dative *ǣc*) have some spellings with an inorganic -*h*-, and the etymology 'red oak' has been accepted for Radnage BUC, which has a similar run of early forms to Stevenage. The first element is probably the dative of *stið* 'stiff, hard, strong', which has not been noted in any other place-name. The senses in which this word is recorded in Old English are not entirely suitable for defining either an oak-tree or a gate; but if the reference is to an oak, then the name falls into line with Broadoak GLO, Fairoak SOM, Harrock LNC ('hoar'), and Radnage BUC ('red'). The adjective is used of plant-leaves in Old English, and perhaps refers to the leaves of the oak rather than to the tree as a whole.

The modern form is due to the substitution of -*v*- for -*th*-, which is fairly common in place-names. Some spellings may indicate association with the personal name Stephen.

Stevenston (AYR, Scotland): Steven's farm (*Stevenstoun* 1246, *Stewynstoun* 1437). We do not know who Steven was.

Stirling (STL, Scotland): unexplained (*Strevelin a.* 1124, *Struelin c.* 1125, *Striuelin* 1136–47, etc.). This name has never been explained satisfactorily, although one presumes that the first element may have some association with the river on which it stands, meaning something like 'flowing water'. A few years ago a good case was made for the suggestion that Bede's *urbs Giudi* may be the earlier name for Stirling, particularly in juxtaposition to *Alclud* (Dumbarton Rock).

Stockport (CHE, England): (*Stokeport* 1188, *Stokeporte c.* 1190, 1260). No convincing translation of this name can be offered. The final element is *port*, discussed under Gosport and Newport, probably in the sense 'market town'. The first element is probably *stoc* (discussed under Basingstoke), which seems to have meant 'dependent settlement'. It has been considered that 'monastery' was one of the meanings of *stoc*, but recent study reveals that there is no firm foundation for this. A form *Stockford*, from about 1285, is not sufficient evidence for the second element being really *ford*.

Stockton-on-Tees (DRH, England): (*Stocton* 1196, *Stoketun c.* 1209, *Stoketone* 1228). This name poses problems similar to those presented by Stockport. Stockton is a fairly common name, and Staughton in Bedfordshire and Huntingdonshire is a variant form. If the first element were *stocc* 'stump', the explanation would be easy, as 'farm built of logs' is a convincing etymology; but the spellings for most of the Stocktons suggest *stoc*, which is not easy to

169

explain as the first element of a compound. Tees is a Celtic river-name, which may mean 'boiling river'.

Stoke-on-Trent (STF, England): dependent hamlet (*Stoche* 1086, *Stoke* 1232). This is one of the commonest English place-names. It is derived from the word *stoc*, discussed under Basingstoke, Stockport, and Stockton. The original meaning of *stoc* was simply 'place'; there is no good evidence for a meaning 'monastery', though that has been suggested for some names such as Halstock DOR, Tavistock DEV. For most of its occurrences in place-names the evidence points to a meaning 'hamlet or farm dependent on a larger settlement'. This is the most probable meaning even when, as in Basingstoke and the present name, the place had become a separate estate by the time of the Domesday Survey. The river-name is discussed under Burton-upon-Trent.

Stonehaven (KCD, Scotland): unexplained (*Stanehyve* 1587, 1592, *Stainhyve* 1600, *Steanhyve* 1629, *Stanehevin* 1637, *Stonhaven* 1690). It may sound incredible but the etymology of this apparently 'easy' name is by no means clear. Early forms rule out *haven* as a second element and Scots *stane* 'stone', too, is made less likely because of the *Steanhyve* of 1629 which roughly corresponds to the modern local pronunciation. The local as well as the standard form have the stress on the second syllable. The suggestion that this is a Norse name is not acceptable.

Stornoway (ROS, Scotland): (?) star bay or rudder bay (*Stornochway*

1511, *Steornaway* 1549), Gaelic *Steornabhagh*. Could be Old Norse *Stǫrnuvágr* 'star bay', from *stjarna* 'star'. *Stjarna* may have been the name of the stream that falls into the bay. Otherwise Old Norse *Stjórnarvágr* 'rudder bay', from *stjórn* 'steerage, rudder' might be considered. Again *Stjórn* could be a river-name. The spelling of 1549 is a fairly good representation of the Gaelic original.

Stourbridge (WOR, England): bridge over the River Stour (*Sturbrug, Sturesbrige* 1255). Stour is probably an Old English river-name meaning 'strong', of which there are at least five examples in England. The river-crossing here was earlier called *Swinford* 'pig ford'. This name occurs in the bounds of a charter dating from about 953, and it may have been extended from the ford to the north-south road which used it. This would explain the application of the names Old Swinford and Kings Swinford to settlements, which are respectively about one mile south and 2½ miles north of the river-crossing. The bridge which replaced the ford and gave name to the town of Stourbridge may have been built at a comparatively late date, since the earliest occurrence of the name which has been noted dates from 1255.

Stourport-on-Severn (WOR, England): this is a modern, artificial name, given to the town which grew up after 1772, when the Staffordshire and Worcestershire Canal was opened. The canal joined the River Severn at this point, and a town grew up which displaced the older shipping places of Wribbenhall, Bewdley, and Bridgnorth. The settlement which was here before the new town grew up was called Lower Mitton. Upper Mitton is still the name of the northern suburb of Stourport. Mitton means 'farm at the river-junction', and refers to the situation of the places in the angle formed by the confluence of the Stour and Severn. It is a fairly common name in the West Midlands, sometimes with the modern form Myton. Severn is an obscure river-name, known in classical times, and possibly pre-Celtic.

Stranraer (WIG, Scotland): (?) broad headland (*Stronyrauer, Stronerawar* 1556). Most likely Gaelic *srón reamhar* 'broad headland' although the headland in question is not easily identified.

Stratford-upon-Avon (WAR, England): ford on a Roman road (*Stretfordæ c.* 700, *Strætford* 985, *Stradforde* 1086, *Stratford* 1221). Old English *strǣt* was a loan-word from Latin *strata*, and places with names containing this element (e.g. Streatham, Stratton, Stretton, Streetly) are usually situated on a Roman road. The road joining the Roman settlements at Alcester and Tiddington crossed the Avon at Stratford. The place is called *Uferanstrætforda* 'higher Stratford' in a charter of 966. This may indicate that there were two settlements. The addition of the river-name is fairly common from the thirteenth century onwards. Avon is a Celtic river-name, of fairly frequent occurrence, identical with the Welsh word *afon* 'river'.

Stretford (LNC, England): ford on a Roman road (*Stretford* 1212). This is the same name as Stratford. The ford was at Crossford Bridge, where the Roman road from Chester to Manchester crossed the River Mersey.

Stroud (GLO, England): marshy land overgrown with brushwood (*Strode* 1200, *Strowde* 1542, *Strood* 1561, *Stroud* 1652). The meaning of Old English *strōd* is inferred from Germanic cognates. Several rivers join at Stroud, and a marshy area probably existed near the junction. The same name has become Strode in Dorset and Somerset and Strood in Kent. The modern pronunciation of Stroud is based on the spelling, though that in the sixteenth century represented the sound Strood.

Sunderland (DRH, England): separate land (*Sunderland c.* 1168). The same name occurs in Cumberland, Lancashire, and Yorkshire, and in Cheshire in the form Sinderland; and it is the first element of Sunderlandwick YOE. The term probably had some precise technical meaning. Its use appears to have been more common in the northern part of the country, but an instance occurs near Worcester in the bounds of a charter of 974. The statement in the Old English translation of Bede, that Bede was born in the *sundurlonde* of the Abbey of Jarrow, is sometimes taken to be a reference to Sunderland DRH, but it may only be a way of saying that he was born on one of the estates of the monastery.

Sutton Coldfield (WAR, England): south farm (*Sutone* 1086, *Sutton Colfeld, Sutton in le Colfeld* 1289, *Sutton Colefyld alias Sutton Coldfeild* 1649). This place is generally said to be so called because it was

171

south of Lichfield, but it is a long way from Lichfield, and Shenstone may in fact be the place referred to. Coldfield ('open land where charcoal was made') is a district-name; it is referred to as *the great wast called Colfield* in 1656.

Sutton-in-Ashfield (NTT, England): south farm (*Sutone* 1086, *Sutton in Essefeld* 1276). It is not certain which settlement this was south of. Skegby has been suggested, but this place has a Scandinavian name, and Teversal is perhaps likely to be an earlier settlement. The district-name Ashfield is discussed under Kirkby-in-Ashfield.

Swansea (GLA, Wales): sea (island) of Sveinn (*Sweynesse* 1153–84, *Sueinesea* 1190, *Sweineshe* 1191, *Swenes* 1208, *Sweynesia* 1214, *Sweynise* 1256, *Swanese* 1291, *Swanesey* 1322, *Swanzey* 1598–1600). Old Norse *Sveinn* (personal name)+*sáer* or *ey* 'island'. There was formerly at the mouth of the River Tawe an island (*Iselond'* 1432, *The Island* 1641). The Welsh name is *Abertawe* 'mouth of the River Tawe' (*Aper Tyui c.* 1150, *Abertawi, Abertaui, Abertawy* 12th cent., *Abertawe* 1191, *Aber Tawy c.* 1300, *Aber Tawy* 14th cent., *Abertawy* 1455–85, *Aber Tawe* 1606, *Aber Tawy c.* 1700). Welsh *aber* 'mouth'+river-name *Tawe*. For *Tawe* see *Tyui c.* 1150, *Taui c.* 1150, *Tauuy c.* 1150, *Tawuy c.* 1200, *Tawe* fl. 1191, *Tawy* 1203, *Tawy* 1336, *Tauwy* 1334, *Tawy* 1449, *Tawey* 1546, *Tawey* 1641). British **Tamoụiā* '(?) water, dark river'.

Swindon (WLT, England): hill used for swine pasture (*Suindune* 1086, *Swindona* 1156). Old Swindon (*Higheswindon, Swyndon super montem* in early records) is on a hill.

Swinton (LNC, England): swine farm (*Suinton* 1258, *Swynton* 1276). The same name occurs in the North and West Ridings of Yorkshire.

Tamworth (STF, England): enclosure on the River Tame (*Tamouuorði, Tamouuorthig* 781, *Tomeworðig* 799). Tame is a Celtic river-name, identical with Taff and Taf in Wales.

The second element of Tamworth is Old English *worðig*, which is a derivative of the word *worð* discussed under Failsworth. It is generally considered to have much the same meaning as *worð*, and is especially characteristic of the south-west of England, where it often has the modern form -worthy (e.g. Highworthy, Langworthy, Smallworthy, all in Devon). Away from the south-west, it is very rare, and the spellings for Tamworth show that in this name it had been assimilated to *worð* by the time of the Norman Conquest. Another Midland instance is *Norðworðig*, the earlier name of Derby. It has been suggested that -*worðig* in the spellings for these two names is due to West Saxon scribal practice, and does not represent the local form. But the earliest spellings for Tamworth are from Mercian charters, and there is every reason to think that they are the true local forms. The meaning 'enclosure' does not seem altogether adequate for Tamworth, which was the seat of the Mercian kings. Possibly at a very early stage of the settlement in the Midlands *worðig* developed a meaning akin to that of *burh*, and was used for sites of considerable importance.

Taunton (SOM, England): farm on the River Tone (*Tantun* 737). Tone is a Celtic river-name, possibly meaning 'roaring stream'. The Tone is a fairly long river, and there are a number of settlements on its banks. Taunton does not seem obviously a name which would distinguish this place from the others, but possibly this was the earliest English settlement on the river. It seems to have been a place of some importance in the early eighth century; King Ine of Wessex is said in the Anglo-Saxon Chronicle to have built some structure here which was destroyed in 722.

Teignmouth (DEV, England): (place at) the mouth of the River Teign (*tenge muðan* 1044, *Teignemudan* 1148, *Tengmuth* 1301, *Tingmouth* 1675). Teign is a Celtic river-name related to Welsh *taen* 'sprinkling'. The spelling of 1044 refers to the river-mouth, not to the settlement.

Tenby (PEM, Wales): little fort (*Dinbych* c. 1275, *Tyneb'* 1291, *Tynebegh* 1292, *Tenebegh* 1349, *Tenby* 1482, *Dinbych y pysgod* 1566, *Tenby y piscoid* 1586, *Tenbi'r Pyscawd* 1612). Welsh *din* 'fort' + *bych* 'small'. This is the same name as *Denbigh* (q.v.), but with an early hardening of Welsh *d*- to English *t*-, cf. *Tintern* from Welsh *Dindyrn*. The Welsh *Dinbych-y-pysgod* is *dinbych* as above + def. art. *y*+*pysgod* 'fish', alluding to Tenby's situation near the sea. Welsh -*ch* has disappeared in the English form, and is only a spelling oddity in *Denbigh*.

Thorne (YOW, England): (place at) the thorn tree (*Torne* 1086, *Thorna* c. 1180). The hawthorn, Old English *þorn*, is one of the commonest trees to be mentioned in place-names. Sometimes the reference may be to a quick-set thorn hedge, but frequently, as in the present instance, it is more likely to be to a single tree of great age and size.

Thornton Cleveleys (LNC, England): farm by the thorn tree (*Torentun* 1086, *Thorneton* 1246). Thornton is a very common name. The origin of the name Cleveleys does not seem to be known. In 1912, in the *Victoria County History of Lancashire* VII, p. 232, it was described as 'a little seaside resort called Cleveleys'. The same account says 'this last name has in common usage superseded the ancient Ritherham or Ritherholme'. The old name meant 'ox meadow'.

Thurso (CAI, Scotland): bull's river (*Thorsa* 1152, *Thorsey* c. 1250, *ad Tursehau* 1200, *Turishau* 1275, *Thorsan* 1276, *Thurso* 1547), Gaelic *Inbhir Thòrsa*. As Ptolemy's name for a neighbouring headland, *Tarvedum* (< *Tarvo-dūnon 'bull-fort') suggests, the earlier Celtic name for the river may have been something like, *Tarvo-dubron 'bull's water'.

This was translated into Old Norse as *pjórsá which, in turn, was before saga-times reinterpreted as *pórsá* 'Thor's river'. Thurso is the settlement at the mouth of that river, as the Gaelic name indicates.

Tilbury (ESX, England): (?) fort by the stream called *Tila* (*Tilaburg* c. 730 Bede's Ecclesiastical History, *Tilaburh* c. 1000, *Tillabyri* c. 1076, *Tiliberia* 1086). A stream-name *Tila* would mean 'the useful one'. Other possibilities are to consider the first element to be the Old English personal name *Tila*, also derived from the adjective *til* 'useful, good', or to be the adjective itself applied directly to the fort. The name Tilbury must have belonged originally to one of the settlements now called East and West Tilbury, which are north-east of the Docks. Bede says that there was a 'city' here in 653, where Bishop Cedd established a missionary centre. Tilbury-iuxta-Clare has similar early spellings and is generally assumed to be identical with Tilbury by the Thames. Although both are in Essex, they are over 40 miles apart, and it is difficult to imagine any connection between the two. Whether the first element be interpreted as a stream-name (there is a small stream by Tilbury-iuxta-Clare, and one by East Tilbury), a personal name, or the adjective *til* applied to the two forts, the double occurrence of the name is slightly surprising. The adjective *til* 'useful, good' may be found in two other Essex names, Tilletsmarsh in Wallasea (Tillet is from *til* and *wereð* 'marsh') and Tilty ('(?) good enclosure'); but it is never possible to say that any place-name contains this word rather than the personal name *Tila*.

Tiverton (DEV, England): estate at the double ford (*Twyfyrde c.* 880 King Alfred's Will, *Tovretona* 1086, *Tuiverton c.* 1148, *Tiverton* 1219, *Twiverton* 1228, *Tiverton alias Twyford Town* 1695). The addition of *tūn* appears to be late. In the ninth century the settlement was defined by the term *twifyrde* 'double ford'. This, or the parallel term *twiford*, has given rise to a number of place-names, including Twerton SOM and many instances of Twyford. In Tiverton, the meaning is probably that the east–west road had to cross both the River Loman and the River Exe.

Todmorden (YOW, England): Totta's boundary-valley (*Tottemerden, Totmardene* 1246, *Todmereden* 1298, *Todmerden* 1439, *Todmorden* 1641). This etymology is generally accepted, and although alternative ones could be suggested, none of them seems any more convincing. It is unusual to find a personal name (or any other defining element) prefixed to a compound like *gemǣre-denu* 'boundary-valley', which seems an adequate name in itself. It would be easier to accept if there were another settlement with a name derived from *gemǣre-denu*, from which this one needed to be distinguished. The valley is probably the one which runs north–west from the town, the head of which is near the Lancashire boundary.

Tonbridge (KNT, England): (?) bridge belonging to the manor (*Tonebrige* 1086, *Tonebricge* 1087, *Thonebregge* 1191, *Tunebrug* 1229). Many roads converge on the crossing of the River Medway here. Tonbridge is probably one of the small class of names which have *tūn* as first element. Others are Tonwell HRT, Tunworth HMP, and Towneley and Townworth LNC. A compound of *tūn* and *brycg* does not seem very meaningful, however, and it might be worth considering Old English *geþun* 'noise, clangor', as a possible first element. This should have given Thunbridge, but *T*- might have been substituted for *Th*- owing to Norman French influence.

Torquay (DEV, England): quay at the place called Torre (*Torrekay* 1591, *Tor Quay* 1765). Tormoham, the parish within which the town of Torquay grew up in the nineteenth century, was earlier *Torre* 'rocky outcrop'. Possibly the quay was built by the monks of Torre Abbey, and named from the Abbey rather than from the parish. In 1412 a French ship laden with wine was seized and brought 'a un lieu appelle le Getce de Torrebaie', and this is probably the first reference to the artificial landing-place later known as Tor Quay. The name had been transferred from the quay to the adjacent settlement by 1668, when there is a reference to 'a small village called Torkay'.

(Y) Trallwng (MTG, Wales), see *Welshpool*.

Tranent (ELO, Scotland): homestead of the streams (*Trauernent c.* 1127, *Treuernent* 1144). From Welsh *tref yr neint*, in which the last element is the plural of *nant* 'stream, valley'. *Tref*, for which see Tredegar MON, is a very important trace of the Cumbric (Welsh) language in Southern Scotland.

175

Tredegar (MON, Wales): farm of Tegyr. The present town is a nineteenth-century industrial development, and was named from the Tredegar family who themselves took their name from the family seat at Tredegar near Newport MON. This is *Tredegyr* 1550, *Tredeger* 1551, *Tredegyr* 1587, *Tredegar* 1632, *Tre Deg Erw* 1833. Welsh *tre* 'farm' + personal name *Tegyr* < British *Tecorix*. The confusion of *-yr* and *-er* is normal in final unaccented syllables. *Tredegar* represents a dialect pronunciation of *Tredeger*. The form *Tre Deg Erw* is straightforward popular etymology which seeks to derive the name from *tre* + *deg* 'ten' + *erw* 'acre'. It has no basis in fact.

Trefaldwyn (MTG, Wales), see *Montgomery*.

Trefdraeth (PEM, Wales), see *Newport* PEM.

Treffynnon (FLI, Wales), see *Holywell*.

Trefriw (CRN, Wales): farm of the hill (*Treffruu* 1254, *Treurow* 1284, *Treffri* 1362, *Treffrewe* 1565, *Trefriw* 1566, *Trefriw* 1757). Welsh *tref* 'farm, town' + *rhiw* 'hill'. The name refers to a very steep hill in the town.

Trefyclo (RAD, Wales), see *Knighton*.

Troon (AYR, Scotland): (the) headland (*le Trone* 1371, *le Trune* 1464). Possibly Welsh *trwyn* 'nose, headland', but the spellings quoted do perhaps argue rather for a Gaelic *an t-Sròn* 'the headland'. Curiously enough, the name of Troon in present-day Arran Gaelic is *an t-Sruthail* 'the current'. This is probably a folk-etymological change.

Trowbridge (WLT, England): (?) bridge made of tree-trunks (*Straburg* 1086, *Trobrigge* 1184, *Treubrigge* 1232, *Trowbrugg* 1230). Trobridge House in Crediton DEV is another instance of this name. Old English *trēow* (discussed under Braintree) is well-evidenced as a first, though it is much more common as the final element of a place-name. As a first element it can be interpreted in several ways. Trowbridge could mean 'bridge by a prominent tree' or 'bridge by a wooden cross', or it could mean 'bridge consisting of a single tree-trunk'. The last sense is possible as regards the size of the River Bliss, but unlikely in view of the number of roads which converge at Trowbridge.

Truro (CNW, England): (?) estate consisting of three hides (*Triueru* 1176, *Treueru* 1229, *Treuru* 1262, *Trywru* 1283, *Truru* 1307). Professor Charles Thomas (who has supplied the above spellings) suggests that the name consists of the Cornish numeral *tri* followed by *erow*, which is a term for a unit of land. Since no precise translation of *erow* is possible, it seems permissible to use the term hide, though it should be emphasised that there is no real basis for this. English names which have this sort of meaning are discussed under Hyde.

Tullibody (CLA, Scotland): hill of the hut (?) (*Dunbodeuin* 1147, *Dumbodenun* c. 1150, *Tullibotheny* 1195). The first element in the present name is Gaelic *tulach* 'hillock'; it seems to have replaced *dùn*, with the same meaning, in the twelfth century. The second element could be connected with Gaelic *bothan* 'cottage, hut', but this is not certain.

Tunbridge Wells (KNT, England): named from Tonbridge. The medicinal properties of the spring here were noticed in the early seventeenth century, and the town grew up later in the century to accommodate the increasing number of visitors.

Tynemouth (NTB, England): (place at) the mouth of the River Tyne (*Tinanmuðe*, *Tine muðan* c. 1121 Anglo-Saxon Chronicle MS E). Tyne is a Celtic river-name which (like Avon) seems not to have a meaning much more specific than 'river'.

Tywyn (MER, Wales): strand, sea-shore (*Thewyn* 1254, *Tewyn* 1291, *Towent* 1294, *Y Tywyn* 14th cent., *Towyn Meronnygh* 1461, *Towyn Myeyonethe* 1529, *Tywyn Myrionydd* 1566, *Tywyn alias Towyn Merioneth* 1763). Welsh *tywyn* 'sand-dune, sandy shore'. The full name is *Tywyn Meirionnydd*, where *Meirionnydd* recalls the name of the cantref. Meirionnydd = 'land of Meirion' < pers. name *Meirion* + territorial suffix -*ydd*. There were two other well-known places with the same name, Tywyn (Tywyn Abergele) in Denbigh, and Tywyn near Cardigan. The word *tywyn* is related to *tywod* 'sand', and should be so spelt according to the rules of Welsh orthography.

U

Uddingston (LAN, Scotland): (?) Oda's farm (*Odistoun* 1296, *Odingstoune* 1475, *Uddistoune* 1492). The first element is obviously a personal name, probably something like *Oda*, as in Odstock WLT (*Odestocke* 1086).

Ulverston (LNC, England): Wulfhere's estate (*Vlurestun* 1086, *Ulverston* 1246). This is a name of the same type as Brighton. The *W-* of *Wulfhere* has been lost owing to Scandinavian influence.

Urmston (LNC, England): Urm's estate (*Wermeston* 1194, *Urmeston* 1212). This name is discussed under Flixton.

Usk (MON, Wales): town on the River Usk (*Isca* Rom. Brit., *Uscha* 1100, *Husca* 1143, *Uisc*, *Uysc*, *Huisc* c. 1150, *Wysc* 13th cent., *Uske* 1205, *Wysc* 14th cent., *Vske* 1504, *Wyske Ryver* 1536–9). *Isca* represents British **Eiscā*, cf. Old Irish *iasc* 'fish', i.e. 'river abounding in fish'. The river gave its name to the town and the lordship. The Welsh name is *Brynbuga* 'hill of Buga' (*Brynbuga* 1450–1500, *Cairuske o.c. Brenbygey* 1536–9, *wrth frynn buga* 1556–64, *Bryn Bygaf* 1566, *Bryn Bvga* 1606). Welsh *bryn* 'hill' + personal name *Buga*. The Roman station was called *Burrium*, probably to be related with Welsh *bwrr* 'thick, stout'.

W

Wakefield (YOW, England): (?) open land where a festival took place (*Wachefeld* 1086, *Wakefeld c.* 1094). The first element is probably Old English *wacu*, 'a watch, a wake'. Wakefield is the traditional capital of the West Riding, and the open land between the River Calder on the South and the great wood of Outwood on the north would be a convenient place of assembly for the southern half of the Riding. There is another Wakefield in Potterspury NTP, and two names of similar meaning are discussed under Mirfield. In medieval times there was a great annual fair at the Yorkshire Wakefield.

Wallasey (CHE, England): island of the British (*Walea* 1086, *Waleie c.* 1150, *Waylayesegh* 1362). At a fairly late date, when the name *Waleie* had ceased to be understood as a compound with *ēg* 'island' as second element, a superfluous Middle English *ey* was added to the genitive of the name, the final meaning being 'island of Walley'. Wallasey is the northern tip of the Wirral, partly cut off from the rest of the peninsula by an inlet of the River Mersey.
Old English *walh* (genitive plural *wala*) is a particularly interesting place-name element. It has been pointed out that the usual translation

of *walh* as 'foreigner' is misleading, and that it was really a word of linguistic meaning, signifying a foreigner who spoke either a Celtic language or Latin. It was eventually used in the sense 'serf', but it is contended that this meant a serf whose speech was Celtic. If this is correct, names containing *walh* become an important part of the evidence for a surviving Celtic strain in the population after the Anglo-Saxon invasions. It has always been recognised that these names had a bearing on the problem, but some authorities have considered that the sense 'serf' is suitable for most of the place-names, and that many of them have therefore no significance as regards the racial origins of the people living at settlements with names like Walton. These problems are discussed further under Wallington, Walmer, Walsall, and Walton. In the case of Wallasey, it is, of course, quite likely that the name is of comparatively late origin and refers to settlers from Wales. Wales is derived from *walas*, the plural of *walh*.

Walmer (KNT, England): pool of the Britons (*Wealemere* 11th cent.). The first element is *weala*, the Kentish and West Saxon form of *wala*, discussed under Wallasey and Wallington. No pool is marked on modern maps; it may have been drained at an early stage in the history of the settlement.

Walsall (STF, England): Walh's valley (*Waleshale* 1163). Old English *walh* (discussed under Wallasey) is recorded as a personal name, but it seems likely that people who bestowed it as a personal name did so with full recognition of its meaning, and it would probably be fair to consider such place-names as Walsall to be evidence for a Celtic strain in the population. *halh*, which is common in this area, is sometimes used of shapeless hollows. J. Gould has recently shown that the earliest settlement at Walsall was probably on low ground.

Waltham Cross (HRT, England): cross near Waltham (*Waltham Crouche* 1360, *Walthamcros* 1365). The settlement was named from the last but one of the 12 crosses set up by Edward I to mark the resting-places of Queen Eleanor's body on its journey from Harby NTT to London. Waltham Abbey ESX (*Waltham* 1062) means 'village in a wood', with *wald* 'woodland, high forest-ground', as first element.

Walton-le-Dale (LNC, England): farm of the Britons (*Waletune* 1086, *Walton in Le Dale* 1318). This is the same name as Wallington GTL. *Dale* refers to the valley of the River Ribble; see Chester-le-Street for this use of French *le* as a connective particle. The addition was probably for distinction from Walton-on-the-Hill, north-east of Liverpool.

Walton-on-the-Naze (ESX, England): farm of the Britons (*Walentonie* 11th cent., *Waletun* 12th cent., *Walton at the Naase* 1545). This is the same name as Wallington GTL. The Naze preserves the final element of an earlier name meaning 'Eadwulf's promontory' (*Eadolfesnæsse* 1049 Anglo-Saxon Chronicle, *Edolfesnes* 1304). This was used of the actual promontory, and also, until the fourteenth century, of a large area including the three parishes of Walton, Kirkby-le-Soken, and Thorpe-le-Soken which belonged to the Dean and Chapter of St Paul's London.

Walton-on-Thames (SUR, England): farm of the Britons (*Waletona* 1086, *Waleton super Thamse* 1279). This is another instance of the name discussed under Wallington GTL.

Ware (HRT, England): the weir (*Waras*, *Wara* 1086, *Ware* 1200). Ware is beside the River Lea. Old English *wer* or *wær* is a fairly common place-name element, occurring by itself (as in this name and Weare DEV, SOM), and as a first or second element; see Edgware GTL and Warrington.

Warlingham (SUR, England): (?) village of Wærla's people (*Warlyngham* 1144, *Warlinggeham* c. 1200, *Warlingeham* 1214, *Werlingham* 1263, *Worlingham* 1291). This is probably a name of the same type as Gillingham, but the series of spellings available starts rather late, and a high proportion of them lacks the medial -*e*- which is a characteristic of Middle English forms for names in -*ingahām*.

Warminster (WLT, England): minster on the River Were (*Worgemynster* c. 912, *Gverminstre* 1086, *Werminister*

1115, *Warmenistre* 1155). Old English *mynster* is discussed under Upminster GTL. The river-name which is the first element of Warminster occurs again in SHR, where it has the modern form Worf. An Old English name related to *wōrian* 'to wander', *wērig* 'tired', has been suggested.

Warrington (LNC, England): farm by the weir (*Walintune* 1086, *Werington* 1246). This name and Warwick almost certainly contain an unrecorded Old English word *wering* or *wæring*, a derivative of *wer*, *wær* (discussed under Ware). Warrington lies beside the River Mersey.

Warwick (WAR, England): dwellings by the weir (*Wærinc wicum* 1001, *Wærincwican* 1016, *Wæring wicum* c. 1050 Anglo-Saxon Chronicle, *Warwic* 1086). The first element is the same as that of Warrington, referring in this instance to a dam across the River Avon. The second element is the plural of *wīc*, discussed under Aldridge.

Watford (HRT, England): ford used by hunters (*Watford c.* 945, *Wathford c.* 1180). The ford was probably over the River Colne. There is another Watford, of identical origin, in Northamptonshire, and the name Huntingford, which has the same meaning, occurs in Dorset and Gloucestershire.

(Y) Waun (DEN, Wales), see *Chirk*.

Wednesbury (STF, England): fortified place sacred to the god Wōden (*Wadnesberie* 1086, *Wodnesberia* 1166, *Wednesbiri* 1227). Wednesbury belongs to the clearly defined class of place-names in which the first element is the name of one of the pagan gods worshipped by the Anglo-Saxons before their conversion to Christianity. Other names which refer to sites of heathen worship are discussed under Harrow-on-the-Hill GTL. Wōden, Thunor, and Tīw are the three gods whose names certainly occur in place-names. The second element of Wednesbury is *burh*, discussed under Aylesbury. This word is frequently applied to an Iron Age hill-fort, and it is possible that the nicely rounded hill at Wednesbury had such a fort, and that the temple to Wōden was built inside it, to be succeeded by a Christian church in a manner similar to the sequence of events postulated for Harrow GTL. The hill at Wednesbury is not such an impressive site as that at Harrow, but it is remarkably conspicuous in any vista of the Black Country.

The change from *Wodnes-* to *Wednes-* is found also in Wednesday, 'Wōden's day' (in which Wōden, because of an equation with Mercury, translates the planet-name in Latin *Mercurii dies*, French *mercredi*).

Wednesfield (STF, England): open land sacred to the god Wōden (*Wodnesfeld* 996, *Wednesfeld* 1251). This name, Wednesbury, and Weoley Castle form a line of place-names west of Birmingham which refer to pagan Anglo-Saxon worship. There may have been temples here which remained in use after most of the Midlands had been converted to Christianity. This would cause such institutions to seem exceptional, and so to be distinctive enough to give rise to place-names.

183

Wellingborough (NTP, England): fortified place of Wændel's people (*Wendlesberie, Wedlingeberie* 1086, *Wendlingburch* 1178, *Wenlingeburc* 1185, *Wendlesburg* 1221, *Wellyngburgh* 1316). The spellings indicate that there were two forms of this name, one meaning 'Wændel's fort', the other being an *-inga-* formation (see *Introduction*, p. 18). The spellings representing the latter are much the more numerous. The personal name Wændel is well-evidenced in place-names but is not recorded in any literary source, and it probably belongs to the earlier stages of the Anglo-Saxon settlement. The nature of the *burh* at Wellingborough is not known. The town lies on gently sloping land which is not obviously suitable for an Iron Age hill-fort.

Wellington (SHR, England): (?) estate associated with Wēola (*Walitone* 1086, *Welintona* 1220, *Weolyntone* 1327). There are other places called Wellington in Herefordshire and Somerset, and the three names have very similar series of early spellings. There is no personal name Wēola on record, but it would be parallel to Old German *Weila*. It is surprising that an otherwise unknown personal name should occur three times in a place-name of the type discussed in the *Introduction*, p. 18, but it is not completely outside the bounds of possibility. A significant word would be preferable, but no suitable word is on record. Derivation from *hwēol* 'wheel', is ruled out by the absence of spellings in *Wh-*. An alternative to the personal name might be a first element *Wēolēahingas* 'dwellers in a place called *Wēolēah*'. *Wēolēah* is a well-evidenced place-name meaning

'sacred grove with a heathen temple', but it is difficult to believe in three *-ingas* formations from this place-name in the counties of Hereford, Somerset, and Shropshire, where *-ingas* was not much used.

Welshpool (MTG, Wales): Welsh pool (*Pola* 1253, *La Pole* 1278, *La Pole Villa* 1286, *Poole* 1411, *Poule* 1445, *Walshe Pole* 1477, *Walsche Poole, Walschpole* 1536–9, *Welshepoole* 1646). Old English *pōl* 'pool, creek'. The name refers to the place where the Lledin brook flows into the Severn. The Welsh name is *Y Trallwng* 'the pool', earlier *Trallwng Llywelyn* 'pool of Llywelyn' (*Trallwg Llywelyn* 14th cent., *y trallwn* 1566, *Trallwng c.* 1700). Welsh *trallwng, trallwm* 'pool'. The name is sometimes found as *Y Trallwng Coch ym Mhowys* 'Red Pool in Powys', probably because Powys Castle near the town is known from its colour as *Y Castell Coch* 'the red castle'. One of the townships of Welshpool was called *Trallwng Gollwyn* or *Gollen* 'pool of Collwyn, Collen' (*Trallung Golloyn* 1309, *Trallwyn-gollwyn* 1597–8, *Trallumgollen* 1681).

Welwyn (HRT, England): (place) at the willows (*Welingum c.* 945, *Welugun* 11th cent., *Welewes* 1203, *Welewen* 1220, *Welwyn alias Welwys* 1626, *Willen, Wellen* 1675). Willian, a village 11 miles north of Welwyn, has the same meaning, and so has Willen in Buckinghamshire.

West Bridgford (NTT, England): ford by the bridge (*Brigeforde* 1086, *Westburgeforde* 1572). There was probably a long period in which both the ford and the bridge were used to cross the River Trent by travellers to and from Nottingham. *West* is for distinction from East Bridgford, about seven miles north-east. Other additions besides *east* and *west* were used to distinguish the two places. West Bridgford was *Brigeford juxta pontem de Notingham* in 1238, *Briggeford atte Briggend* in 1361. This suggests that the significance of Bridgford had been forgotten, and it was just a meaningless term for the settlement on the other side of the bridge from Nottingham. East Bridgford was sometimes called *-on Hyll*, *-super montem* in the sixteenth and seventeenth centuries.

West Bromwich (STF, England): dwelling among broom (*Bromwic* 1086, *Westbromwich* 1322). This is a similar name to Aldridge. *West* is for distinction from Castle Bromwich WAR, about eight miles east.

West Kirby (CHE, England): village with a church (*Kirchebi c.* 1165, *Westkirkeby* 1289). This is a Norwegian name identical with Kirkby. *West* is for distinction from Kirkby near Liverpool.

Weston-super-Mare (SOM, England): west farm (*Weston* 1266, *Weston super Mare* 1349). This type of name is discussed under Sutton GTL. *Super Mare* was perhaps added by government clerks to distinguish this place from Weston Zoyland in the same county.

Weybridge (SUR, England): bridge over the River Wey (*Webrug* 1086, *Waibrigge c.* 1180, *Weybrigge* 1294). Wey is a pre-English name, identical with Wey in Dorset and Wye in Derbyshire and Wales. It is of unknown meaning and may be pre-Celtic. The earliest reference to the settlement at Weybridge is probably the one in Domesday Book, though the name occurs in a number of forged charters which purport to be earlier than this. The actual bridge is mentioned as a boundary mark in a survey of Chertsey and Thorp which is of uncertain date but may be pre-Conquest.

Weymouth (DOR, England): (place at) the mouth of the River Wey (*Waimuda* 1130, *Weymuthe* 1258). The river-name is discussed under Weybridge.

Whickham (DHR, England): village with a quick-set hedge (*Quicham* 1196). Names in *-hām* probably go back to an early stage of the Anglian settlement in Northumberland and Durham. They are fairly common in the two counties, but Whickham is a rather isolated example, and although it is not recorded until 1196 it may be one of the earliest English settlements in the Newcastle area.

Whitburn (WLO, Scotland): white stream (*Whiteburne, Witburn* 1296), from Old English *hwīt* 'white' and *burna* 'stream'.

Whitby (YON, England): Hvíti's village (*Witeby* 1086, *Whitby* 1138, *Hvítabýr* 12th cent., Heimskringla). This is an old Norse name of the same type as Corby. Whitby replaced an earlier Old English name *Streoneshalh*, probably meaning 'lovers' nook', which occurs also as a lost name in Worcestershire, and as a surviving name in Strensall YON. The great synod of A.D. 663, now generally referred to as the Synod of Whitby, is stated in the early accounts to have been held at *Streoneshalh*. Historians writing in the eleventh century

185

identified this with Whitby, and modern excavations have uncovered the monastic buildings.

Whitehaven (CMB, England): harbour by the white headland (*Qwithofhavene c.* 1135, *Witenhauen* 1278, *Wythauene, Whytehauene* 1279, *Whittofthaven* 1329). This is an Old Norse name. The hill of white stone which forms one side of the harbour was called *Hvíthofuð* 'white head'. The addition of *hafn* 'harbour', to this resulted in a triple compound, and the middle element of this was eventually dropped, as frequently happens with these compounds. There was a 'black headland' somewhere on this stretch of coast which is called *Swartahof c.* 1125, *Suarthoved* late 12th cent., *Swarthow* 16th cent.

Whitland (CRM, Wales): white land (*Alba Domus* 1191, *Alba Landa* 1214, *Whitland* 1309, *Blaunchelande* 1318, *Blancalanda* 1329, *Whytland* 1349, *Whiteland* 1352, *Whitelond* 1443). Old English *hwīt* 'white' + *land* 'land'. This and the Latin forms *Alba Domus* 'white house', *Alba Landa* 'white land' are ecclesiastical and monastic translations of Welsh *Tŷ Gwyn* 'white house', traditional site of the meeting at which Hywel Dda promulgated the Welsh Laws, in the tenth century, and later the site of a Cistercian monastery. ([*yr*] *ty gwyn ar daf* 13th cent., *y ty gwyn* 14th cent., *Hendygwyn* 1561, *Hendy Gwyn* 1603). Welsh *hen* 'old' + *tŷ* 'house' + *gwyn* 'white' [or the pers. name *Gwyn* with the same meaning] + *ar* 'on' + *Taf* (river name). For *Taf* cf. *Taph* 1191, *Tafe* 1594–5, *Tave* 1687–8. British **tamos* '(?) dark, (?) water'.

Whitley Bay (NTB, England): white wood or clearing (*Wyteleya* 12th cent., *Hwyteleya* 1198). This is a fairly common name, particularly well-evidenced in the West Riding. It is impossible to say exactly what it means; a precise interpretation would involve a decision as to whether *lēah* (discussed under Barnsley) refers to a clearing or to a wood. Here, as with other names which are repeated a number of times, something might be achieved by a detailed study of all the examples.

Whitstable (KNT, England): (place) at the white post (*Whitstapel* 1197). The name is first recorded as that of a hundred (the administrative division intermediate between estate and shire). This occurs in Domesday Book with the spelling *Witenestaple*. This seems to be a clear instance of the use of a post to mark the meeting-place of the hundred court; see Barnstaple. The settlement (as opposed to the hundred) does not appear to be mentioned in records until the late twelfth century, and it seems possible that it grew up relatively late on the site of the ancient meeting-place.

Wick (CAI, Scotland): bay (*Vik* 1140, *Wik* 1530), from Old Norse *vík* 'bay'.

Wickford (ESX, England): (?) ford by the Romano-British settlement (*Wicforda c.* 975). Old English *wic* is discussed under Aldridge. Although it is one of the commonest suffixes in English place-names and occurs frequently by itself, it is rare as a first element, except in the compound discussed under West Wickham GTL. It is possible that some of the few names in which it is found as the defining element date from an early stage of the Anglo-Saxon settlement, and that in some of them *wīc* retains its association with Latin *vicus*, from which it is derived. A Roman farm-site has recently been discovered at Wickford, and another name of this type, Weekley in Leicestershire, is adjacent to a Romano-British settlement.

Widnes (LNC, England): wide promontory (*Wydnes c.* 1200). The name refers to the round promontory which juts out into the Mersey.

Wigan (LNC, England): (?) (homestead of) Wigan (*Wigan* 1199). The only suggestion available for this name is that it is a shortened form of a Welsh name *Tref Wigan*, in which the final element is a personal name. There is another Wigan in Anglesey, which may be of identical origin. *Tref Wigan* would be the later type of Celtic compound, and the name would be post-Roman. British names are unusually frequent in this part of Lancashire; for example, Ince, which adjoins Wigan, is a British name meaning 'island, water-meadow', and both the district-name Makerfield and the village-name Eccleston have British first elements.

Wigston Magna (LEI, England): Wīcing's estate (*Wichingestone* 1086). This is a name of the same type as Brighton. The personal name is the Old English form of the word *viking*, and it was probably used by the Anglo-Saxons before the Viking invasions. Magna was probably prefixed to distinguish this place from Wigston Parva, about 10 miles south-west. Wigston Parva is in origin a completely different name

meaning 'rocking-stone', but when the spellings had become identical it may have been felt necessary to distinguish them from each other.

Wigtown (WIG, Scotland): dwelling-place (*Wigeton* 1266, *Wygton* 1328). Probably from Old English *wīc-tūn* 'dwelling-place, homestead, manor'. If it is the same as Wigton CMB, on the other hand, which is *Wiggeton* in 1163 and *Wigeton* in 1262, it may be 'Wicga's farm'.

Willenhall (STF, England): Willa's sheltered place (*Willanhalch c.* 733 charter of King Æthelbald of Mercia, drawn up at this place). This name is different from Willenhall in Coventry WAR, which has -*l*-, not -*ll*-, in the early spellings, and probably has *wilegn* 'willow', as first element. It is difficult to define the meaning of *halh* in Willenhall. The town is in a slight hollow and the site is well watered. It is not an obvious 'valley' site, but the reference could be to its lying in a hollow. The sense 'river-meadow', discussed under Bramhall, is possible but not inescapable.

Willington (DRH, England): estate associated with Wifel (*Wyvelintun c.* 1190, *Wyuelington* 1296). This is a name of the same type as Addington GTL.

Wilmslow (CHE, England): Wīghelm's tumulus (*Wilmislowe, Wilmislawe* 1260). Old English *hlāw* or *hlǣw* usually refers in place-names to a burial mound. The mounds in question may be prehistoric, as in Lewes, or they may be the tumuli of pagan Anglo-Saxons, as appears to be the case in Taplow (discussed under Hounslow GTL). It would be pleasant to think that Wīghelm was one of the earliest English settlers in Cheshire and was given a burial mound here from which the settlement was named. The more prosaic explanation would be that Wīghelm was a landowner whose estate was conveniently distinguished from its neighbours by the presence of a prehistoric tumulus.

Winchester (HMP, England): Roman town called Venta (*Ouénta c.* 150 Ptolemy, *Venta Belgarum* 4th-cent. Antonine Itinerary, *Uintancaestir c.* 730 Bede's Ecclesiastical History). This is a name of the same type as Cirencester. *Venta* is a Celtic name applied to several of the towns of Roman Britain, including Caerwent.

Windsor (BRK, England): windlass bank (*Windlesora c.* 1060, *Windesores* 1086, *Nova Wyndelesor et Vetus* 1242). This place-name occurs at least five times, Broadwindsor and Little Windsor DOR, Windsor WAR, and Winsor DEV, HMP having the same etymology. The reference is probably to a device by a road for helping laden carts along steep, muddy stretches. New Windsor (*niwan Windlesoran* 1110 Anglo-Saxon Chronicle) was the name given to the settlement which grew up near Windsor Castle, built in the late eleventh century.

Winsford (CHE, England): Wine's ford (*Wyneford bridge c.* 1334, *Wynsfurth brygge* 1475). This is a name of the same type as Bedford. The ford carried the road from Chester to Middlewich over the River Weaver.

Wisbech (CAM, England): back, or low ridge by River Ouse (*Wisbece*

1086, *Wisbitch* 1588). Place-name studies are rendered more than usually difficult in the Fens by the drastic alterations in river-courses which have taken place since the names arose. The first element of Wisbech may be considered to be either the river-name Ouse or the river-name Wissey; both rivers once flowed to Wisbech. It has not yet been clearly established whether Ouse and Wissey are different names, or are variants of the same river-name. Opinions about the origin of Ouse include a statement that it is Celtic, a statement that it is certainly not Celtic but may be pre-Celtic, and a statement that it is Germanic and derives from the same stem as Wissey.

Wishaw (LAN, Scotland), see *Motherwell*.

Witham (ESX, England): (?) village near a river-bend (*Wit ham c.* 925 Anglo-Saxon Chronicle). The only suggestion available for the first element of this name is that it is Old English *wiht* 'curve, bend'. This suits the topography, as there is a bend in the River Brain immediately south of the town. Place-names containing this element usually have some Old English spellings in *Wiht-* and some Middle English spellings in *Wight-*, however, and as these are not evidenced for Witham the etymology cannot be regarded as certain.

Witney (OXF, England): Witta's island (*Wyttanige* 969). The River Windrush divides into numerous branches here, and the land round Witney is very marshy. The area south of the town, now called The Moors, is referred to as *wittan mor* 'Witta's marsh', in a charter of A.D. 969. The site of the town is a circular raised area surrounded by the 275-foot contour, and this constitutes the 'island' of the place-name.

Woking (SUR, England): Wocc's people (*Wocchingas c.* 712, *Woccingas* 796, *Wokinge* 1154, *Okkyng* 1474, *Woakeing* 1693). This is a name of the same type as Barking GTL.

Wokingham (BRK, England): homestead of Wocc's people (*Wokingeham* 1146, *Wokkyngham* 1284, *Okingham* 1600). This is a name of the same type as Gillingham. The *Woccingas* from whom Wokingham is named are almost certainly the same group which gave rise to the name Woking SUR, about 14 miles east.

Wolstanton (STF, England): Wulfstān's estate (*Wlstanetone* 1086, *Wulstaneston* 1199). This is a name of the same type as Brighton.

Wolverhampton (STF, England): high farm associated with Wulfrūn (*Heantune* 985, *Wolvrenehamptonia c.* 1080, *Wulfrunehanton* 1169). Wolverhampton stands high in relation to the ground west, north, and east of the town. The earliest record of the name is in a charter of A.D. 985 by which King Æthelred gave land here and at Trescott to a lady named Wulfrūn. In A.D. 996 Wulfrūn gave a number of Staffordshire estates to a monastery which she had founded at Wolverhampton. Wulfrūn was the mother of Wulfrīc Spott, the founder of the monastery of Burton-upon-Trent, and it is clear from his will that the family owned an enormous number of estates in the Midlands. Wulfrūn's name was not prefixed to

the place-name until the spellings had become liable to confusion with those for a number of other names, some of which are discussed under Hampton.

Worcester (WOR, England): Roman town of the people called *Weogora* (*Weogorna civitas* 691, *castra Weogernensis* 737, *Weogorna cæstre* 789, *Wigraceaster* 904, *Wirecestre* 1086, *Wircestre* 1350, *Worcetre* 1396, *Worcester alias Wurcestre* 1487). The difficulties presented by this name are very similar to those encountered in the name Leicester. There are a great many Old English spellings; some of these are Latinised, but the series leaves no doubt that the Old English form of Worcester was *Weogernaceaster* or *Weogornaceaster*. Immediately west of Worcester there was an estate called *Weogorenaleage* in a charter of 816. This name means 'wood' or 'clearing of the people called *Weogora*'. One suggestion is that the first element was the genitive of a folk-name formed from a Celtic place-name, the Celtic place-name being related to the river-name Wyre in Lancashire, and to a Gaulish river-name *Vigora*, possibly meaning 'winding river'. Either the Celtic place-name or the folk-name derived from it occurs in Wyre Forest, some 14 miles north-west of Worcester, and in Wyre Piddle, about 8 miles south-east. If all these names are connected, we have to think of a district-name applied to a territory at least 20 miles in length. There are a number of winding rivers in this area, but the larger ones have well-established pre-English names, which seems to preclude any of them being

189

originally called *Weogor*. Possible candidates are the Avon (which besides being the most dramatically winding of them all might have obtained its present Celtic name by a mistaken assumption on the part of the Anglo-Saxons that when the natives said 'the river' they were giving the name of it), or Piddle Brook (which has a name of Germanic origin). But these are both on the southern edge of the area. A full collection of field-names for Worcestershire might lead to the identification of a river formerly called Wyre.

Workington (CMB, England): estate associated with Wyrc (*Wirkynton c.* 1125, *Wirkyngton c.* 1130, *Workington* 1564). This is a name of the same type as Addington GTL. The type is less common in Cumberland and Westmorland than in most parts of England; most of the examples in Cumberland are in the west of the county, between Workington and Rottington.

Worksop (NTT, England): Wyrc's valley (*Warchesoppe, Werchesope* 1086, *Wirkesop* early 12th cent., *Wyrshop* 1340, *Worksoppe alias Worsoppe* 1571). Old English *hop* (discussed under Bacup) is not common in Nottinghamshire, but occurs also in Warsop, about seven miles south of Worksop. Both places are beside rivers, at points where a small side valley opens out of the main river-valley.

Worthing (SSX, England): Weorð's people (*Ordinges* 1086, *Worthing* 1244). This is a name of the same type as Barking. The cluster of *-ingas* names in this part of Sussex is discussed under Lancing.

Wrexham (DEN, Wales): Wryhtel's pasture (*Wristlesham* 1161, *Wrexham* 1186, *Gwregsam* 1291, *Wrightesham* 1294, *Wrechtessham* 1294, *Wryghtlesham* 1316, *Wrexam* 13th cent., *Wrexham treuly caullid Wrightelesham* 1536–9). Old English *wryhta* 'workman' (> pers. name *Wryhtel*) + *hamm* 'enclosure, water-meadow'. In common with other early English names in eastern Flintshire and Denbighshire it was given a Welsh pronunciation and appearance, i.e. *Gwrecsam*. There was also an antiquarian form, cf. *K[aer] Vantell= Gwryxam* 1604–12. As far as is known there is no basis for the form *Caer Fantell*, which is presumably Welsh *caer* 'fort' + *mantell* 'mantle'.

(Yr) Wyddgrug (FLI, Wales), see *Mold*.

Y

Yarmouth (NFK, England): (placc at) the mouth of the River Yare (*Gernemwa* 1086, *Gernemuta Magna* 1254). Yare is a Celtic river-name which appears in Ptolemy's Geography with the spelling *Gariénnos*. It may be related to Welsh *gair* 'word', and have some such meaning as 'babbling river'.

Yeovil (SOM, England): (place on the) River *Gifl* (*Gifle c*. 880 King Alfred's Will, *Givele* 1086). The River Yeo, on which Yeovil is situated, was earlier called *Gifle*. The river (as opposed to the settlement) is referred to by this name in a charter of A.D. 933. The same river-name occurs in the modern form Ivel in Bedfordshire and Huntingdonshire. It is a Celtic name, meaning 'forked river'. The Yeo has several head-streams. Yeovilton SOM and Ilchester DOR are also named from it, but Yeovil may have been the earliest settlement on its course. The modern form of the river-name is probably a fairly recent back-formation from Yeovil, rather than a corruption of *Gifl*.

York (YOE, England): estate of Eburos (*Ebórakon c*. 150 Ptolemy, *Eburacum* 4th cent. Antonine Itinerary, *Eforwicceaster c*. 893, *Eferwic* 10th cent., *Eoforwic c*. 1060, *Jeorc, Jeurc* 13th cent., *York* late 13th cent.). *Eburacum* is a Celtic place-name of a type well evidenced in Britain and in Gaul. Most of these names were formed by the addition of the suffix *-ācon* to a personal name, and mean 'estate of x'. Some have river-names or significant words as a base, however, and it is possible that *Eburacum* means 'yew-tree estate'. The later British form would be something like *Evorōc*. Germanic-speaking people may have become familiar with this in the late fourth or early fifth century. York was from the end of the second century the most important military centre in Roman Britain, and it has been argued convincingly that when Germanic mercenaries were employed at the end of the Roman period to protect Romano-British towns from Picts, Scots, and Saxons, those who were active in the north-east were probably quartered at York. If the English adaptation of *Evorōc* to *Eoforwic* goes back to this early period, it is possible that mercenaries heard the civilian settlement outside the military fort referred to as 'the *vicus*', and that this influenced the development of the second element to *wic*. The first part of the name was doubtless associated with the Old English word *eofor* 'boar'. It is impossible to say how old the English form *Eoforwic* is. Bede and some other relatively early English sources give the Romano-British name, but this is probably due to learned knowledge of classical sources and does not mean that anyone actually spoke of York as *Eburacum* in Bede's day. York was intensely Scandinavianised during the period after 965, when it was the centre, first of a Danish kingdom, and later of a kingdom founded by Norwegians from Ireland. Old English *Eoforwīc* was then adapted to Old Scandinavian *Jórvík*, which became modern York.

Y Waun (DEN, Wales), see *Chirk*.

Acton: oak estate (*Acton* 1181). The GTL example of this name is an outlier. Others are concentrated in the west midland counties, with a few (modern forms Aighton, Aughton) in LNC, YOE, YOW.

Addington: estate associated with a man named Ead(d)a or Æddi (*Eddintone* 1086, *Adingeton* 1203, *Adington* 1247). This type of name is discussed in detail in the *Introduction*, p. 20.

Alperton: estate associated with Ealhbeorht (*Alprintin* 1199). This is a name of the same type as Addington.

Barking: Berica's people (*Berecingum* c. 730 Bede's Ecclesiastical History). The element -*ingas* is here added to a personal name, probably that of a leader (see *Introduction*, p. 16). Barking is some distance from other examples of the same type.

Barnes: the barn (*Berne* 1086, *Bernes* 1222, *La Berne* 1244, *Barnes* 1387). The plural ending is comparatively late (as in Staines) and should be disregarded for the etymology. Other places named from an outstanding barn are Barns NTB and Berne DOR. A spelling of 979 given in reference books is from a forged charter.

Barnet: land cleared by burning (*Barneto* c. 1070, *La Barnette* 1248). The name belongs to several places, some of which (Chipping alias High, East, New, and Friern Barnet) have distinguishing prefixes. Probably Barnet was originally the name of the whole strip of land, about three miles long and two miles broad, over which these settlements extend. It refers to the clearing of woodland by burning the trees, and the group of place-names in -ley to the northwest of Barnet indicates the wooded nature of the area in pre-Conquest times. Some of the prefixes are self-explanatory; Chipping means 'market', and Friern means 'brothers', with reference to the Knights of St John of Jerusalem who owned Friern Barnet.

Battersea: Beadurīc's island (*Badrices ege, Batriceseie* a. 1066, *Batriseye* 1366, *Battersea* 1595, *Batrichsea alias Battersea* 1700). Chertsey SUR and Witney OXF are similar names. The pre-Conquest forms for Battersea are either from dubious charters or from a set of boundaries of Battersea and Wandsworth; none of these can be precisely dated.

Beckenham: Beohha's village (the phrases *Biohhahema mearc* and *Beohhahammes gemæru* 'the boundary of Beckenham', occur in charters of

193

862 and 973). This is a name of the same type as Amersham.

Bermondsey: Beornmund's island (*Vermundesei c.* 712, *Bermundesye* 1086, *Bermonsey* 1450, *Barmesey* 1450, *Barmsey* 1617). This is a name of the same type as Battersea and Chertsey; all three refer to sites on marshy land beside the Thames. *Beremundeseye* developed naturally to *Barmsey*, but the longer form was restored in modern times, probably because people became aware of the spellings in medieval records.

Bethnal Green: the village-green at Blīða's river-meadow (*Blithehale* 13th cent., *Blithenhale* 1341, *Blethenale-grene* 1443, *Bednalgrene* 1568, *Beth-nall alias Bednall grene* 1576). Old English *halh* may mean 'meadow' here, as suggested under Northolt. The personal name is derived from the same stem as the river-name discussed under Blythe NTB, and it could be a river-name if there was formerly a stream here.

Bexley: box wood (*Byxlea* 814). This is the same name as Bexhill SSX.

Brentford: ford over the River Brent (*Bregunt ford* 705, *Bregentforda* 781). Brent is a Celtic name meaning 'holy'. The ford must have been where the Roman road to Silchester and Bath crosses the stream, just above its junction with the Thames.

Bromley: forest-clearing where broom grows (*Bromleag* 862). There are other examples of this name in Essex, Hertfordshire, and Stafford-shire.

Camberwell: unexplained (*Cambre-welle* 1086, *Camerwella* 1175). The final element is *welle*, perhaps in the sense 'spring', rather than 'stream.' The first element is found also in Camerton CMB and YOE, but no satisfactory suggestion has been made about it. The form was probably *camer-*, with *-b-* developing as in *cucumber*, earlier *cucumer*.

Carshalton: farm by the river-source, noted for watercress (*Aultone* 1086, *Cresaulton* 1235, *Kersalton* 1239, *Carshalton* 1323). The original name, Old English *ǣwiell-tūn*, modern Alton, occurs in Dorset, Hampshire, and Wiltshire. The existence of four places with this name in the southern part of the country probably led to confusion, and a distinguishing pre-fix was therefore felt to be desirable. Watercress was produced at Car-shalton in the thirteenth century, when a grant of property there mentions a *kersenaria*, i.e. a water-cress-bed, and there are still water-cress-beds by the River Wandle, which rises at Carshalton. Sometimes other early spellings are quoted but these are either from spurious charters, or wrongly identified with this place.

Cheam: (?) village near the tree-stumps (*Cegham* 967, *Ceiham* 1086, *Cheiham* 1199, *Cheyme* 1569). The word assumed to be the first element is only on record in this place-name, though cognates can be found for it in Scandinavian languages; the two earliest spellings usually quoted are from forged charters.

Chelsea: (?) landing-place for chalk or limestone (*Celchyth* 789, *Caelic-hyth* 801, *Cealchithe c.* 1073, *Chelc-hede* 1086, *Chelchee* 1214, *Chelchuthe* 1300, *Chilchith* 1319, *Chelceheyth* 1519, *Chelshith* 1535, *Chelseye* 1523, *Chelsyth alais Chelsey* 1556). The second element is *hȳð* as in Erith. The first may be 'chalk,' but this necessitates a rather forced etymology and conflicts with the early spelling *Caelichyth* The only alternative suggestion is *cælic*, 'cup, chalice', which is not otherwise noted in place-names, but which might have had a topographical use. In Chelsea, Putney and Stepney *-hithe* has become *-ea*, *-ey*, perhaps partly by assimilation to names like Battersea.

Chingford: shingle ford (*Cingefort* 1086, *Chingelford c.* 1243, *Shingelford* 1346, *Shingford* 1541, *Chengeford* 1544). The ford was probably a crossing-place on the river Lea. The soil is gravelly.

Chislehurst: gravelly wooded hill (*Cyselhyrst* 973). The one-inch map shows a spot height of 339 near Chislehurst Church, which is about at the centre of a hill marked by the 300-foot contour.

Chiswick: cheese farm (*Ceswican c.* 1000, *Chesewic* 1181, *Chiswyk* 1537, *Cheeswick* 1638). This is a fairly common name, ocurring also in the modern forms Cheswick, Keswick. Old English *wīc* (discussed under Aldridge STF) is frequently compounded with words for farm produce; Butterwick is another fairly common example.

Coulsdon: Cūðrǣd's hill (*Cudredesdune* 967, *Cuðredesdune* 1062, *Colesdone* 1086, *Cullesdona c.* 1115, *Coulesdon* 1346). This is a name of the same type as Basildon, but in this case the *dūn* is a hill-spur south of the town. The development from *Cuðredesdune* to *Culesdona* is due to Norman influence. A shortened form, such as *Curesdune*, was probably

current at the time of the Norman Conquest, and the Norman tendency to confuse *-r-* and *-l-* transformed this to *Culesdone*.

Croydon: (?) saffron valley (*Crogedene* 809, *Croindene c.* 980, 1086, *Cruendon* 1242, *Croydene* 1261). Croydon is usually considered to derive from *denu* 'valley' (confused in this instance with *dūn* 'hill') and *croh*. The word *croh* is recorded in Anglo-Saxon texts dealing with plants and medicine, and is derived from Latin *crocus*. Some of the spellings for Croydon have *-n-* in the first element, which indicates an alternative form, perhaps derived from an adjective *crogen* 'growing with saffron', a type of formation which is common with tree and plant names. For the problems arising from this etymology see *Introduction*, p. 21.

There are several other place-names which may contain *croh*, one of them being Crowhurst in Sussex which is about 10 miles from Croydon. Croham Farm and Crohamhurst in the parish of Croydon, however, can be shown from early spellings such as *Crawehum* (1225) to have *crāwe* 'crow', as first element.

The 'valley' of Croydon is that of the River Wandle.

Dagenham: Dæcca's village (*Dæccanham* in a charter purporting to date from the late seventh century, which is a forgery, but which may contain place-name spellings copied from genuine Anglo-Saxon charters, *Dakeham* 1194, *Dakenham* 1261, *Daginham* 1262, *Dagenham* 1274). This is a name of the same type as Amersham.

195

Deptford: deep ford (*Depeforde* 1293). There was a deep ford over the river Ravensbourne, which was superseded by the bridge. The same name occurs in Wiltshire, and in that instance also the -*t*- is a late development. In Deptford GTL it occurs from the fifteenth century, in Deptford WLT from the sixteenth.

Dulwich: marshy meadow where dill grows (*Dilwihs* 967, *Dilewisse c.* 1211, *Est Dilewissh* 1340, *West Dilwysh* 1344, *Suthdilewysshe* 1354, *Dulwich* 1530). The plant has a medicinal use. The final element is Old English *wisce*, well-evidenced in place-names, but not common.

Ealing: Gilla's people (*Gillingas c.* 698, *Ilingis c.* 1127, *Gilling* 1243, *Yelyng* 1512, *Elyng* 1553, *Ealing alias Yealing* 1622). This is a name of the same type as Barking GTL.

Edgware: Ecgi's weir (*Ægces wer c.* 975, *Eggeswera* 1168, *Heggwere* 1202, *Edgeware* 1495). Old English *wer* also meant 'a fishing-enclosure in a river'. The earliest reference to Edgware occurs in a set of boundaries, and this enables the precise position of the weir or fishing-enclosure to be ascertained. It was where Watling Street crosses the Edgware Brook.

Edmonton: Ēadhelm's estate (*Adelmetone* 1086, *Edelmintone* 1211, *Edelmeston* 1214, *Edmenton* 1369, *Edelmeton alias Edmonton* 1464). This is a name of the same type as Alfreton DRB, but there seem to have been variant forms with an inflected personal name (as in Brighton SSX) and with -*ingtūn* (as in Addington GTL).

Eltham: (?) swan meadow (*Elteham, Alteham* 1086). This may be a shortened form of the compound which has become Elvetham HMP, for which there is an Old English spelling *ylfethamm*, certainly meaning 'swan meadow'. Alternatively the spellings available for Eltham may represent an Old English *Eltan hām*, 'Elta's village', which would be a name of the same type as Amersham BUC.

Enfield: Ēana's open land (*Enefelde* 1086). In this name, as in Cuckfield, *feld* refers to an open space in predominantly wooded country.

Erith: (?) gravelly landing-place (*Earhyð c.* 960). Erith is on the south bank of the Thames. Old English *ēar* is an ancient word only recorded once with the general meaning 'earth, ground', the reference being to a corpse lying in the earth. It has cognates with more precise meanings in Scandinavian languages, including Swedish *ör* 'gravel', and two Old Norse words *aurr* 'gravel, loam', and *eyrr* 'sandbank'. Earith HNT, on the bank of the River Ouse, has the same derivation as Erith GTL. Apart from these two names the element has only been noted in Yarmouth IOW, where 'muddy' seems the appropriate meaning. Only close acquaintance with the river-bank at Erith could enable a firm etymology to be given.

Finchley: forest-clearing frequented by finches (*Finchelee c.* 1208). Settlements in this area were probably made by clearing woodland, see Barnet GTL.

Finsbury: Fin's manor-house (*Vinisbire* 1231, *Finesbire* 1235). Finsbury seems likely to be a late Old English name, and 'manor-house' is probably a fair translation of *burh* (discussed under Aylesbury BUC).

Fulham: Fulla's land in a river-bend (*Fulanham c.* 705, *Fullanhamme c.* 900 Anglo-Saxon Chronicle). This type of name is discussed under Evesham WOR. Twickenham is another example on the River Thames.

Gidea Park: (?) the Folly (*La Gidiehall'* 1258, *Guydie hall parke* 1668). It is thought that the first element of this name is Old English *gydig* 'mad, insane, giddy', referring to a foolish building venture, in somewhat the same way as French *folie* in the common minor name The Folly. Another possibility is that *gydig* was a stream-name, referring to the small stream west of Gidea Park. There is another Giddy Hall in Essex (in Little Clacton) and a Giddeahall in Wiltshire (in Yatton Keynell), but there are no spellings for these earlier than the sixteenth and eighteenth centuries respectively, and they are probably named after the *Gidiehall'* which has become Gidea Park.

Goodmayes: (*Goodmayes* 1456). This is a name of relatively late origin, derived from a surname. John *Godemay* paid tax in Ilford in 1319.

Greenford: green ford (*grenan forda* 845, *Greneforde* 1066, *Greneford Magna* 1254). The name presumably refers to a crossing-place on the River Brent, but it was not part of a known ancient road, like Brentford. *Magna* is for distinction from *Parva Greneford*, the old name of Perivale.

Greenwich: green port (*Grenewic* 964, *Grenawic* 1013 Anglo-Saxon Chronicle). The place is referred to in the Anglo-Saxon Chronicle because a Danish army camped there for several years. The selection of this site for a military camp may indicate that it was an established trading place, with facilities for landing goods from the river. See Ipswich, Norwich, Sandwich, Woolwich, for other instances of *wīc* in the sense 'harbour, port'.

Hackney: Haca's island (*Hakeneia* 1198). This is a name of the same type as Battersea and Bermondsey GTL.

Ham, East and West: river-meadow (*Hamme* 958). This may be a relatively late instance of Old English *hamm* (discussed under Buckingham). The earlier sense 'land in a river-bend' is not strikingly appropriate here.

Hammersmith: hammer smithy (*Hamersmythe* 1294). Old English *smiðõe*, 'metal-workers' shop' is fairly well-evidenced in place-names see Smethwick STF for names of similar significance.

Hampstead: homestead (*Hamstede* 959, *Hamstede* 978). This is the compound noun which occurs with a defining element in Berkhamsted and Hemel Hempstead.

Hampton: farm near a bend in a river (*Hamntone* 1086). The first element of this name is *hamm*, discussed under Buckingham. Hampton is to the west of a great loop of the Thames, which encloses Hampton Court and Wick. The bends of the river to the north of Hampton

197

have given rise to the names Ham and Twickenham.

The name Hampton does not always derive from *hamm-tūn*. In many instances it goes back to *hāmtūn*, a compound term for a type of settlement (see Littlehampton), or *hēan tūne* 'high farm' (see Wolverhampton).

Harlington: estate associated with Hygered (*Hygereding tun* 831, *Herdintone* 1086, *Herlyngdon* 1362, *Herlyngton alias Herdyngton* 1564). This is a name of the same type as Addington. Development to Hardington would have been more normal. There is another instance of interchange of *d* and *l* in this part of the country, in the name Charlton, in Sunbury, which was *Chardynton* in 1294, *Charlyngton* in 1539.

Harold Wood: Harold's wood (*Horalds Wood c.* 1237). This place is believed to have been named from Earl Harold, who was King of England before his defeat at the Battle of Hastings in 1066. The nearby manor of Havering belonged to Earl Harold before the Conquest.

Harrow-on-the-Hill: heathen temple (*Gumeninga hergae* 767, *æt Hearge* 825, *Harghe* 1299, *Harowe* 1369, *Harowe atte Hille* 1398, *Harowe on the Hill* 1426). This is one of a class of place-names, numbering between 40 and 50, which refer to the heathen practices of the Anglo-Saxons during the first two centuries of their occupation of this country, and which constitute the main evidence for any study of Anglo-Saxon paganism. There were two Old English words for a heathen temple, one being *hearg*, from which Harrow

is derived, and the other *wēoh*, which occurs in at least 15 names including Wye KNT, Weoley near Birmingham, and Weedon Beck and Lois NTP. Other place-names in this category contain the names of heathen gods, and these are discussed under Wednesbury.

The prominent hill at Harrow is the obvious site of the heathen temple, which (since it is called *Gumeninga hergae* in 767) was apparently the sanctuary of a group of people known as the *Gumeningas*, a name of the type discussed under Barking. It was probably the most impressive site of Germanic heathen worship in England. The hill is today crowned by a Christian church, the earliest stonework of which belongs to the church consecrated by St Anselm in 1094. This may be the successor of a church of the early seventh century, which would be the direct successor of the heathen temple. Pope Gregory the Great, in 601, advised the Roman missionaries who were converting south-east England not to destroy heathen sanctuaries but to convert them into Christian churches 'in order that the people may the more familiarly resort to the places to which they have been accustomed'.

Harrow Weald: woodland near Harrow (*Weldewode, Welde* 1282, *Waldis in Harwes* 1303, *Harewewelde* 1388, *Harrow Weelde* 1553). Old English *wald* originally meant 'wood', and usually has this meaning in place-names. Because a number of great forests with names containing this word (such as those of the Weald in Kent and the Cotswolds) were on high ground which was gradually cleared of trees, the word developed new meanings such as 'hill, down, open country, high moorland'. The Anglian form was *wald*, which gives -wold in modern names. The Saxon and Kentish form was *weald*, which causes many of the southern names containing it to end in -weald or -wield.

Hatch End: district by the gate (*le Hacchehend* 1448). The gate may have belonged to Pinner Park.

Hayes: brushwood (*linga hæse* 793, *Hæse* 831, *Hesa* 1086, *Heys* 1498, *Hayes* 1524, *Heese alias Hayes* 1643). This is derived from Old English *hǣs*, a somewhat rare term, not recorded except in place-names, but identified from cognates in other Germanic languages. The mysterious prefix *linga* in the reference of 793 has never been explained.

Hendon: (place) at the high hill (*Heandun c.* 975). The old village of Hendon clustered round the church of St. Mary, which stands on a prominent hill, visible for many miles from the west and south-west.

Hillingdon: Hilda's hill (*Hildendune c.* 1080, *Hillendone* 1086, *Hyldedon* 1236, *Hylingdon* 1274). The personal name was probably masculine. The place is encircled by the 150-foot contour, with lower ground all round.

Holborn: stream in the hollow (*Holeburne* 1086, *Howeborne* 1551, *Holbourne* 1567). The depression is still visible in part of the course of Farringdon Road. The spelling of 1551 shows that the loss of -*l*- represented in the modern pronunciation goes back to the sixteenth century.

Loss of -*l*- before a consonant occurred in a number of words in the early modern period.

Hook: hook-shaped hill (*Hoke* 1227). Only a close study of local topography could reveal the precise meaning of this name. The word *hōc* is very common in Surrey place-names.

Hornchurch: church with horn-like gables (*Monasterium Cornutum* 1222, *Hornechurch* 1233, *Hornedechirche* 1291). The figure of a bull's head with horns, fixed to the eastern gable of the church, does not appear to be very ancient, and this and the Prior's seal of 1385, which has a horned bull's head, probably only reflect local knowledge of the meaning of the name.

Hornsey: (?) enclosure in the grey wood (*Haringeie* 1201, *Haringesheye* 1243, *Harynsey* 1401, *Harnesey* 1524, *Haryngey otherwise Harnesey* 1557, *Hornsey* 1564). Harringay and Hornsey are different developments of the same name. The older form *Harringay* was applied to the manor-house until it was demolished *c.* 1870; specialised use for a manor-house is often the case when an older form of a name survives along with a more developed form. The original base appears to have been Old English *Haring-gehæg* with the same second element as Bushey, and a first element which could be either an uninflected personal name or a name for a wood derived from *hār*, 'grey'. The -*s*- of such spellings as *Haringesheye* may be intrusive or may indicate an alternative form *Hǣringes-gehæg*, in which the first element was in the genitive. *Haringesheye* developed regularly to Hornsey; Harringay represents the uninflected form.

Hounslow: (?) the hound's tumulus (*Hundeslawe* 1217, *Houndeslowe* 1341, *Hounslawe* 1406). The same name occurs in Berkshire in charter boundaries of the mid-tenth century, which refer to two Bronze Age tumuli south of White Horse Hill as *hundes hlæwe* and *hafeces hlæwe* ('hawk's tumulus'). This suggests that such names could be applied to prehistoric barrows in some manner, perhaps jocular, which is now difficult to understand. An alternative interpretation of Hounslow would take *Hund* to be a man's name, and the *hlāw* to be his burial-mound. Names of this type are known. Taplow BUC means 'Tæppa's tumulus', and refers to a barrow in the old churchyard from which were recovered the rich grave goods of a seventh-century Saxon prince.

Ickenham: Tica's village (*Ticheham* 1086, *Tikenham* 1203, *Ikeham* 1203, *Ikenham* 1236, *Iknam* 1452, *Icknam* 1737). This is a name of the same type as Amersham. The loss of initial *T-* is due to confusion with the final *-t* of *at*, see Elstree.

Ilford: ford through the River Hyle (*Ilefort* 1086, *Hyleford* 1300). The lower stretch of the River Roding, in the neighbourhood of Loughton and Ilford, was called *Hile* in 958, *Hyle* c. 1250, *Iuell* 1577. This is a Celtic river-name which means 'trickling stream'. It occurs also in Ilam STF. The ford was where the Roman road to Chelmsford (now A12) crossed the river.

Isleworth: Gīslhere's enclosure (*Gislheresuuyrth* '677' charter granting lands to the nunnery of Barking, *Gistelesworde* 1086, *Istleworth* 1231, *Thistelworth* 1313, *Isleworth vulgo Thistleworth* 1675). The earliest spelling for this name is from a forged charter, but the spellings of the place-names in it, particularly this one, show that the forger had a very ancient document from which to copy them. The name was transformed before the date of the Domesday Survey by the loss of *r* and the development of *t* between *s* and *l*. The occasional form *Thistelworth* is probably due to association with the word *thistle*.

Islington: Gīsla's hill (*Gislandune* c. 1000, *Iseldone* 1086, *Islyngton* 1464, *Iseldon otherwise Islyngton* 1554). The name has been associated with the *-ingtūn* type (see Addington GTL), but the original second element was *dūn*, 'hill'. Nearby Highbury is also named from the elevation. The loss of *G-* is paralleled in Isleworth, which contains a related personal name.

Kensington: estate associated with Cynesige (*Chenesitun* 1086, *Kensinton* 1221, *Kensington* 1235). This is a name of the same type as Addington GTL.

Kenton: farm associated with Cœna (*Keninton* 1232, *Kenyngton* 1307). This is a name of the same type as Addington.

Keston: Cyssi's stone (the boundary of the estate is referred to in charters granting land at Bromley as *Cystaninga mearc* 'boundary of the people of Keston', in 862, *Cysse stanes* *gemæro* 'boundary of Keston', in 973). This is a name of the same type as Boston.

Kingston-upon-Thames: royal estate (*Cyninges tun* 838, *Kyngeston super Tamisiam* 1321). There was a royal residence at Kingston in the Anglo-Saxon period. King Æthelstan was crowned here in 925, and King Æthelred in 979.

Lambeth: landing-place for lambs (*Lambhyð* 1041 Anglo-Saxon Chronicle, *Lambeth* 1255). Rotherhithe is a similar compound, with *hyð* and *hrȳðer* 'cattle'. The names refer to traffic in animals on the River Thames.

Lewisham: Lēofsa's village (*Levesham* 1086). This is a name of the same type as Amersham BUC. Earlier references are contained in the bounds of Bromley in Anglo-Saxon charters; in one of these, dated 862, occurs the phrase *Liofshema mearc*, 'the boundary of the people of Lewisham'.

Leyton: farm on the River Lea (*Lugetune c.* 1050, *Leyton* 1226). See Luton BDF, which is an identical place-name higher up the same river. The places are 28 miles apart, and this and the different development must have prevented confusion between them.

Merton: farm by the pool (*Meretone* 1086, *Mareton* 1176, *Martin* 1605, *Mirton alias Marten* 1679). The same name occurs in Devon, Norfolk and Oxfordshire. This place is sometimes identified with *Merantun*, mentioned in the Anglo-Saxon Chronicle under the year 786, but this identification is very doubtful.

Mitcham: large village (*Michelham* 1086, *Michham* 1178). This settlement was presumably larger than Clapham and Streatham, which are the other settlements with names in -*hām* in the immediate vicinity.

Morden: hill in the fens (*Mordone* 1086). The same name occurs in Cambridgeshire and Dorset, and (in the modern form Mordon) in Durham. The translation 'hill in the fens' seems more satisfactory than 'marshy hill'. Morden occupies a sort of promontory, overlooking lower ground to the north, west, and south.

Mottingham: village of the family or followers of Mōda (*Modingeham* 1044). This is the same type of name as Gillingham KNT. The bounds of Bromley mentioned under Lewisham refer to *Modingahema mearc*, 'boundary of the people of Mottingham'.

New Malden: hill marked by a cross (*Meldone* 1086, *Maldon* 1225). This is another example of the name discussed under Maldon ESX.

Northolt: (?) north river-meadows (*Norðhealum c.* 960, *Northala* 1086, *Northold* 1593, *Northall alias Northolt* 1631). The second element is the plural of *halh*, possibly used in the sense 'river-meadow' (discussed under Bramhall), though the use of the word in that sense is most commonly found in the north of England. North- is by contrast to Southall. The corruption to -holt is similar to that in Arnold.

Northwood: north wood (*Northwode* 1435). This was originally the name of a wood situated to the north of

201

Ruislip. The present town dates mainly from the construction of the railway about 1880.

Orpington: estate associated with Orped (*Orpedingtune* 1032, *Orpinton* 1086). This is a name of the same type as Addington.

Paddington: estate associated with Padda (*Padington c.* 1050). This is a name of the same type as Addington GTL.

Penge: chief wood (*Penceat* 1067, *Pange* 1204, *Penge* 1206, *Pengewode* 1472). This is a Celtic name; other evidence for the survival of Celtic speech south of London during the period of the Anglo-Saxon settlement is discussed under Caterham SUR and Croydon GTL. British **penno-*, 'head, end', can have various meanings in place-names, cf. Penrith CMB. Pencoyd HRE contains the same elements as Penge, but a translation '(place at) the end of the wood' may be more appropriate there. Penge was originally a wood which provided swine pasture for the manor of Battersea, so 'chief wood' seems more satisfactory.

Pinner: bank resembling a pin (*Pinnora* 1232). The second element is *ōra*, discussed under Bognor SSX. Nower Hill in Pinner means 'at the bank', but the original *pinn-ōra* is perhaps more likely to have been the curiously shaped ridge on which Pinner Park stands. The Pinn River is a 'back-formation'.

Poplar: (place at) the poplar tree (*Popler* 1327). The word *poplar* came into English from French, so this

must be a name of post-Conquest origin.

Putney: Putta's landing-place (*Putelei* 1086, *Puttenhuthe* 1279, *Putneth* 1474, *Putney alias Puttenheath* 1639). This development of *hȳð* is discussed under Chelsea GTL.

Richmond-upon-Thames: when Henry VII rebuilt the palace after a fire in 1501 he called it Richmond after his earldom of Richmond in Yorkshire. The earlier name was *Shene* (*Sceon c.* 950, *Shene otherwise called Richemount* 1502). This is the plural of an Old English word *scēo* 'shelter'.

Romford: (?) wide ford (*Romfort*, 1177, *Rumford* 1199). An element *rūm* occurs in a number of names, including Rumworth LNC, Runcorn CHE, Rumburgh SFK. It is probably the Old English adjective *rūm* 'spacious', but some doubt arises from the absence of spellings with *Rome-* or *Rume-*, in which the medial *-e-* would represent the case ending of *rūman*, the oblique form of the adjective. If the first element is in fact the adjective, it appears to be used in an uninflected form. Alternatively, the names could contain the noun *rūm* 'room, space', possibly in an unrecorded sense 'clearing'. Romford is on the Roman road from London to Colchester. A stretch of the River Beam has been re-named Rom from the town-name.

Ruislip: (?) rushy place where the River Pin could be jumped across (*Rislepe* 1086, *Ruslep* 1227, *Reslepe* 1328, *Ruysshlep* 1341, *Ryselypp* 1530, *Ruislip* 1597). There seems little doubt from the early spellings that the final element of Ruislip is Old English *hlȳp* 'leap', although some authorities prefer *slǣp* 'slippery place'. Other names which certainly contain *hlȳp* are Birdlip GLO, Hartlip KNT, Hindlip WOR, Clerkenleap WOR, and in all of these the first element refers to a creature or a person presumably seen frequenting a place where an obstacle could be crossed by leaping. Ruislip is out of line with these as regards the first element, but the suggested compound of *rysc* 'rush', and *hlȳp* 'leaping-place', is not unreasonable.

Shoreditch: the ditch of the bank (*Soreditch c.* 1148, *Soresdic* 1183, *Schoredich* 1236). The nature of both the bank and the ditch is unknown. The first element cannot be the shore of the Thames (as has been suggested), unless the place-name refers to the northern end of a very long ditch. Old English **scor(a)* can refer to a steep slope, as well as to the seashore or the bank of a river.

Sidcup: seat-shaped hill (*Cetecopp'* 1254, *Setecoppe* 1301, *Sidycope* 1407). There is another Sidcup in Lincolnshire and the name occurs as a field-name elsewhere. The material points to an Old English compound *sete-coppe*, parallel to Old Norse *set-berg* 'flat-topped hill', which is the source of Sadberge DRH, Sedbergh YOW, and Sedbury YON. A similar idea is expressed by the Celtic names discussed under Caterham. The ground slopes away on all sides of Sidcup High Street.

Southall: (?) south river-meadows (*Suhaull'* 1198, *Sudhale* 1204, *Southall* 1415, *Southold* 1578, *Southolt* 1710).

This name is the counterpart of Northolt, and the problems associated with it are discussed under that name.

Southwark: southern defensive work (*Sudwerca* 1086, *Suðgeweorke c.* 1100 Anglo-Saxon Chronicle). Old English (*ge*)*weorc* (discussed under Newark NTT) means 'fort' here. The place was earlier called *Suþriganaweorc*, 'fort of the men of Surrey', which occurs in an early tenth-century list of places where earthworks had been made as centres for the defence of the kingdom of Wessex against the Danes. The later name, *Suðgeweorc*, may be a shortened version, or it may be a remodelled name referring to the position south of London Bridge. The name 'The Borough' for Southwark goes back at least to 1677; *borough* is sometimes used to denote the suburbs of a city.

Stanmore: stony pool (*Stanmere* 1086, *Standemore* 1562, *Stanmore* 1574). There are still pools here, and there are outcrops of gravel on the clay soil which would provide a stony bottom.

Stepney: Stybba's landing-place (*Stybbanhyþe c.* 1000, *Stibenhede* 1086, *Stepenhithe* 1370, *Stebunheth alias Stepneie* 1591). This name is an exact parallel to Putney GTL.

Stoke Newington: new farm at the tree-stumps (*Neutone* 1086, *Neweton Stoken, Stokneweton* 1274, *Stokenewington* 1535). This is the very common place-name discussed under Newton Abbot DEV. *stoccen*, 'of the stocks', was prefixed to distinguish the main settlement from *Neweton Barrewe*, an earlier name of Highbury.

203

Stratford: ford on a Roman road (*Stratford* 1177, *Stratford atte Bowe* 1279). See Stratford WAR, Stretford LNC. The ford was where the Roman road to Colchester crossed the various branches of the River Lea. Later a bridge was built which was called *Bowe* from its arched shape.

Streatham: village by the Roman road (*Estreham* 1086, *Streteham* 1247). The first element is *strǣt*, discussed under Stratford WAR. The Roman road ran from London to Brighton, and the section from Streatham to Old Croydon is closely followed by the A23. 'Pre-Conquest' forms for Streatham given in reference books are from forged charters.

Surbiton: south grange (*Suberton* 1179, *Surbeton* 1263, *Surbiton* 1597). The place was named in distinction to Norbiton, 'north grange', on the other side of the Hogsmill River. Both places were presumably grange farms of the royal manor of Kingston. The second element of both names is Old English *beretūn*, literally 'barley farm', which is a term of similar meaning to *berewīc*, discussed under Berwick.

Sutton: south farm (*Sudtone* 1086, *Sutton* 1164, *Suthtona* 1174). Names in which *tūn* is qualified by an adjective of direction (i.e. *ēast, norð, sūð, west*) are very common in England. It is sometimes easy to locate the settlement (presumably either earlier or more important) in relation to which such places are named, but the answer is not always obvious. This Sutton is thought to be named in relation to Carshalton.

Teddington: estate associated with Tuda (*Tudintun* 969, *Tudingtune c.* 1000, *Todinton* 1274, *Tudington* 1274, *Tedinton* 1294, *Tedyngton* 1428). The early spellings which certainly refer to this place suggest that it is a name of the same type as Addington. An Anglo-Saxon will of about 970 mentions a place called *Tudincgatun*. If this were certainly Teddington the etymology would be less simple, but the identification is far from certain. The vowel-change from -*u*- to -*e*- is due to its position between *t* and *d*.

Tottenham: Totta's village (*Toteham* 1086, *Tottenham* 1254). This is a name of the same type as Amersham BUC.

Twickenham: Twicca's land in a river-bend (*Tuican hom, Tuiccanham* 704, *Tuicanham, Tuicanhamme* 793, *Twikenham* 1291, *Twicknem* 1651). The final element is *hamm* (discussed under Buckingham and Hampton), referring to the position of this settlement in a loop of the River Thames. The place was sometimes called *Twitnam* or *Twittenham* in the seventeenth and eighteenth centuries.

Upminster: higher minster (*Upmynstre* 1062). Old English *mynster* often refers to a church served by several clergy, rather than to a monastery. It is difficult from the Ordnance Survey map to see the relevance of the prefix *upp*, which normally means 'higher up than something else'. A similar name to Upminster is Upchurch KNT, but there the church is so situated that its spire was accounted a sea-mark. The town of Upminster does not rise much above 60 feet, and there is appreciably higher ground to the north and east. Perhaps the site is more impressive in reality than the contours on the map suggest.

Uxbridge: bridge of the tribe called Wixan (*Oxebruge c.* 1145, *Wixebrug' c.* 1145, *Uxebrigg* 1200, *Woxebruge* 1219, *Wyxebrigge* 1220, *Woxenbrugge alias Uxbridge* 1398, *Wooxbryge* 1547). In the list of regions in the eighth-century document known as the Tribal Hidage, the territory of the people called *Spalde* (see Spalding) is preceded by areas called *East wixna* (*land*) and *West wixna* (*land*). These regions can hardly be in Middlesex, but it is generally assumed that detached portions of the people called *Wixan* settled in Middlesex, giving rise to the names Uxbridge and Uxendon. Whitsun Brook in Flyford Flavell, Worcestershire, is *Wixenabroc* in a set of Old English boundaries, and this is clearly a reference to another detached portion of the *Wixan*. The Anglo-Saxons were acutely aware of tribal identity, irrespective of whether the tribe was settled in a compact block or had split into scattered units. There is good evidence in place-names that if a small group broke away from the main body their tribal origin was recognised and remembered by their new neighbours. To take one example, Exton in Hampshire is *Eastseaxnatun* in a charter of 940; this means 'farm of the East Saxons', and presumably refers to people from Essex who had moved to Hampshire.

Wallington: farm of the Britons (*Waletona juxta Mordon c.* 1080, *Wallyngton* 1377, *Wallington alias Waleton* 1713). The first element is *wala*, genitive plural of *walh*, which is discussed under Wallasey. This compound normally develops into Walton, and in the present instance the substitution of Wallington is comparatively modern. The name Walton does not always have this origin. It can derive from *weald-tūn* 'farm in a wood', *wealltūn* 'farm by a wall', or (in Anglian territory) *wælletūn* 'farm by a spring'. In many instances no certainty is possible, but it is usually considered that in Saxon territory a substantial proportion of Middle English spellings with *Wale-* (as opposed to *Wal-*) indicates Old English *w(e)alatūn* 'farm of the Britons'. Evidence for the coexistence of English and Celtic speakers in this area is discussed in the Introduction, p. 22.

Walthamstow: (?) guest-house (*Wilcumestowe c.* 1075, *Welcomstowe c.* 1115, *Walcumstowe* 1398, *Walthamstowe* 1446). The second element is *stōw* (discussed under Bristol), possibly in the sense 'place where people assemble'. The first element may be Old English *wilcume*, 'a welcome person or thing'. An alternative etymology is 'religious foundation of a woman named Wilcume'. Walthamstow had connections with Waltham Abbey, and the name Waltham has influenced its development.

Wandsworth: Wændel's enclosure (*wendles wurðe a.* 1066, *Wendleswurthe* 1067, *Wandesorde*, *Wandelesorde* 1086, *Wanneswor th* 1393, *Wandlesworth vulgo Wunsworth* 1675). The personal name is discussed under Wellingborough NTP.

205

Wanstead: place by the hill called The Wen (*Wænstede c.* 1055). The first element is probably Old English *wænn*, 'tumour', used in a topographical sense. Cf. the etymology suggested for Pudsey yow. Old English *stede* is discussed under Ashstead SUR.

Wembley: Wemba's forest-clearing (*Wemba lea* 825, *Wembanlea* 10th cent., *Wemlee* 1387, *Wembley* 1535, *Wymeley alias Wemley* 1562). This is a name of the same type as Barnsley. Names containing *lēah* are comparatively rare in Middlesex.

West Drayton: (?) estate where sledges are used (*Draitone* 1086, *Westdrayton* 1465). The place-name element *dræg* is very common in the names Draycot or Draycote and Drayton or Dreyton. The word is not on independent record in Old English, and its meaning is uncertain. It is related to *dragan* 'to draw, to drag', and the two main senses which have been suggested are 'portage' (i.e. 'place where boats are dragged overland') and 'dray, sled'. West Drayton is situated in marshy ground by the River Colne, and it is reasonable to suggest that sledges were used for some work on the manor. *West* is for distinction from Drayton in Ealing.

West Wickham: village associated with an earlier Romano-British settlement (*Wichamm* 973, *Wicheham* 1086, *Westwycham* 1284). A recent study of all the known place-names derived from Old English *wīchām* (numbering about 30) has shown that all except four of them are situated on or not more than a mile from a Roman road, and that over half of

them are on the same site as, or adjacent to, a known Romano-British habitation site. The name only occurs in parts of the country affected by the earliest phases of the Anglo-Saxon settlement. This distribution suggests that the compound *wīchām* may have been in use among Germanic mercenaries employed in Britain at the end of the Roman period, and that *wīc* in this name may have a direct reference to the *vici* (the smallest administrative units) of Roman Britain. The word *wīc* is a loan-word in the Germanic languages from Latin *vicus*. It was later employed as one of many Old English words for a settlement, and it developed a variety of meanings, some of which are discussed under Aldridge, Greenwich, and Nantwich. The direct connection with Roman *vici* is only likely in the compound *wīchām* and in some of the rather rare names (apart from those formed from this compound) in which *wīc* is used as a first element. This last point is discussed under Wickford. Other evidence for the coexistence in the West Wickham–Croydon area of Anglo-Saxons and earlier inhabitants is discussed under Croydon. *West* is for distinction from East Wickham in Bexley.

Westminster: west monastery (*Westmynster c.* 975); so named because it lay to the west of London. The Anglo-Saxon charters (some forged and some genuine) which refer to the monastery say that the site was called *Thorney*, 'island overgrown with thorn-bushes'. This name referred to an island formed by two branches of the Tyburn at its outfall into the Thames. It has been commemorated in Thorney Street, which dates from 1931.

Willesden: hill with a spring (*Wellesdone* 1086, *Wilesdune* 1185, *Wullesdon* 1248, *Willesden* 1290, 1535, *Wylsdon* 1563, *Willesdon alias Wilsdon* 1658). The inferior spelling *Willesden* was adopted *c.* 1840 by the London and Birmingham railway, and so ousted *Wilsdon*, which had been usual until then.

Wimbledon: Wynnman's hill (*Wunemannedune c.* 950, *Wimeldon* 1202, *Wimbeldon* 1211). Wimbledon Common occupies a large raised area. It is generally agreed that the first element of Wimbledon is an uninflected personal name, but opinions differ as to its form. Much depends on whether the spelling of *c.* 950, which occurs in a fourteenth-century copy of an Anglo-Saxon will, is regarded as hopelessly corrupt or only slightly so. If it is taken seriously it indicates a name such as *Wynnman*, and the later development must be ascribed to French confusion of *-n-* and *-l-* (giving *Wimeldoun* for *Wimendoun*) and the insertion of an inorganic *-b-* (see Camberwell GTL).

Woodford: ford by the wood (*Wdefort* 1086, *Wudeforde* 1225). This is a fairly common name. The ford was probably across the River Roding.

Wood Green: village green by the wood (*Wodegrene* 1502).

Woolwich: port from which wool was exported (*Uuluuich* 918, *Wulleuic* 964, *Wolewic* 1089). Other names in which *wic* has the sense 'port' are listed under Greenwich.

For Further Reading

General
Wainwright, F. T.: *Archaeology and Place-Names and History*. London, 1962.

England
Ekwall, Eilert: *The Concise Oxford Dictionary of English Place-Names*, Fourth Edition. Oxford, 1962.
Cameron, Kenneth: *English Place-Names*. London, 1961.
Gelling, M: *Signposts to the Past: Place-Names and the History of England*. London, 1978.
Place-Names in the Landscape. London, 1984.
Reaney, P. H.: *The Origin of English Place-Names*. London, 1960.
English Place-Name Society Publications. Cambridge, 1923– . Especially vols. 25 and 26; Smith, A. H.: *English Place-Name Elements*. Cambridge, 1956.

Scotland
Watson, W. J.: *The History of the Celtic Place-Names of Scotland*. Edinburgh, 1926.
'Notes on Scottish Place-Names' in the journal *Scottish Studies*. Edinburgh, 1957– .

Wales
Charles, B. G.: *Non-Celtic Place-Names in Wales*. London, 1938.
Williams, Ifor: *Enwau Lleoedd* (Place-Names). Liverpool.
Thomas, R. J.: *Enwau Afonydd a Nentydd Cymru* (The Names of Welsh Rivers and Brooks). Cardiff, 1938.
Pierce, G. O.: *The Place-names of Dinas Powys Hundred*. Cardiff, 1968.